AF605818

Spelling in Spanish Heritage Language Education

Related Works

Outcomes of University Spanish Heritage Language Instruction in the United States
Melissa A. Bowles, Editor

Innovative Strategies for Heritage Language Teaching: A Practical Guide for the Classroom
Marta Fairclough and Sara M. Beaudrie, Editors

Spanish as a Heritage Language in the United States: The State of the Field
Sara M. Beaudrie and Marta Fairclough, Editors

The Changing Landscape of Spanish Language Curricula: Designing Higher Education Programs for Diverse Students
Alan V. Brown and Gregory L. Thompson

Spelling in Spanish Heritage Language Education

AMÀLIA LLOMBART-HUESCA

GEORGETOWN UNIVERSITY PRESS / WASHINGTON, DC

Library of Congress Cataloging-in-Publication Data

Names: Llombart-Huesca, Amàlia, author.
Title: Spelling in Spanish heritage language education / Amàlia Llombart-Huesca.
Description: Washington, DC : Georgetown University Press, 2024. | Includes bibliographical references and index.
Identifiers: LCCN 2023029394 (print) | LCCN 2023029395 (ebook) | ISBN 9781647124397 (paperback) | ISBN 9781647124403 (hardcover) | ISBN 9781647124380 (ebook)
Subjects: LCSH: Spanish language—Orthography and spelling. | Spanish language—Study and teaching. | Heritage language speakers.
Classification: LCC PC4143 .L58 2024 (print) | LCC PC4143 (ebook) | DDC 461.52—dc23/eng/20231106
LC record available at https://lccn.loc.gov/2023029394
LC ebook record available at https://lccn.loc.gov/2023029395

♾ This paper meets the requirements of ANSI/NISO Z39.48-1992 (Permanence of Paper).

25 24 9 8 7 6 5 4 3 2 First printing

Printed in the United States of America

Cover design by Martha Madrid
Interior design by click! Publishing Services

Contents

Illustrations

Figures

Tables

Acknowledgments

I am deeply grateful to the many people who have accompanied me in this journey. These people have helped me and supported me in different ways, and they are not presented here in order of importance. I might also fail to recognize some people, but I hope they know I am grateful for their presence in my personal and/or academic life.

I want to thank Eve Zyzik for reading portions of my manuscript, as well as for joining me in my research and inviting me to join hers. Your work ethic is truly an inspiration for me.

I also thank Israel Sanz for reading portions of the manuscript. Your helpful and kind comments and suggestions are greatly appreciated.

I want to express my gratitude to the anonymous reviewers who have offered suggestions to improve this book, as well as to editor Hope LeGro for her support and help in taking this project forward.

I would like to express my appreciation to the audiences of the American Association of Teachers of Spanish and Portuguese, Southern California Chapter (AATSPSoCal). Your regular presence at my research presentations and workshops has encouraged me to keep working in this field. Your questions and comments have made me consider things I was not considering and have sparked ideas to explore.

I also want to thank my colleagues in the Department of English & Modern Languages at Cal Poly Pomona. Your efforts to balance research, teaching, and administrative tasks are an inspiration to me and help me keep going. I particularly thank the members of the College of Letters, Arts, and Social Sciences' writing group for their encouragement and the comments to portions of my manuscript. I also value my university, Cal Poly Pomona, for fostering and encouraging a Teacher-Scholar model, which has been crucial in shaping the research and teaching journey that has led to the completion of this book.

I would like to extend a heartfelt appreciation to my students. Thank you for your patience with me while I try to figure it out, for your questions, for your insights, and for the way you have opened to me. Syndy, Lilia, Jenny, Elizabeth, Krystal, Óscar, José, Xitlali, Ruby, Jazz, Samantha, Vanesa, Yesenia, Alison, Kimberly and many others.

Special thanks to my family. My parents, for instilling a love for education and for making it easier for me than it was for them. My sisters, Maru and Laia, for sharing the stresses and joys of academic life.

And finally, a special place for my husband, Javi, and my children, Unai and Ainara. Sorry for all the time I stared at a computer instead of looking at you.

Introduction

In recent decades, there has been a growing interest in the linguistic and educational development of Spanish Heritage Language Learners (henceforth, SHLLs)—Spanish-language students who grew up in a Spanish-speaking home in the United States. Until recently, linguistic research on SHLLs focused primarily on identifying grammar aspects in which SHLLs' speech differs from that of monolingual Spanish speakers, as well as on sociolinguistic issues related to language maintenance and development in this student population, such as language and identity and linguistic prejudice. Research on SHLLs' literacy development has predominantly centered around the acquisition of standard forms and the development of formal academic registers. However, spelling has only recently started to receive attention, despite the fact that its acquisition and development have been identified as a major obstacle for SHLLs as well as for their instructors, who struggle with finding effective strategies to address this issue (Carreira 2002; Mikulski 2006; Beaudrie 2012).

Who Is This Book's Audience?

It is my hope that instructors of courses for SHLLs (sometimes called Spanish for Spanish Speakers or Spanish for Native Speakers) at both secondary school and college levels, as well as professors of writing/composition courses in Spanish postsecondary programs with a high enrollment of SHLLs, will benefit from reading this book and incorporate its recommendations. I believe it will also appeal to professors who teach curriculum and methods of teaching Spanish to prospective Spanish teachers in Spanish teaching credential programs or postsecondary preservice programs, as well as those who teach courses related to bilingual speakers' literacy development.

Teaching spelling to SHLLs can be challenging for instructors due to the lack of attention it has received in their preparation as Spanish teachers. This book aims to address this gap by providing instructors with an understanding of the cognitive skills underlying spelling and the role that age and bilingualism play in the spelling learning process of their students. It also offers a thorough description of the different types of spelling errors students make and an analysis of their causes, as well as some guidelines, recommendations, and practical ideas for spelling activities. While reading about spelling development, instructors will also gain insights into the connections between spelling, vocabulary building, and reading fluency and will find ways to help students develop these different skills at the same time.

I also hope researchers in the fields of SHLLs' education, literacy acquisition and development, and of bilingual education will find this book of interest. Researchers will find a summary of the fundamental aspects of spelling acquisition and development that will serve as a foundation for advancing ongoing research in this area. In essence, the book offers a comprehensive toolbox for research on spelling for researchers who specialize in heritage language education, bridging the gap between linguistics, education, and cognitive psychology.

Spelling in Spanish Heritage Language Learners' Education

The fact that research on SHLLs' spelling is at an incipient stage should not be interpreted as a lack of interest in the topic. Some researchers started discussing this aspect of literacy in heritage language education in the early 2000s. In 2001, writing on the linguistic needs of heritage learners of Russian, Kagan and Dillon (2001, 512) asserted that "they also need extensive work on orthography, unlike non-heritage learners" and that "in that sense, the instruction they need is similar (though not identical) to the instruction Russian children receive in elementary school." One year later, García (2002) devoted a few lines to the spelling difficulties of bilingual teachers, and that same year Carreira (2002) published a study on SHLLs' difficulties with stress marks. However, it was perhaps Beaudrie's (2012) corpus-based analysis of the most frequent spelling errors in SHLLs' writing that led the way for other studies on spelling in SHLLs to take place in the last decade.

Knowledge about how SHLLs develop and improve their spelling skills is certainly sought in the teaching sector, as both teachers and students acknowledge that spelling poses a significant challenge to these students. Most important, difficulties with Spanish spelling are pervasive throughout SHLLs' education, even at the most advanced levels. In fact, as will be discussed later in this book, spelling difficulties are particularly resistant to instructional interventions as students advance in their Spanish courses.

Another common observation found in articles and teaching conferences is that instructors of SHLLs' courses struggle when attempting to teach spelling, which causes frustration to teachers and students, as well as time wasted in tedious spelling lessons and repetitive activities. SHLLs produce orthographic errors that are not seen in students who are learning Spanish as a second/foreign language (henceforth, L2/FL), which baffles many Spanish teachers, who are used to the learning progress L2/FL students follow (Potowski and Carreira 2004).

In my experience organizing, attending, and presenting at conferences for Spanish teachers, and talking with prospective and current Spanish secondary school and college language instructors, I have seen that instructors are not given adequate training and good resources for understanding the spelling patterns of SHLLs, nor effective strategies for addressing their challenges. Because spelling is typically developed in the first years of elementary education, it is not (yet) thoroughly covered in programs directed to prepare secondary school teachers and college-level language instructors. Some teaching credential programs and Spanish master's programs have started to include principles of heritage language education, instead of focusing exclusively on the teaching of Spanish as L2/FL, but there is still not enough attention to spelling in the research arena to have trickled into pedagogical proposals and materials. In fact, some pedagogical proposals made in textbooks work against what we know about spelling development. More awareness, research, and dissemination of the topic are certainly needed.

In my view, the reason there is not more research or publications on spelling in SHLLs' education is the disconnect between the academic backgrounds of education researchers. On the one hand, there is a growing field of research on SHLLs, which is typically conducted by researchers with a background in linguistics, including applied linguistics and/or sociolinguistics, which has naturally veered toward linguistic aspects of language production, such as phonological and morphosyntactic variation. On the other hand, there is a large body of research on the acquisition of orthography and spelling development, which is typically conducted by specialists in education and psycholinguistics and which has focused mainly on monolingual and bilingual children at the elementary school level. In addition, research conducted on bilingual students at a secondary school level has focused on improving spelling in English because English literacy is an education priority in the United States. Few studies have focused on the spelling needs of SHLLs in Spanish at the secondary and college levels.

This research gap extends to a gap in the Spanish language curriculum. The inclusion of spelling in Spanish within the "Common Core Language Arts / Literacy standards" (Spanish version) for K–12 levels (NGA Center for Best Practices and Council of Chief State School Officers 2012) suggests that education specialists are aware of the spelling needs of students and are well versed in the topic. The problem is that these standards are made with students who enroll in a primary school dual-immersion program in mind. After sixth grade, the Common Core standards barely make any references to spelling, because this skill has been addressed in previous years in the dual-immersion system. Most SHLLs, however, receive their education in English and take their first "Spanish for Spanish Speakers" course in high school or, in a few cases, in middle school. No curricular guidance exists to address spelling in secondary education for those students who begin their Spanish education at that level. In this book, I hope to offer some understanding of how SHLLs acquire and develop spelling in Spanish in the typical school setting in which they start taking Spanish courses.

Finally, addressing spelling acquisition and development in SHLLs who start taking their courses at the secondary level is crucial not only as a goal in itself. Spelling is intricately connected to reading, directly and indirectly, in ways that go beyond the old adage that we learn how to spell by reading a lot. For example, attention to spelling facilitates vocabulary retention by creating stronger connections between meaning, written form, and pronunciation. And some activities that help improve spelling are also helpful for developing other skills, such as reading fluency and metalinguistic awareness, which, in turn, help students expand their vocabulary. As SHLLs in secondary courses start reading books in Spanish, they will encounter many new words. Therefore, addressing spelling, both separately and alongside reading activities, also has the potential to make reading an opportunity to greatly increase students' vocabulary.

Why Do We Need to Learn about the Spelling Development Process to Teach Spelling?

Encountering spelling errors in written language causes very visceral reactions in readers. You may have seen how spelling errors made by high-profile personalities, from Dan Quayle's "potatoe" incident to Tony Blair's "toomorrow" gaffe to Donald Trump's frequent misspellings on social media posts, are the target of scorn and are often used to lower the author's credibility. In general, spelling errors negatively impact the perception people have of writers and their communicative abilities (Kreiner et al. 2002; Pan, Rickard, and Bjork 2021). In a meta-analysis study, Graham, Harris, and Hebert (2011) found that teachers gave lower scores on content quality to student papers that contained misspelled words than to the same papers with no spelling errors. In college courses' online forum discussions, arguments in posts that contain spelling errors are more likely to be questioned than are correctly spelled posts (Jeong, Li, and Pan 2017). An advertisement with spelling and punctuation errors creates a perception of an inferior business and lower-quality employees, and people are less inclined to use the service being advertised (Mozafari et al. 2019). Likewise, spelling errors on a resume are immediate red flags for questioning the candidate's abilities. For example, Martin-Lacroux and Lacroux (2017) show that spelling errors in a candidate application have a stronger influence on recruiters than the amount of professional experience.

This aversion to poor spelling is an effect of an aversion to what we *think* it reflects. Martin-Lacroux (2017) found that recruiters attributed bad spelling in candidates' applications to lack of soft skills (e.g., credibility, politeness, rigor, and conscientiousness), cognitive abilities (e.g., intelligence and communication skills), or general culture. I have given conference talks and workshops on spelling in SHLLs' education, and I often hear comments attributing students' bad spelling to the fact that they do not read, and I have even heard comments blaming the parents of these students for not having raised their children in rich literacy environments that encouraged avid reading. Although there is a connection between reading and spelling, I believe these sorts of statements result from an oversimplistic understanding of this connection, for many reasons that I hope will become clear throughout this book. The statements might also reflect the personal background of the person who makes such comments. Teachers who grew up in an environment rich with reading opportunities and/or raised their own children in such an environment might have a particular perspective on learning and literacy. I hope to share in this book how a teacher might understand their students from a different perspective and give them the necessary skills to succeed regardless of their home learning environment.

It is also important to recognize that the assumptions that SHLLs have poor reading habits and that those are to blame for their weak Spanish spelling skills do not make sense in the United States because SHLLs are typically not taught in Spanish but in English. In fact, as we will see in the next chapter, writing proficiency in Spanish is significantly higher in SHLLs who were born in a Spanish-speaking country and were schooled in Spanish before moving to the United States than in those who were born in the United States and were schooled in English (Gatti and O'Neill 2017).

In addition, because SHLLs' oral skills are typically very high, their spelling skills do not conform to instructors' expectations of how they ought to write. Almost twenty years ago I started teaching advanced Spanish courses that had a mix of SHLLs and L2/FL learners of Spanish, and a colleague "warned" me about some students who speak fluently "like you and I" but then write "like five-year-old children do." I soon understood what she was referring to: SHLLs' spelling. SHLLs made spelling errors that this colleague had not seen in other adult, educated, fluent Spanish speakers—who had grown and been educated in a Spanish-speaking country. The mismatch in expectations is also the result of teachers' training and experience with teaching Spanish as L2/FL. When L2/FL students learn a word, for example, the verb *hacer*, they learn its meaning, its pronunciation, its written form, and its conjugation at the same time. They will always write *hacer* with the letter *h* and will do so in every verb form (*hice*, *hago*, *haré*) because they are aware of which verb they are writing and especially because they need to think about its conjugation. They might make a grammar mistake and write or say *hacía* instead of *hice*, but whichever form they write, it will begin with an *h*. In contrast, SHLLs who have used various forms of *hacer* in oral speech for years, having naturally acquired the word at home, once they start writing may sometimes not write it with an *h*. This is why teachers trained in teaching Spanish to L2/FL learners see their expectations, or "implicational hierarchies," break down when working with SHLLs (Potowski and Carreira 2004). According to these L2/FL-based implicational hierarchies, a student who can conjugate *hacer* "should" also know how to spell it. That is simply not true for SHLLs. This book looks at SHLLs' spelling production and spelling errors not as an oddity but as something to be expected given the specific juncture of language acquisition setting and educational context of SHLLs. It also looks at their spelling production as something that needs to be thoroughly understood, because the strategies that have worked in other types of students will not necessarily apply to SHLLs.

Overview of the Book

This book aims to illuminate a lesser-discussed aspect of language learning for SHLLs: spelling acquisition. I address the teaching and development of spelling within the overall field of SHLLs' education by reviewing key aspects of a large body of general research on spelling development and of a smaller number of studies that have been conducted specifically targeting SHLLs' spelling. I also present the findings of my research conducted on a corpus of essays written by SHLLs, and I conclude with specific pedagogical recommendations on how to improve SHLLs' spelling.

In Chapter 1 I present a general overview of SHLLs and their education goals. I look at various attributes that have been included in several definitions in the literature on heritage languages and that are present—in different degrees—in the various profiles of SHLLs. The chapter also presents an overview of the goals that have been proposed for SHLLs courses and programs, as well as the possible role of spelling instruction within SHLLs' education.

A comprehensive review of our current understanding of the different elements involved in the spelling acquisition and development process is presented in chapter 2. Here, I look at the cognitive skills involved in the acquisition and development of spelling and the learners' typical progress through the acquisition of different types of spelling rules, as well as the effect that age and bilingualism have on this development. Age is an important factor to consider; because SHLLs typically do not start taking Spanish courses until secondary education, or even college, they have missed the natural progression and milestones of these cognitive skills. In addition, bilingual and monolingual learners differ in terms of access to written language in ways that go beyond simple negative spelling interference.

Chapter 3 offers an overview of the Spanish spelling system. The goal is to provide an explanation beyond the mere presentation of the Spanish sound-letter correspondences and delve into the underlying factors that drive these connections. I explain the different types of sound-letter correspondences and the way they are intertwined with the phonological and morphological systems of the language, to show that spelling acquisition is more than learning a mere convention and is a linguistic endeavor. The chapter also looks at how Spanish spelling deals with linguistic change, both from a dialectal variation perspective and language change across time, in a way that is of particular relevance to SHLLs.

In chapter 4 I describe thoroughly the spelling errors SHLLs make, in terms of both relative frequency and accuracy, including an analysis and classification of the different types of spelling errors, with the goal of understanding their different underlying causes. In addition to reviewing previous studies on spelling errors in SHLLs, this chapter describes and analyzes a corpus of 125 essays written by SHLLs, which I refer to as the LH corpus, as well as the results of several studies I have conducted in the past few years. I discuss these findings in relation to the different ways instructors and researchers elicit students' spelling—such as through essays versus targeted exercises—and the spelling sequences where students make more errors, both in absolute terms, that is, the sequences that account for the greatest percentages of misspellings in a text, and in terms of accuracy, that is, sequences that seem especially difficult to spell. In particular, I look at how SHLLs' spelling errors compare and differ from those monolingual and bilingual children make when learning how to spell in elementary school.

Chapter 5 is devoted to the issue of stress marks ("acentos"), which many researchers have identified as the most challenging aspect of spelling and the major source of spelling errors. I start with an overview of the stress-marking rules and their underlying logic and then present the most productive stress patterns in Spanish. The chapter also includes a review of studies on SHLLs' difficulties with stress-marking, including their difficulties when attempting to identify the stressed syllables in Spanish. The chapter ends with a proposal on how to address stress marks in the SHLLs' classroom, which differs—or augments—current practices and proposals.

Last, in chapter 6, I present a set of strategies and approaches for developing and improving SHLLs' spelling skills that are not commonly used in textbooks. The activities I propose not only align with the specific characteristics of SHLLs' spelling and target the most frequent spelling errors, as described in previous chapters, but also target some less-visible skills underlying the proficiency of spelling, such as decoding skills and phonological and morphological awareness.

Personal Fascination and Professional Interest

My interest in the acquisition and development of Spanish in SHLLs is both personal and professional. I have mentioned earlier the mismatch between

SHLLs' spelling skills and teachers' expectations about their students' spelling abilities—expectations that are based on other linguistic skills SHLLs possess, such as their oral fluency and their grammatical proficiency. I have also discussed that this mismatch derives from our experience with educated native speakers' spelling skills—educated in Spanish, that is—or our experience with students of Spanish as a L2/FL. However, this mismatch has never been odd to me, as I grew up with a similar experience—in another language. While I grew up speaking Spanish and Catalan at home, most of my school education was in Spanish, which was also the language in which I learned how to read and write. Like many SHLLs, I entered school able to speak two languages, but I learned the alphabet, the sounds of the letters, and how to read my first words in only one of them. In third grade I had the chance to attend a school that taught all of its classes in Catalan—except for a Spanish language arts class. I have a strong memory of the first day of class when the teacher asked us to write what we did over the summer, and I thought, "I have never been taught how to write in Catalan; how am I going to do it?" I was amazed when I saw that the Catalan words I was thinking came out of the pencil on my paper. I also remember my first spelling mistake in that essay, one that reflected some Spanish interference in my Catalan pronunciation of the word. After that year, I took some Catalan language arts and literature courses in middle and high school, and eventually pursued a bachelor's degree in Catalan language, where I barely had the need to write in Spanish. However, my spelling skills remained much better in Spanish than in Catalan, and I definitely feel more confident when writing in Spanish. (I wish my Catalan spelling was better, and if I were teaching Catalan instead of Spanish or lived or worked in another environment where I used Catalan more often, I would work on that skill.) This experience with partial literacy in my home language has helped me to be more flexible with my assumptions about the meaning of bad spelling. In Catalonia many people my age and older have difficulties with Catalan spelling because they were born before Catalan was allowed in schools. Bad spelling in Catalan, then, is not so strongly attached to negative values. In fact, I have great respect for those who write in a language they have not been able to study at school.

When I started teaching SHLL courses, my students' experiences with Spanish spelling resonated with my own experience with Catalan spelling. Not only did I not dislike my students' misspellings, but I also became fascinated by them, to a point that I decided to devote my research to the subject. I see a misspelled word, and I think about the cognitive process behind that particular spelling. In fact, even when I see that a student spelled a word correctly on the board, I actively seek out alternative (incorrect) spellings other students may have used. One time when I did not ask for alternatives, a student raised her hand and said, "OK, I understand why this word is spelled with a *z*, but I wrote it with an *s*; can you tell me why I wrote it that way?" That student had become interested not only in knowing the correct way to spell a word or the reason for that spelling but also in her own learning process and her own understanding of the language. I am interested in finding the best ways to help students improve their spelling, and I cannot do that successfully if I just dislike misspellings and stop there. I will be even less helpful if I bring my own assumptions about students' reading habits or their carelessness into my teaching. Instead, I have developed a genuine intellectual interest for misspellings and, as always, feel a genuine respect for my students and where they are in their learning process.

After reading this book, I hope the reader will join me and make no more mentions of *horrores de ortografía*! (I am guilty of having done this in the past, thinking it was "clever.") It is also my hope that this knowledge will enable readers to adopt a different perspective about SHLLs' spellings. Spelling errors are fascinating and provide us with valuable insights about learners and the way the language is represented in their minds.

ONE

Spanish Heritage Language Education

Who Are Spanish Heritage Language Learners?

Valdés's (2001, 38) seminal definition of a heritage language learner as "a language student who is raised in a home where a non-English language is spoken, who speaks or at least understands the language, and who is to some degree bilingual in that language and in English" has been often quoted and questioned. Defining and characterizing heritage language (HL) learners are not without problems, and the high heterogeneity of this group is often acknowledged in the literature, which has found that variability among bilinguals is greater than among monolingual speakers (de Swart 2013; Rothman and Treffers-Daller 2014). SHLLs are found within a large range of students, from those who have been schooled in a Spanish-speaking country, speak a prestige variety of the language, and possess some academic skills, to receptive bilinguals with no or little productive abilities in a stigmatized variety of Spanish (Valdés 1997).

Given the great variability of HL learners, Zyzik (2016, 19) proposes that we "move away from definitions" and, rather, "situate the HL learner in a category that exhibits prototype effects." In order to create the prototype, Zyzik assembled the various attributes that have been included in several definitions in the literature on HL learners. Each of these attributes is scalar or gradient, and the different profiles of HL learners emerge from the combination of different degrees in each of these attributes.

Early Exposure to the Heritage Language in the Home

Zyzik (2016) explains that although this attribute could be seen as a categorical (yes/no) one, this exposure may happen at different degrees, depending on the number of hours the HL is spoken per week, the percentage of time that adults in the home speak the HL, the number of speakers who regularly use the HL to the child, or trips to the family's country of origin. In fact, language ability among young HL speakers is positively correlated with the number of different speakers who regularly address them in the HL (Gollan, Starr, and Ferreira 2015). Similarly, Mikulski (2010) found that both predominant use of Spanish with family and multiple trips abroad were associated with higher language proficiency.

Some Degree of Bilingualism

The concept of heritage language is understood only in the context of bilingualism in a home language and a majority or societal language (English, in our case). HL speakers are found in a bilingual continuum along different levels of competence in each of the two languages (Silva-Corvalán 2001).

Dominance in a Language Other Than the Heritage Language (the Majority Language)

Language dominance is a compound construct that draws on diverse conceptual dimensions (skills) and domains (contexts of language use). In the context of bilingualism, it is used to refer to the "asymmetries of skill in, or use of, one language over the other" (Birdsong 2014, 374). Language dominance is found in a continuum from an unbalanced bilingualism in one language to the other, with some degrees of balanced bilingualism in between, that is, similar levels in proficiency and use of the two languages (Gertken, Amengual, and Birdsong 2014). Language dominance is a fluid construct that shifts over time. For many SHLLs, the dominant language during childhood is Spanish, and some children are even exposed to Spanish literacy in the home, when they are read to by their parents (Carreira and Kagan 2011), but when they start attending school in English, language use typically shifts to the majority language, often leading to a language shift at home (Montrul and Potowski 2007, 303). This shift in language use and exposure typically results in halted acquisition and attrition of grammatical features, especially semantically complex ones (Silva-Corvalán 1994a, 1994b; Polinsky 2008). Relative language dominance is an important feature of SHLLs, as Spanish-language dominance has been found to correlate with vocabulary knowledge in that language (Zyzik 2021a).

Limited Proficiency in the Heritage Language

The proficiency in the HL has been characterized as what Hulstijn (2011, 2019) labels as "Basic Language Cognition"—the ability to produce spoken language in situations of everyday life, common to all adult native speakers, regardless of age, literacy, or educational level. It is also an implicit knowledge, as a consequence of having been acquired in a naturalistic context in early childhood.

Speaking and listening are the language skills that HL learners perceive as their stronger skills (Jensen and Llosa 2007; Carreira and Kagan 2011). Writing proficiency, on the other hand, is somehow limited, because HL learners are typically schooled in English and not in their heritage language. Gatti and O'Neill (2017) found that writing proficiency is significantly higher in HL learners born outside the United States than in those born there. And within HL learners born outside the United States, the age of arrival and the number of years of schooling they received in their country of origin also correlate with writing proficiency. While becoming or staying proficient in English does not require parental use of English in the home, staying proficient in Spanish requires support in both school and at home (Duursma et al. 2007).

Ethnic/Cultural Connection to the Heritage Language

HL learners have an ethnic and/or cultural connection to the language, which we do not see in L2/FL learners. This connection is understood as a cluster of sociocultural variables that include attitudes, motivation, and social and ethnic identity. As with language dominance, the sociocultural connection to the HL is neither static nor monolithic but, rather, varies throughout the lifespan of the individual as well as across learners and is influenced by the individual's interactions and the family's and community's social practices (see He 2006, 2010). The ethnic community has also been considered a key element of the HL learner's status (Cho, Cho, and Tse 1997; McCarty et al. 1997; Cho 2000; Yamauchi, Ceppi, and Lau-Smith 2000). As a consequence, the affective and cultural needs of HL learners differ from those of L2/FL learners.

In sum, the prototype HL learner, "although difficult to define in terms of sufficient and necessary characteristics, can be understood as exhibiting a cluster of attributes" (Zyzik 2016, 29):

- Early exposure to the HL
- A certain degree of bilingualism
- Dominance in a language other than the HL
- Proficiency of the HL that is limited to basic language cognition and implicit knowledge
- Ethnic/cultural connection with the HL

Zyzik explains that in this model, some HL learners may be closer to the prototype and others may be more distant. For example, students who have overheard the HL at home but have had few opportunities to speak it will be situated in the periphery of the prototype but still included. Similarly, students who were schooled in a Spanish-speaking country and have recently arrived in the United States—and who, therefore, are more dominant in Spanish than English and have more advanced literacy skills than the prototypical HL learner—will also be found in the periphery but included in the prototype.

What Are the Goals of Heritage Language Instruction?

In the last few decades, the number of courses of Spanish for heritage language learners (Spanish for Native Speakers, Spanish for Spanish Speakers, Spanish for Heritage Speakers) has grown exponentially. Those courses may be found in a course sequence ranging between two and five courses, or as single courses. In those secondary and postsecondary schools where such courses do not exist, SHLLs enroll in different levels of Spanish L2/FL (Beaudrie 2011).[1] In addition, Spanish bachelor's and Spanish teaching credential programs may also have many SHLLs.

The reasons SHLLs study Spanish may include one or more of the following: to fulfill a language requirement, to connect with their roots, to communicate with monolingual family members, to increase participation in community affairs, or to make professional use of Spanish in local service professions or at the national or international levels (Carreira and Armengol 2001; Carreira 2004). According to Valdés (1997), there are four goals of Spanish for SHLLs courses: Spanish language maintenance, acquisition of the prestige variety of Spanish, expansion of bilingual range and development of linguistic competence, and transfer of literacy skills.

Spanish-Language Maintenance

It is well known that societal bilingualism in the United States is maintained through immigration and not through transmission across generations. The role of heritage language education in the maintenance of the language across generations is not clear. However, for those who believe that these courses could have a role in language maintenance, Valdés (1997) suggests they explore what levels of linguistic development and what kinds of linguistic interactions, readings, and classroom activities contribute to positive attitudes toward the use of Spanish. Language maintenance seems to be closely related to the attitudes toward the language held by speakers and the community. However, many heritage speakers may reject Spanish "because they have internalized messages about its inferiority or undesirability" (Potowski and Carreira 2004, 430), which stem from an accepted linguistic hierarchy that traditionally has privileged English monolingualism and marginalized US Spanish and its communities (see, e.g., MacGregor-Mendoza 2000; Leeman 2012). Many SHLLs also display insecurity about their Spanish-language skills, which are often compared to those of monolingual Spanish speakers and dismissed for including certain nonstandard forms and/or English interference. Therefore, for Spanish courses to have an effect on SHLLs' willingness and enthusiasm to use and maintain the language, they need to address not only the students' linguistic needs but also their affective and cultural needs, such as building students' linguistic self-esteem, allowing them to reconnect with their culture, and giving them opportunities to assert their identity (Carreira 2004). For example, Webb and Miller (2000) make their case for getting to know the students' linguistic proficiency, motivation, academic preparedness, and cultural connectedness, as well as some emotional and societal factors, and they offer a framework to engage in this discovery.

In addition, as a way to counteract students' internalized negative messages about their Spanish-language skills, some researchers have proposed employing a critical pedagogy that helps them to develop a critical awareness toward linguistic prejudices, such as the stigmatization of certain language varieties and of bilingual practices that assume monolingual norms (Carreira 2000; Martínez 2003; Leeman 2005; Holguín-Mendoza 2018; Beaudrie and Wilson 2022). A basic premise of critical language awareness pedagogies is that when students view language variation as natural and recognize the value of all language varieties, while also becoming aware of the sociopolitical forces that underlie language ideologies, they will be empowered to make their own decisions about language use. Sociolinguistic awareness has also been researched in implementations of service-learning activities, where students' linguistic performance in the classroom is connected with the language presence in their communities (Leeman, Rabin, and Román-Mendoza 2011; Petrov 2013; Lowther Pereira 2015; Llombart-Huesca and Pulido 2017).

Acquisition of the Prestige Variety of Spanish

This has been a widely debated topic in the literature of SHLLs' education. Potowski and Carreira (2004, 430) state that "it is generally agreed that a primary goal of formal education, in any language, is to prepare students to function in formal circles of discourse." What has been debated is exactly which prestige variety should be taught (Villa 1996, 2009). In addition, there exists a concern that the focus on a standard variety of Spanish may be easily interpreted as a disdain for students' own varieties and increase their linguistic insecurity (Villa 1996; Krashen 1998; Bernal-Enríquez and Hernández-Chávez 2003; Leeman 2005; Callahan 2010).

In addition, there is the issue of how second-language varieties and registers are learned. Valdés (1997) explains that adding a new register of the L1 is not analogous to learning an L2. In the latter process, learners know when they are listening/reading the L1 or the L2. However, this is not the case when they are adding a new linguistic variety to the learner's own variety of the same language, because the prestige or standard variety includes many features that are also present in the nonstandard variety, as well as other features that are not (Craig

1988). Valdés explains that because speakers of nonprestige varieties are aware of the existence of common features in both varieties, they often use nonstandard or even stigmatized forms when attempting to speak a standard or prestige variety, under the assumption that they also belong to the prestige variety. I would also add that something that complicates matters is that, at times, the learner might be unsure whether a certain feature belongs to the specific geographic variety of the instructor or if it is common to most Spanish speakers. For example, if the instructor uses forms that the students do not use, such as *vosotros* (instead of *ustedes*) or *vos* (instead of *tú*) and also *haya* (instead of *haiga*), students might not necessarily know that *haya* is the form that is considered standard in all Spanish-speaking areas but that *vosotros* and *vos* are only used in some areas.

Expansion of Bilingual Range and Development of Linguistic Competence

A metasynthesis conducted by Gironzetti and Belpoliti (2018) of teaching-oriented studies on SHLLs found that many of them have focused on grammatical competence, such as the verb system (e.g., Fairclough 2005; Potowski, Jegerski, and Morgan-Short 2009; and, more recently, Pascual y Cabo and Montrul 2021) as well as vocabulary (e.g., Tocaimaza-Hatch and Walls 2016; and, more recently, Zyzik 2021a, 2021b). An overarching debate when discussing linguistic competence relates to the explicit versus implicit nature of the linguistic competence of SHLLs. The dichotomy between these two types of linguistic knowledge, as well as the question of their interface, is a fundamental topic in the field of second-language acquisition (see Ellis 2011), and it has also been studied in the HL learning field. For example, Bowles (2011) and Correa (2011) show that contrary to what is the case for L2/FL learners, SHLL's knowledge of Spanish is primarily implicit in nature, which is a consequence of having acquired the language naturalistically in early childhood. Not only that but also SHLLs make less use of the explicit knowledge they may learn (Montrul 2009; Correa 2011).

Llombart-Huesca (2021) argues that we need to look at implicit and explicit knowledge in the context in which they are developed. The explicit knowledge developed in a language that was first acquired implicitly at home is qualitatively different from the explicit knowledge learned by an L2 student without an implicit foundation. The role of the explicit metalinguistic knowledge is also different for both types of students. For the L2 learner, it is the starting point toward the development of an implicit knowledge, a process that has been studied in the second language acquisition (SLA) field. However, for L1 speakers, explicit knowledge is developed based on the implicit knowledge they already possess, a process that pertains to the language arts field. In language arts classes, children develop an explicit knowledge of their own language as part of their literacy development and also for general intellectual growth, that is, to know things about their own language. The problem arises when instructors use explicit knowledge in SHLLs courses with the same goal that an L2/FL course would have. In fact, it has been widely documented that SHLLs do not do well with language materials that make use of explicit knowledge (Potowski, Jegerski, and Morgan-Short 2009), do not use them in the same manner as L2/FL learners do (Torres 2013), or feel confused by them (Beaudrie 2009).

Development of Literacy Skills

Literacy development has been another main area of focus of the publications on pedagogical implementation and empirical studies in the HL field (Gironzetti and Belpoliti 2018). Most studies conducted in this area aim at advanced literacy skills and adopt a discourse-linguistic perspective (see Edstrom 2006; Achugar and Colombi 2008; Cordero 2008; Colombi 2009). In recent years we have observed a turn to a multiliteracies approach, such as "learning by design," based on Mary Kalantzis and Bill Cope's work (e.g., Cope and Kalantzis 2000; Kalantzis and Cope 2004), which has been touted as particularly fitting for SHLLs (Zapata 2017; Elola, Padial, and Guerrero-Rodríguez 2021; Parra Velasco 2021). In this framework, the curriculum must be built on relevant materials that are connected to the learners' personal world and community, and learners must be given the tools to develop not only traditional academic literacy skills but also multiple literacies in a multimodal environment in which learners can express their personal and community identities.

The attention to spelling issues in the SHLLs literature is relatively recent, and in the last decade we have witnessed an increase in studies on the spelling proficiency of SHLLs. One set of studies are error analyses that, using naturalistic data gathered through essays written by students, aim to uncover the most frequent errors in SHLLs' writings, findings that could help instructors deploy a more targeted approach (Beaudrie 2012; Bahr et al. 2015; Belpoliti and Bermejo 2020a; Contreras-Wise 2020). Another set of studies have an experimental (or quasi-experimental) design that calls for participants to perform tasks with words selected by the researcher with the purpose of investigating a specific aspect of spelling development (Carreira 2002; Llombart-Huesca 2017a, 2019; Beaudrie 2018; Llombart-Huesca and Zyzik 2019). Other studies have looked at the effects of instructional interventions in spelling development—specifically the accent placement aspect (Carreira 2002; Beaudrie 2017; Fernández Parera and Lynch 2021).

Why Teach Spelling in the SHLL Classroom?

Spelling has often been viewed as a trivial aspect of the language arts curriculum and has not experienced the variety of instructional methods that have been researched and implemented in the teaching of reading and writing (Brown 1990; Adams 1990). Although in recent years spelling has received greater recognition as a fundamental aspect of literacy, the widespread use of spell-check on computers and phones may have lessened the motivation to develop research-based strategies for effective spelling teaching. In a multiliteracies approach, where nonacademic materials are used and created, and where the process of "meaning-making" is considered the priority, it is also easy to relegate spelling as a mere last-minute editing issue. Within the field of SHLLs education, the teaching of spelling might seem unattractive for additional reasons. As mentioned earlier, studying one's heritage language carries some emotional elements that we do not see in L2 teaching and in L1 language arts courses in monolingual contexts, as many SHLLs display insecurity about their language skills. With spelling being an area that gives these students great difficulties, some instructors may prefer to focus on other aspects of the language that help build confidence in their language skills and positive emotions toward the process of further developing them.

However, there are many reasons to lend a space to the teaching of spelling in SHLLs courses. It is important to understand that contrary to common belief, spelling is not simply the "cherry on top" of good writing or a mere editing issue. Spelling, "though belonging to the written domain and related to school-type activities, is an authentic linguistic act" (Ravid and Gillis 2002, 73). Spelling is not merely a convention; instead, it is tightly connected with phonology and morphosyntax, and the development of orthographic skills is intertwined with the development of metalinguistic awareness in these two areas. The connection between spelling and morphosyntax necessarily involves an attention to meaning. What's more, the skills behind the acquisition and development of spelling also lie beneath literacy development in general, and they help to improve other crucial literacy aspects, such as reading fluency, reading comprehension, and vocabulary growth.

In addition, fluent spelling enables writers to devote their attention to higher-level aspects of composition (Westwood 1999), since the attention students devote to spelling as they are writing is likely to interfere with other aspects of writing (Berninger 1999; Graham and Santangelo 2014). Uncertainty about the spelling of words can further influence the words students choose, as they may avoid using words they cannot spell (Graham and Harris 2005, cited in Graham and Santangelo 2014). In the SHLLs' context, Fernández Parera and Lynch (2021) found that students who were enrolled in a course section that did not provide explicit instruction in spelling wrote longer essays on average than students enrolled in a section of the same course that did, which these authors believe may be because students were told "not to worry" about spelling. Although this outcome could be seen as an incentive to not focus on spelling in the SHLLs' class, we could also envision the scenario in which students would "not worry" about spelling and write longer essays because they have developed and automatized good spelling.

We also need to be aware of the way spelling is regarded on a societal level, as the mark of a well-educated person, and the fact that spelling errors often negatively impact the perception readers have of writers (Kreiner et al. 2002; Mozafari et al. 2019; Pan, Rickard, and Bjork 2021). Kreiner et al. (2002) found that the presence of spelling errors caused adults to give lower ratings to authors' writing abilities and in some cases lower ratings of their intellectual ability. Spelling also has consequences in the employment sector, both in hiring practices and promotion decisions, as reviewed by Pan, Rickard, and Bjork (2021). In the context of Spanish in the United States, one of the main reasons fluent Spanish speakers study Spanish in college is to prepare themselves to use Spanish for professional and academic purposes, and part of this preparation is the development of advanced literacy competencies (Colombi 2002). SHLLs seem well aware of their spelling difficulties and perceive spelling development as an important goal for their Spanish-language education (Carreira 2002; Mikulski 2006; Callahan 2010). Poor spelling adversely affects SHLLs' chances of being hired for a job that uses Spanish professionally—for example, in translation, media, or marketing (Carreira 2002). Lack of early literacy in Spanish puts SHLLs at a competitive professional disadvantage compared to professionals from Spain and Latin American countries who immigrated to the United States as adults and who have strong Spanish-writing skills (Llombart-Huesca 2017b). Although spellcheckers work decently for those who can spell fairly well, rudimentary spelling skills are insufficient for using a spellchecker, and there are many spelling errors in Spanish that are not caught by spellcheckers, as will be discussed in chapter 6. In addition, there are many situations in which a professional might not be able to use a spellchecker, such as a teacher writing something on the board in front of a class.

Reflection Questions

1. Carreira (2004, 11) gives several student profiles, some of which are presented here.[2] When reading these profiles, you may imagine them as corresponding to students in a secondary school or at a college level. Discuss how they would fit in Zyzik's (2016) prototype framework. Would they be close or far from the prototype?

   Juan
   a. Born in Chicago.
   b. Parents born in Mexico. Speaks English and Spanish at home. His parents speak mostly in Spanish to him, and he responds in either Spanish or English. He speaks English to his younger sister.

c. English dominant but understands Spanish and is able to communicate in everyday situations, can read and write Spanish, hesitates when reading certain words and makes some grammatical and spelling mistakes. Sometimes helps parents to translate letters from English to Spanish. Listens to music in both English and Spanish. He is used to hearing Spanish on TV and radio at home.
d. Participates in Mexican cultural events with his family, such as Quinceañeras, Día de los Muertos, and Posadas.
e. Considers himself "Mexican American."

Maria

a. Born and raised in Omaha, Nebraska.
b. Parents were born in Texas and grandparents were born in Mexico. Does not speak Spanish at home, only with grandmother who visits twice a year from Mexico, with whom she wishes she could communicate better.
c. Understands Spanish but speaks haltingly. Feels uncomfortable around adult Spanish speakers when they try to engage in conversation in Spanish. Does not read or write Spanish.
d. Participates in some Latinx/Hispanic cultural and community events.
e. Considers herself "Chicana."

Luisa

a. Born in Buenos Aires, arrived in the United States at age fourteen with her parents and sister.
b. Parents are Argentinian. Speaks only Spanish at home, both to parents and sister. In the last year, she has started using some English with her sister. Does not speak or write English at the same level as most of her peers.
c. Reads and writes Spanish at grade level.
d. Sometimes participates in Latinx/Hispanic community events. These are mostly Mexican, and she is unsure about how much she identifies herself with that community. At a school Hispanic Month event, she was happy to be able to represent Argentina.
e. Considers herself "Argentinian."

Pablo

a. Born and raised in Chicago.
b. Dad is Cuban, mother is American of non–Hispanic/Latin American descent. Speaks English at home. Dad occasionally uses Spanish to address to him.

   c. English dominant but has some basic level of Spanish acquired during summers in Miami with relatives. Can read and write Spanish with difficulty.
   d. Does not participate in Latinx/Hispanic events, except when he goes to Miami.
   e. Considers himself "American."

2. Connect the different SHLLs' profiles with your own experience, either as a SHLL yourself or as a Spanish instructor—or both.

3. If you have had any experience as a SHLL yourself, as a SHLL teacher, or both, or have observed SHLLs courses as part of your teacher preparation work, reflect on the attention given to spelling in those courses.

Notes

1. Beaudrie's (2011) study is based on data from colleges and universities in the southwestern United States.
2. The profiles have been slightly modified from Carreira's (2004) original text.

TWO

How Do We Learn How to Spell?

More Than Just "Learning the Rules": Cognitive-Linguistic Components of Spelling

When students, and sometimes teachers, talk about spelling errors and improving someone's spelling, they often mention "spelling rules." Some students lament that they do not know the spelling rules or that they forgot them, or they say they need to learn them. However, learning and developing spelling go beyond learning "spelling rules," that is, the specific phoneme-grapheme correspondences (PGCs) that have been established in a language. In order to learn how to spell, students also need to develop some metalinguistic awareness and skills. We understand metalinguistic awareness as the ability to reflect on and manipulate the structural features of language, as well as to be able to shift the focus from meaning to form. More specifically, an awareness of the phonological and morphological systems of the language plays a crucial role in the development of spelling skills (Defior et al. 2015). In addition to the decoding of orthographic, phonological, and morphological information, spelling has also been shown to benefit from whole-word visual information, which is developed through the repeated exposure to the printed word (Ehri 1980, 2014; Seymour 1992). Moreover, when "learning the spelling rules," learners internalize different PGCs in different ways, depending on factors such as their level of complexity or predictability. And the process of learning how to spell is also affected by learners' factors, such as age and bilingualism.

This chapter describes the effect of phonological and morphological awareness and of the visual representation of written words on the acquisition and development of spelling, as well as the ways in which learners internalize different types of rules. It also explains how the factors of age and bilingualism intervene in this process.

Spelling and Phonological Awareness

One of the first complexities of spelling children encounter is that spelling is based on the correspondences between phonemes and graphemes, while what we hear and what we naturally produce when we talk are not the phonemes themselves but rather sounds that are pronounced differently depending on what the previous or subsequent sound is, or on whether they appear at the beginning of the syllable or at the end. Phonemes are abstractions of the actual sounds we produce. For example, the "t" we produce and hear in the word *tea* or *time* is not the same as the "t" in *cat* or *pot*. But the difference between these two pronunciations of /t/ (called allophones of /t/) is not relevant to spelling, because we assign the letter *t* to the phoneme /t/ regardless of its specific pronunciation (or allophonic realization). Therefore, spelling does not actually assign a grapheme to a sound, but to an abstraction of a sound—the phoneme (see figure 2.1).

Another difficulty regarding sounds and their connections with graphemes comes from the fact that some phonemes have a very similar sound but correspond to different letters, as is the case of /i/ and /I/ (beat, bit), in English, or /p/ and /b/ (peso, beso), in Spanish. To make things more difficult, children rarely hear sounds in isolation but in tight and long strings of sounds comprising several words. While most literate adults have no difficulty in segmenting words into each individual sound, to a preliterate child sound sequences such as /tr/

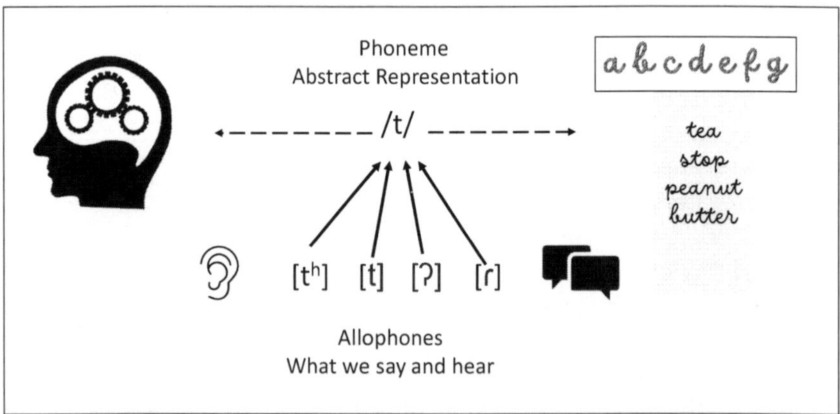

FIGURE 2.1. Phonemes and allophones

In English, /d/ and /ð/ are different phonemes because they can appear in the same position within a word and, therefore, distinguish between two otherwise identical words: *this* and *diss*, for example. In Spanish, [d] and [ð] are different allophones of the same phoneme because they appear in different places of a word: [d] appears in word-initial position and after a nasal consonant, and [ð] appears in the remaining contexts. Therefore, [d] and [ð] will never distinguish between two words.

or /pl/ could be units of sounds, just like /tʃ/ (ch in chat) or /oʊ/ (o in so), which we consider units of sound, instead of sequences containing two units.

Therefore, in order to learn how to write and to know which grapheme to assign to each phoneme, children need to develop an awareness of the phonological abstractions of the sounds they hear and produce and disregard the small differences between the different pronunciations of a phoneme (e.g., perceive the "t" in both *tea* and *cat* as /t/). Phonological awareness (henceforth, PA) also allows children to discriminate between similar sounds, such as telling /i/ (*b<u>ea</u>t*) apart from /ɪ/ (*b<u>i</u>t*), for example, as well as to break down sequences of sounds into discrete units (e.g., notice that there are two sounds in /tr/ and one in /tʃ/). Discrete, identified sounds can then be encoded into graphemes in accordance with the language-specific PGCs. Because phonemes are language specific, English-speaking children will develop an awareness of the sound differences that are relevant to English, and Spanish-speaking children will develop an awareness of the differences that are relevant to Spanish. For example, in English, [d] and [ð] correspond to two different phonemes, /d/ and /ð/, respectively; for this reason, English-speaking children become aware of the two sounds as different and are able to clearly distinguish between them. This distinction will be helpful when spelling *<u>d</u>ose* and *<u>th</u>ose*. However, since in Spanish [d] and [ð] are two allophones of the same phoneme—two ways to pronounce /d/—Spanish-speaking children will develop an abstraction of these two sounds and not pay attention to their difference, which will allow them to easily assign the same letter to those two sounds, as in *<u>d</u>os* and *la<u>d</u>o*.

Since PA aligns with both the phonological system of the language itself—independently from writing—and with the orthographic system, one could wonder whether PA is a natural linguistic skill children acquire as part of their language acquisition process, or a literacy skill that must be learned at school. It is a little bit of both. Children initially develop PA implicitly, through natural language acquisition, as a result of hearing words that are distinguished by a single phoneme (Defior 2004; Defior et al. 2015). For example, when small children hear words like *peso* and *beso*, they develop an awareness of /p/ and /b/ as two sounds whose difference is worth noticing and should be conceptualized as separate. For that reason, larger vocabularies in children have been correlated with higher PA. In addition, engaging in certain preliteracy activities in the home, such as rhyming songs and playful tongue twisters, helps to make this implicit knowledge increasingly explicit. Think, for example, of *itsy-bitsy spider*; *she sells seashells*; *a, e, i, o, u el burro sabe más que tú*; or singing the ABCs. Although PA starts as an implicit and intuitive ability that naturally evolves in a rich linguistic environment at home, it is later supported and strengthened at school through literacy practices, which include letter knowledge, learning how to read and write, sorting words by their sounds, reading aloud, and so on. These school literacy practices assist in further developing this conceptualization of sound strings into a series of discrete, distinguishable phonemes.

Therefore, PA and early stages of literacy have a reciprocal influence: PA has a crucial role in the acquisition of reading and writing (Ziegler and Goswami 2005), but literacy also assists in developing PA through awareness of word segmentation, phoneme discrimination, and conceptualization of sounds (Ehri and Wilce 1980; Cataldo and Ellis 1988; Burgess and Lonigan 1998). When children are learning how to read and write, the sight of written words modifies the way they conceptualize the phonological constituents of the spoken words (Ehri 2014). As Olson (1994, 85) puts it, "learning to read is learning to hear speech in a new way." Most adults who learned how to read and spell at an early age have a hard time perceiving sounds in a way that is not mediated by their awareness of phonological units—the phoneme—instead of a purely phonetic perception—the specific allophone of a phoneme—as well as by orthography. Kemp (2016) gives the example of adults' puzzlement when children spell the word *natural* as *nachrel*, a spelling that reveals that the child is paying attention to the aspirated pronunciation of *t* in that word, instead of the abstract concept of /t/. Ehri and Wilce (1980) exemplify the effect of orthographic-mediated perception with the case of adults who believe they hear the *t* in *pitch* but not in *rich*.

The effect of having underdeveloped PA can be seen in both reading and spelling. Low PA is manifested as a difficulty to perceive speech sounds accurately, because phonemes are less securely represented in the perceptual system of the student (Brady 1997; Post, Foorman, and Hiscock 1997; Post et al. 1999). Low or underdeveloped PA may result in the following types of misspellings (Bruck and Treiman 1990; Treiman 1991; Jiménez González and Jiménez Rodríguez 1999; Leal, Matute, and Zarabozo 2005; Llombart-Huesca 2019; Zhang et al. 2021):

1. Misspellings that are more closely related to a purely phonetic perception of sounds than to a phonological one; for example, writing *nachrel* for *natural*, in English

2. Substitution of one grapheme for another that represents a similar sound; for example, writing *rebtil* for *reptil* (Zhang et al. 2021), or *monito* for *bonito*, in Spanish
3. Simplification of diphthongs or consonant clusters; for example, writing *nive* for *nieve*, in Spanish (Leal, Matute, and Zarabozo 2005)

Several studies have shown that PA develops quickly once literacy instruction begins, especially in languages with transparent orthographies such as Spanish (Mann and Wimmer 2002; Anthony and Francis 2005). For that reason, the probability of finding spelling errors due to low PA in Spanish decreases after just one year, especially those involving vowels. Justicia et al. (1999) and Borzone de Manrique and Signorini (1994, 1998), in studies with monolingual children schooled in Spanish, observed that Spanish vowel errors are unlikely to occur once students develop PA and move beyond the initial stages of spelling.

The need to develop PA in the classroom as a separate activity from learning how to read and write has been a subject of debate, but it is agreed that this need is variable and affected by different factors, such as the child's sociocultural environment and the language. With respect to the first factor, although many children arrive at school with well-developed PA skills and ready to learn how to read and write, children who grow up in conditions of poverty and restricted access to rich preliteracy environments seem to benefit from early literacy practices that promote the development of PA in the school setting, which has the potential to close the gap in literacy achievement (Lonigan 2007; Phillips, Menchetti, and Lonigan 2008).

With respect to language, because of the relative transparency and simplicity of the Spanish orthographic system, it seems that PA instruction is less crucial in the development of literacy in Spanish than it is in English (Borzone de Manrique and Signorini 1994; Vernon and Ferreiro 1999; Zamudio Mesa 2008). The most frequent syllables in Spanish simply consist of one consonant followed by one vowel; therefore, phonemes "are ready to be discovered as letters are learned" (Ziegler and Goswami 2005). In addition, names of letters themselves are very common syllables found in Spanish words. For example:

Letter *a*: a-trás, te-a-tro
Letter *be*: be-so, ca-be-za
Letter *ce*: ce-na, ma-ce-ta

Goldenberg and colleagues (2014) conducted an interesting study comparing literacy and PA skills in Spanish in three groups of Spanish-speaking students: Mexican school students learning to read in Spanish, students in the United

States in a bilingual program (learning to read in Spanish), and students in the United States in an English immersion program (learning to read in English). Because US schools place greater emphasis on the development of PA than schools in Mexico do, both groups of students instructed in the United States showed higher PA skills in Spanish in first grade than did children in the Mexican schools. Even those who were learning to read in English! What is interesting here, however, is that within two years Mexican children caught up with or even surpassed US children in reading skills, though remaining behind the US children in PA. Therefore, it seems that PA training prior to literacy might not be necessary in Spanish, since the activities involved in learning to read and write in this language seem to be sufficient. However, as the authors warn, it is possible that children in a US school context—even in a dual immersion program—are in disadvantage with respect to Mexican children because of the lower amount of Spanish input they receive in a bilingual context, which will be reduced even further when moving into an exclusive English literacy environment. For that reason, these students might benefit from receiving an explicit focus on PA to compensate for the reduced input. In chapter 4 we will examine some misspellings in SHLLs' writings that are likely to be due to difficulties in PA, and in chapter 6, we will see some activities aimed at strengthening PA in SHLLs in the areas in which they are most likely to need it.

Spelling and Morphological Awareness

Successful spelling and reading development are also connected to another component of metalinguistic awareness: morphological awareness (Titos et al. 2003). The term "morphological awareness" refers to speakers' sensitivity to the morphological structure of words and their ability to think and talk about that structure (Carlisle 1995; Kuo and Anderson 2006). Morphological awareness (henceforth, MA) should not be understood as the application of declarative knowledge about morphemes. Instead, it is an intuitive and insightful introspection into the word (Masny 1987; Ravid and Gillis 2002; Ravid and Tolchinsky 2002; Kuo and Anderson 2006; Dillon 2009). To demonstrate MA, a child does not need to be able to divide words into roots and affixes, or state the part of speech of a word, but simply have an intuition that the two words in pairs such as *imagine-imagination* or *flor-florero* are related, while *verde* and *verdad* are not, or that while *singer* contains a "smaller word" (*sing*), *finger* does not. Likewise, MA will allow us to have the intuition that *mirar* and *mirada* are related, whereas *mirar* and *ver* are not, despite the meaning connection.

MA is an important contributor to the development of good reading and spelling skills (Carlisle 1995, 2000; Champion 1997; Defior and Alegría 2005; Nagy, Berninger, and Abbott 2006; Defior et al. 2008; Kirby et al. 2012). Typically, less-skilled readers and writers have more difficulties in naturally noticing spelling patterns that are related to the morphological structure of words (Elbro and Arnbak 1996; Nunes, Bryant, and Bindman 1997).

Let us see an example of how MA helps writers to spell more accurately. Children might produce and use the following words correctly in oral conversation as a result of natural language acquisition: *libros*, *casas*, *vez*, and *lunes*. However, a certain degree of MA will allow these children to recognize that *libros* and *casas* pattern together and separately from *vez* and *lunes* and that they are the plural form (i.e., express "more than one") of *libro* and *casa*. This sensitivity or awareness will make it easier for children to spell the final /s/ of *libros* and *casas* more accurately and consistently than the final /s/ in *lunes* and *vez*. Similarly, Defior and colleagues (2008) observed in Spanish children in Andalusia, a Spanish region where the final *-s* in words is typically not pronounced, that children grades 1 through 3 were more likely to write the word-final *-s* when it was a morpheme (in plural nouns/adjectives or in second-person singular verbs) than when it was part of the root. This was observed only in low-frequency words, when children could not simply rely on memory and had to resort to their sensitivity to the morphological structure of the words.

MA also has an effect on reading fluency and reading comprehension. In English, it is easier to read made-up words as *debrification* and *impraginize* than the made-up words *taginilegafe* or *lipegatineck*, because we recognize the affixes *de-*, *-ic-*, *-tion*, *im-*, and *-ize*. Similarly, in Spanish, the made-up words *pelifeador* and *impabrigante* are easier and quicker to read than *lofimentope* and *lapigamine*, because they include real affixes (*-dor*, *im-*, *-ante*). Not only are the words with real morphemes easier to read but also easier to "understand." While knowing that those are not real words, we can guess that *debrification* is some sort of process and that *impraginize* is an action, as we imagine that *pelifeador* and *impabrigante* are probably people who do something. Most relevant, the effect is also seen in real word reading. Readers recognize words with high-frequency suffixes more quickly than words with low-frequency suffixes, both in English (Baayen, Wurm, and Aycock 2007) and in Spanish (Lázaro 2012). Words with large morphological families are also recognized more quickly than words with smaller morphological families (Schreuder and Baayen 1997).

MA is developed through literacy activities, because extensive reading, writing, and exposure to a rich vocabulary allow children to develop an awareness of repeated orthographic patterns that are associated to a meaning—that is, morphemes (Mahony, Singson, and Mann 2000; Verhoeven and Perfetti 2011). For example, an avid reader will be more likely to have encountered many words that contain the suffix *-eza* (*belleza*, *tristeza*, *aspereza*, etc.) and, therefore, to have an intuition about the meaning and the spelling of words with that morpheme: they refer to qualities, and they are spelled with *-z*. While some children will develop MA naturally through extensive reading and writing, other children might require more targeted instruction. A study on morphological interventions in English found that although morphological instruction did not have a noticeable effect on reading comprehension or reading fluency, it produced positive effects for phonological awareness and decoding skills, vocabulary, and spelling (Goodwin and Ahn 2013). Some intervention studies (Arnbak and Elbro 2000; Nunes, Bryant, and Olsson 2003; Kirk and Gillon 2009) have shown that training in segmenting words into morphemes results in spelling accuracy improvement. Other studies, such as that of Bowers and Kirby (2010), found that training focusing on connecting morphologically related words results in an increase in vocabulary.

The contribution of MA to reading and spelling is particularly significant during the middle school years (Carlisle 1995, 2000; Deacon and Kirby 2004), for two main reasons: at that time, students have abandoned decoding strategies (sounding words out), and in those years their vocabulary increases enormously through classwork content—lessons on math, social studies, and other subjects. However, some studies have shown that students are sensitive to Spanish suffixes in as early as second grade (Lázaro et al. 2017). Some theories have proposed that both skills (PA and MA) are at play simultaneously from an early age and that young children use their sensitivity to the morphological structure of words to make spelling decisions. For example, children as young as six are more likely to spell *rock* correctly in *rocking* and *rocky* than in the non-morphologically-related word *rocket* (Deacon and Bryant 2006). Regardless of the exact age when MA starts to have an effect on spelling, there seems to be a consensus that this effect increases with age. It has also been observed that MA also has a facilitative effect in reading and writing in adults with low literacy skills (Tighe and Binder 2015). In chapter 6 we will see some activities that allow students to improve their spelling—together with reading accuracy and vocabulary—by strengthening their MA.

The Orthographic Code: What Rules Are More Difficult to Learn?

Not all PGCs are equal, and children internalize them at a different pace in a hierarchical, developmental progression. Phoneme-grapheme correspondences can be divided into two main types: consistent PGCs and inconsistent PGCs. Consistent PGCs are subject to a rule. This rule can be context-independent or context-dependent. Context-independent consistent PGCs are simple correspondences, in which one phoneme is always represented by the same grapheme, independently of the context. For example, in Spanish, the phoneme /l/ is always represented by the letter *l*, independently of the sound that precedes it or follows it. In context-dependent consistent PGCs, one phoneme may be represented by two or more graphemes, depending on the context of the phoneme within the word. For example, in Spanish, the sound /k/ is represented by *c* when it precedes *a, o, u* and by *qu* when it precedes *e, i*. In these cases, writers can successfully and consistently write a word by applying this contextual rule, even if they have never seen the word before. On the other hand, inconsistent PGCs are those in which a phoneme is represented by two or more graphemes but there is no rule to inform the choice and the writer just needs to learn the spelling of the word. For example, *b* and *v* are used to represent /b/, and we find these graphemes in the same context of a word, as in before any vowel. Inconsistent PGCs are assumed to have a dominant grapheme, which is the most frequent grapheme associated with that phoneme. Spelling proficiency in consistent PGCs are likely indicators of the development of phonological codification processes, whereas inconsistent PGCs require the use of lexical knowledge—that is, the visual knowledge of the written word (Alegría and Mousty 1994).

It is not surprising that context-independent consistent PGCs, that is, simple PGCs, are the first ones acquired by children. The answer is not as clear when we compare the degree of difficulty between context-dependent consistent PGCs and inconsistent PGCs, and it seems that it depends on the language. In transparent (shallow) orthographies, such as Spanish, context-dependent consistent PGCs are acquired first, as observed in elementary school children in Uruguay (Carbonell de Grompone et al. 1980) and Spain (Defior, Martos, and Herrera 2000; Defior, Jiménez-Fernández, and Serrano 2009). However, in opaque (deep) orthographies, such as French, in earlier stages of spelling development, children perform their best when spelling words with inconsistent PGCs in their dominant letter, compared to spelling words with consistent spellings that are context-dependent (Alegría and Mousty 1994; Martinet, Valdois, and Fayol 2004). This result suggests that in such languages, "children start with a simplified set of rules, probably acquired through classroom instructions and sufficiently powerful to allow autonomous reading and spelling" (Alegría and Mousty 1996, 332). These simplified rules include one-to-one correspondences and dominant graphemes for inconsistent PGCs, which are typically the first ones that teachers present in the classroom. The contrast between children's performance with different types of PGCs in shallow orthographies versus deep orthographies is further confirmed by Carrillo, Alegría, and Marín (2013), who compared children's performance in inconsistent PGCs in their nondominant grapheme with their performance in context-dependent consistent PGCs. Whereas children learning Spanish spelling were more accurate in words with context-dependent consistent rules, children learning French spelling made fewer errors in inconsistent PGCs in their nondominant grapheme.

In the context of English-Spanish bilingual children, two studies conducted with children in dual language, transitional bilingual, or Spanish immersion programs in the United States found that these children were less accurate with words that have context-dependent PGC rules than with words with inconsistent PGCs (Arteagoitia et al. 2005; Ford, Invernizzi, and Huang 2018); that is, they followed the pattern observed in French.

Engraving Words in Our Minds

Every time children write or read a word, the image of that written word gets increasingly engraved in their minds, and through intensive and extensive exposure to written words, they develop a mental lexicon comprised of images of those words (Morton 1980; Valle-Arroyo 1989; Defior, Justicia, and Martos 1996). These visual representations of written words stored in our minds allow us to read and write with accuracy, fluency, and ease (Glushko 1979; Ehri 1980; Coltheart et al. 1993). Adult writers do not typically read and write by "sounding out" words, as children do when they start reading and writing their first words. This would be a very slow process that would not allow us to read and write long and complex texts. In addition, it would not produce very accurate results, due to the many complex PGCs and inconsistencies. Even in cases when applying a rule would achieve the correct spelling, as in /k/ → *c* (*a*, *o*, *u*) and *qu* (*e*, *i*), having to retrieve the rule would certainly slow down the reader/writer. Therefore, adult writers spell by using a lexical mode, that is, by matching what they are writing with the mental image of the written word. This "matching" produces the well-known feeling that a word "looks right." This visual matching is also behind the bad feeling a misspelled word produces in many people—like *wen yoo reed* this.

Similarly, when adults read, they do not need to decode each letter into its sound. Rather, they identify the whole word by matching it with the stored image of that word. For adults, reading words is more about "saying" the words that we "see." However, when readers encounter an infrequent or an unknown word, this recognition strategy is not available, and they need to resort to a phonological strategy (Meyer, Schvaneveldt, and Ruddy 1974; Morton and Patterson 1980; Coltheart et al. 1993; Besner 1999). In those cases, the effect of poor phonological awareness can be more easily observed, because readers cannot decode the word correctly and they stumble through it, mispronounce it, say a similar one, or simply skip it altogether. The visual mental lexicon explains why real (known) words can be read more quickly than pseudowords. (If you flash a long word for half a second on a screen, the audience will most likely be able to read it. Follow it by a made-up word of the same length for the same amount of time, and they will not. In the first case, readers were merely identifying and "saying" the word, while in the second case, they were forced to decode it, and that requires extra time.)

The facilitative effect on reading and writing of accessing the images of written words stored in our minds is more obvious in languages with an opaque orthography. For example, in English, children are introduced to "sight words" (words like *one, they, here*) right from the beginning, since decoding these words would be an unrewarding task. But the effect also applies to languages with a transparent orthography in which words could be read accurately by phonological decoding, such as Italian and Spanish (Barry and De Bastiani 1997). Visualization of written words not only helps children to spell words with no spelling rule, such as spelling *hombre* with *h*. Based on a study involving French, a language with an opaque orthography, Alegría and Mousty (1994, 1996) suggest that the development of a visual memory of written words also facilitates spelling by helping automatize the application of spelling rules. Therefore, it is extremely important to encode a vast number of written words into our mental visual lexicon (Ehri and Rosenthal 2007). For example, reading many words spelled with *que* and *qui* could help not only to remember the spelling of those specific words but also to automatize the /k/ → *qu, c* rule.

How are the images of words strongly engraved—encoded—in our minds? According to Share's "Self-Teach" hypothesis, it is fundamental to go through a successful decoding stage in which accurate orthographic representations are acquired (Share 1995, 2004). A key element is the need to do a thorough letter-by-letter decoding of the word. According to Share (1995, 1999), visual exposure is not enough; there needs to be reading aloud. It is what children say, and not only what they see, that leads to successful orthographic learning. In addition, the first exposures to the new (or unfamiliar) word have the strongest effect in engraving the visual representation of the word in the reader's mind, and a "decoding (or spelling) error on the very first attempt at a new word should be more detrimental to long-term orthographic learning than should an error committed at a later point" (Share 2004, 278).

Do High School Students Learn Spelling in the Same Way as Primary School Children?

Spelling is acquired and developed through a combination of the naturally developing cognitive skills presented in the preceding discussion and pedagogical interventions that in a more or less direct manner tap into these skills at the school grade and child's age in which the contribution of these skills has greater potential. Therefore, when looking at the spelling and reading development of SHLLs, we need to consider the possible effect of age, since SHLLs typically do not start taking Spanish courses until high school, or even college, and might miss the natural progression of these cognitive skills.

While the cognitive-linguistic skills behind the acquisition and development of spelling are the same for children and adults, there are differences in the approaches and compensatory strategies employed in reading and in making spelling decisions by these two groups of learners. Greenberg, Ehri, and Perin (2002) observed that adults and children behave differently when they encounter difficulties in reading a word by sight—either because they do not know the word or because they cannot identify it. In those cases, children are more likely than adults to deploy their phonological decoding strategies to overcome these difficulties, while adults tend to get stuck in trying to identify that word using their visual memory. As a result, they might mispronounce the word, say a similar one, and even skip it altogether.

Similarly, in writing, when in a dictation activity adults need to write a word they do not know, they are less likely to resort to encoding the word by going over each sound-letter correspondence. In my Spanish for Spanish Speakers class, I have often observed that when dealing with pseudowords (made-up words that sound like they could be actual Spanish words) in spelling and reading activities, some students write or read a real word that is similar to the pseudoword used, despite the fact that students had been told those were words I had invented and that they do not exist. The search for a real word to substitute a pseudoword (or an unknown word) is consistent with a tendency for students with underdeveloped metalinguistic skills to focus on meaning and lexical elements over formal aspects of language. Focusing attention on meaning is the default linguistic strategy of speakers (Cazden 1974; Hakes 1980) because language is primarily used to convey meaning. In sum, phonological decoding/encoding is a difficult strategy for low-literacy adults for two reasons: first, because it goes against the natural tendency of adults for whole-word strategies and, also, because it requires keeping attention away from meaning, which is the natural focus of attention for students with weak metalinguistic skills.

In addition to differences in the cognitive strategies deployed by young children and adults, some affective elements seem to be at play. When comparing children and low-literacy adults with a similar reading level as those children, Greenberg, Ehri, and Perin (2002) noticed that all children completed all the tasks (with or without errors), while many adults left words blank, which might be the result of embarrassment and fear of making mistakes.

In fact, a related nonlinguistic or cognitive individual factor that has an effect on literacy development is that of academic self-concept, which encompasses "the perceptions, knowledge, views, and beliefs that individuals hold about themselves as learners" (Chapman and Tunmer 2003, 7). Academic self-concept has been shown to influence students' academic performance. Students who believe they have the ability to accomplish an academic task are more likely to persevere and overcome learning challenges, which allows them to perform better, while those who have low self-concept tend to avoid tasks that they consider too difficult, which does not allow them to become more proficient (Pajares 2003). The relationship between self-concept and achievement is a reciprocal one. While self-concept contributes to performance, achieving high levels of performance also contributes to developing a positive self-concept (Hamachek 1995).

Beaudrie (2018) conducted the first study that investigates the impact of self-concept on the literacy performance in SHLLs. This author found that self-perceptions of spelling were associated not only with spelling scores but also with writing scores. This association was not found in reading, however, where students felt the most competent, in a way that did not match their actual level of performance.

Does Being Bilingual Help or Hinder SHLLS' Spelling?

Finally, we cannot forget that the population under discussion is bilingual in Spanish and English and that, typically, SHLLs have developed their literacy skills in English before they started developing their literacy skills in Spanish in middle or high school. Bilingual and monolingual children differ in terms of access to written language in these two ways:

1. Differences in their linguistic knowledge prior to learning how to read and write. Successful reading and writing are greatly influenced by vocabulary (Adams 1990; Dale, Crain-Thoreson, and Robinson 1995). Since bilingual children typically have smaller vocabularies in each language than monolingual children do, they have a potential disadvantage when learning how to read.
2. Possible cross-linguistic transfer of skills (Laurent and Martinot 2010). Since some literacy skills and strategies are universal, once they are acquired in one language, they will transfer to the other languages of the learner without the need for instruction specifically targeting those languages (Durgunoğlu 2002). Phonological awareness is one such transferable skill, and bilingual children appear to have superior PA in early stages of literacy development in comparison to monolingual children (Campbell and Sais 1995; Gottardo et al. 2001; Durgunoğlu 2002). Earlier in this chapter, we saw an example of this transfer mentioned in Goldenberg et al.'s (2014) study, which showed that Spanish-English bilingual children in the United States who had received PA instruction *only in English* had higher levels of PA *in Spanish* than did children in Mexico, where little emphasis on PA is given. However, this bilingual superiority must be qualified, as it is affected by several factors:

a. Age of bilingual exposure: A study found that Spanish/English bilinguals exposed to their second language before the age of three outperformed those exposed to it at the age of three to six years (Kovelman, Baker, and Petitto 2008).
b. Language proficiency: The effect of bilingualism on PA also seems to require a threshold proficiency level in each of the two languages, below which no advantage (or only a moderate advantage) is observed (Cummins 1979; Bialystok, Luk, and Kwan 2005; Chen et al. 2008).
c. Literacy: The bilingual advantage disappears when formal teaching appears, probably because teaching provides "an equalizing experience for all the children, removing any initial advantage that the bilinguals might have demonstrated" (Bialystok 2002, 187).
d. Limitations of phonological awareness: The advantage of bilinguals' superior PA is also limited by the limitations of PA itself. PA is not the only thing that counts in literacy. One example of the limitations of the advantage of PA transfer in bilinguals can be seen in Goldenberg et al.'s (2014) aforementioned study. Although US bilingual children showed greater PA in Spanish than Mexican monolingual children did, within two years Mexican children caught up with or surpassed US children in reading skills while still remaining behind the US children in PA.

Morphological awareness has also been found to be a language-general skill that transfers across languages in bilingual speakers. A study conducted with college-age SHLLs showed a strong correlation between the results obtained in an MA task in English and those obtained in the same task in Spanish (Llombart-Huesca 2017a). In addition, MA developed in one language not only enhances literacy development in that language but its contributions transfer to literacy in the other language as well (Wang, Cheng, and Chen 2006; Deacon, Wade-Woolley, and Kirby 2007; Ramírez et al. 2010).

While phonological and morphological awareness skills seem to be universal and their benefits transfer across languages, the orthographic patterns are specific to each language. Therefore, using the spelling patterns of one language when writing in the other language is likely to produce errors. Indeed, the few studies that have examined the English spelling development of elementary school students who are bilingual in Spanish and English and had learned to read initially in Spanish indicate that there is an influence of Spanish on English spelling (Fashola et al. 1996; Zutell and Allen 1988). Durgunoğlu, Mir, and Ariño-Martí (2002) give these examples: **rid* (*read*), **nid* (*need*), **favret* (*favorite*),

thet* (*that*), **stor* (*store*).[1] Negative spelling transfer also occurs in the other direction, such as in using English consonant clusters when spelling Spanish words (scuela* for *escuela*, **spero* for *espero*) and English consonant doubling (**differente* for *diferente*). (We will take a closer look at these types of misspellings in chapter 4.)

However, these results have been obtained in studies that specifically look for errors. If we look at the overall students' spelling proficiency and not only at their errors, we see that knowledge of English spelling is also beneficial in cognate pairs that share the same letter. More specifically, students are more accurate in writing *s* or *c* in Spanish in cognate words, such as *cerámica, policía, situar*, than in noncognate words, such as *calcetín, ciruela, semana* (Llombart-Huesca and Zyzik 2019, Llombart-Huesca 2022). In more general terms, we should not lose sight of everything that goes right thanks to transferring spelling patterns from one language to another. First, we need to appreciate the fact that someone who starts writing later in life in a language they speak when they already write in another language does not need to start at the beginning. As many errors as SHLLs might produce when writing their first Spanish sentence in high school, these students are not illiterate. Not only do they already have the understanding that letters are used to represent sounds, and have developed an awareness of words—as to not represent many words in one entire string—many sounds are represented with the same graphemes in the two languages. It is easy to take for granted the commonalities between languages and focus only on the errors, but we should also value and appreciate the bulk of spelling development that was already conducted in the other language.

Reflection Questions

1. Phonological awareness allows us to distinguish between very similar sounds. Match the Spanish sounds in sets A and B based on their similarity—and the likeliness that they could be confused with one another. A sound from set A may be matched with more than one sound in set B. (The sounds are expressed in letters, with their phonetic symbol in parentheses.)

Set A	Set B
b ([b])	i ([i])
ñ ([ɲ]	m ([m])
e ([e])	ch ([tʃ])
d ([d])	p ([p])
u ([u])	t ([t])
	o ([o])
	ni ([ni])

2. Think of nursery rhymes you know in English and/or Spanish. What individual sounds or syllables do they seem to encourage children to pay attention to? Now, are these nursery rhymes in Spanish translated versions of the English ones? Do you think the rhymes or sound patterns are lost in the translation?

3. Read the following pseudowords aloud. Read them as if they were in Spanish.

   deteí puigado biugado graupar pruetilación colifiando
   colifeando polefeación leteriedo pentenimiento

   How did you feel while you were reading them? Was it difficult? Was it more difficult (or at least less easy) than reading words like *releí, cuidado, ciudadano, caudal, cruelmente,* and *cotilleando*? If reading the pseudowords was more difficult or slow, that's normal! This is because you could not simply recognize them and "say" them; you had to decode them and sound them out letter by letter.

4. Dictate the pseudowords from the previous activity to a person who has not seen them and ask that person to write them down. (This person should know Spanish.) Look at their spelling errors and see if you can find some pattern and understand the cause of the error. For example, were there more errors in diphthongs? If so, what were those errors? Inversion of the two vowels (as in writing *piugado* for *puigado*)? Shortening—eliminating one of the two vowels (as in writing *pugado* for *piugado*)? Were there errors consisting of writing one letter for another that sounds very similar (as in writing *b* for *p*)? This is just a first look at possible errors that happen due to difficulties with phonological awareness. In the next chapters we will take a more systematic look at the different types of misspellings.

5. Let us now look at morphological awareness. First, match the given word with the word of the three-word series that would be more conducive to noticing a spelling pattern. Then, indicate the morpheme that is shared between the given word and the word you selected from the three-word series.

   Example: hacer: deshacemos, realizar, fabricar → deshacemos; hac-
   a. ves: vez, mirar, hablas
   b. cocer: cocina, coser, hervir
   c. belleza: bonito, elegancia, tristeza
   d. educación: misión, comunicación, docencia
   e. enrojecer: rojizo, ruborizar, amarillear

f. pescar: pez, pescado, pesar
g. cantaba: miraban, contar, cantidad

6. For each of the following made-up words, indicate which ones contain real morphemes. For those, write real words that include these morphemes. The first set is in English, and the second one is in Spanish.

   Example:
   praginize: → *-ize*: *terrorize, realize, personalize*
   lipegatinock→ No real morphemes

   English pseudowords:
   a. sutiness ______
   b. frimelify ______
   c. sythlation ______
   d. pirpiligute ______
   e. brimable ______

   Spanish pseudowords:
   a. pindez ______
   b. labiridad ______
   c. luptade ______
   d. pondini ______
   e. abregancia ______

7. Test your visual memory!
   Step 1: Find a partner to help do this activity.
   Step 2: Take twenty to thirty seconds (approximately) to read the following pseudowords. Then, stop looking at them.

   labizunda dustiagán hisullo layesando
   pacelluco iceyano lavicudo

   Step 3: Ask your partner to read them to you while you write them down.
   Step 4. Review and notice any errors. If you made any errors, they were probably on

   - *b/v*: *labizunda, lavicudo*. Did you misspell *b* or *v* in these words? The appearance of *b* and *v* in the sequence *la_i* was done on purpose, to confuse you. But real words can also be confusing, like when we find *lavar* and *laboratorio*, *maya* and *malla*, *casa* and *caza*.

- *h*: *hisullo, iceyano*: Did you write *isullo, hiceyano?*
- *s/c/z*: *labizunda, hisullo, layesando, pacelluco, iceyano.* Did you write *labisunda? hizullo? layezando? paselluco? iseyano?*
- *ll/y*: *hisullo, layesando, pacelluco, iceyano.* Did you write *hisuyo? lallesando? paceyuco? icellano?*

Those graphemes are not subject to any contextual rule, as we will see in more detail in the next chapter. Therefore, "knowing a rule" will not help. Phonological awareness would not help either, because those misspelled words are pronounced the same as the original ones (*hisullo, hisuyo, isullo,* and *isuyo* sound the same in most Spanish language varieties).[2] Morphological awareness would not help either, because these pseudowords are not related to any words we know. The only way we can know whether we should write *s* or *z*, *y* or *ll* is to visually remember those words with the right spelling. Misspelled words **labar, *isimos,* or **yubia* (instead of *lavar, hicimos, lluvia*) look bad (or hurt our eyes) because we have seen and written them many times throughout our lives and they are strongly engraved in our minds, while we cannot have this effect with the pseudowords that we have seen only thirty seconds of our life. Also, you will probably find it more difficult if you try the exercise one more time, because now you have seen the misspelled words you wrote and the ones I suggested as possible misspellings. If all those alternative spellings are dancing in your mind and there is not one word that looks or feels right, you will be closer to understanding the experience of adults/young adults learning how to spell words that they have not been reading and writing since childhood. For SHLLs, many words are as loosely engraved in their minds as those made-up words are in ours now. Add to this the fact that they have probably misspelled them before, and the image of those misspelled words has entered their minds.

8. Reflect on the effects of a mental visual lexicon on your own reading and writing practice. When you write, how often do you think of a spelling rule to decide what letter to write? When you doubt how to spell a word, do you find yourself writing it in different ways to decide which one "looks" better? Do words with spelling errors pop up over other words at a first glance? Do you notice the same effect in Spanish and English?

Notes

1. The use of * before a word indicates the word is misspelled.
2. In the next chapter we will discuss different pronunciations in different language varieties and the effect they may have on learning the spelling of certain PGCs.

THREE

The Spanish Spelling System

From Speaking to Writing

It is well accepted that being able to speak Spanish fluently and accurately is not enough to teach students how to speak Spanish. Spanish teachers need to have an explicit knowledge of Spanish grammar and to know things such as how to place verb forms in a larger system of tense, aspect, and mood, or quickly classify pronouns into matrices of functions and persons. Teachers also know that this explicit knowledge they have about Spanish grammar is not necessarily what they will teach to students but the basis to understanding their students' development of accurate and fluent expression, as well as to creating activities that target different grammar elements and proficiency skills.

My contention is that a similar explicit understanding of the orthographic system needs to be developed for teaching spelling successfully. Many Spanish teachers can spell accurately and with ease because they have been reading and writing for many years. This chapter offers a description of the Spanish orthographic system to gain an explicit understanding of its different phoneme-grapheme correspondences (PGCs), as well as of the way spelling interacts with the two linguistic components we looked at in the previous chapter: phonology and morphology. This description also considers the relationship between spelling and language variation, both geographical and social (language varieties) and historical (etymology). However, as it happens with grammar, this explicit knowledge about the spelling system is not necessarily what should be taught to students. After all, as we saw in the previous chapter, knowing the orthographic code is only one aspect of spelling development. Therefore, the description offered in this chapter is meant as a presentation of the underpinnings of the Spanish orthographic system, which will serve as the basis to understanding students' production and development of Spanish spelling (chapter 4), as well as the basis to creating activities that target different spelling rules (chapter 6).

Orthography is a system that assigns a graphic/visual representation of oral speech. Therefore, oral language is first, and writing is second. Literate adults often conceive words as written words, which are pronounced in a certain way. However, it would be more accurate to conceive words as oral words (the way we say them), which are spelled in a certain way. In fact, languages were first oral languages before systems were created to represent them in writing, and there are languages for which no writing system has been created. While this difference does not seem to be essential to consider in our daily lives, we need to keep it in mind when we think of the learners who are developing their spelling skills or the learner who is doubting the correct way to spell a word. Typically, children speak for four to six years before they start writing or reading. For them, language is only oral, and words are only spoken words. When they receive literacy instruction—that is, when they learn how to recognize some letters, start sounding out some written words, write their first letters and words, and so forth—they reproduce the natural relationship between oral language and written language: written language aims to represent oral language, not the other way around.

The oral-to-written direction of literacy is also important for understanding language variation and the effect it has on the process of learning how to spell. Although Spanish spelling is the same for all language varieties,[1] Spanish

Some Examples of Writing Systems

Ideographic

Chinese characters: 光 = light; 书 = book.

Phonographic

Japanese Syllabary: てりやき (*teriyaki*), where て = te, り = ri, や = ya, き = ki.

Cyrillic alphabet (in Russian)

абвгдежзийклмно. . . .; for example, "Дом" (*house*), pronounced /dom/.

Greek alphabet

αβγδεζηθικλμνξοπ. . . .; for example, κόρη (*daughter*), pronounced /kori/.

Latin alphabet

abcdefghijklmnopqrstuvwxyz.

pronunciation is not the same. Therefore, spelling offers different challenges to different speakers. And this is not only true for those well-known cases of dialectal variation, such as "yeísmo" (pronouncing *y* and *ll* with the same sound) or "seseo" (pronouncing *c, s, z* as /s/), but also other cases of language variation that include stigmatized varieties, as well as for relaxed and spontaneous pronunciations.

In the remainder of this chapter, I present the different types of spelling rules we find in Spanish, first examining vowels and then consonants. The chapter continues with two specific sounds in Spanish that present a certain degree of complexity in terms of spelling and ends with an examination of silent letters, beyond *h*. Because the use of stress marks has been found to be the most difficult aspect of the Spanish spelling system, it is discussed separately, in chapter 5.

Different Types of Spelling Rules in Spanish

As just noted, languages are naturally oral, spoken languages.[2] Humans have devised ways to transfer these spoken words into graphic representations, that is, writing. Writing takes two basic forms: ideographic and phonographic. In an ideographic system, symbols directly express the meanings conveyed by the spoken sounds. Examples of ideographic systems are Aztec pictograms, Egyptian hieroglyphs, or Chinese writing systems. In phonographic systems, symbols represent sounds that by themselves do not have meaning. These may be individual sounds or syllables. Examples of languages that use symbols to represent entire syllables are Japanese and Cherokee. Alphabets are systems that use symbols (letters or graphemes) to represent individual sounds (phonemes). The alphabet used in English and Spanish is the Roman (or Latin) alphabet, but there are other alphabets, such as Cyrillic and Greek. Within a given alphabet, languages have their own orthography with their own PGCs. For example, the phoneme /f/ is always represented by the letter *f* in Spanish (e.g., *forma, farmacia, pilaf*), whereas English has three different graphemes to represent it: *f, ph*, or *gh* (e.g., *form, pharmacy, laugh*).[3]

As discussed in chapter 2, Spanish is considered to have a shallow orthography because the relationship between graphemes and phonemes is relatively transparent, that is, in most cases, each phoneme is represented by only one grapheme. In contrast, English (like French or Swedish) is said to have a deep orthography, because in many instances several graphemes are used to represent the same phoneme, which makes the PGCs fairly opaque.

In Spanish, when it comes to reading, there is a complete one-to-one correspondence between phonemes and graphemes. Therefore, a given word or a given sequence of letters can only be read one way (according to the speaker's specific language variety, of course). That means that when we encounter a Spanish word, we know how to read it, even if we have never seen or heard the word before—as long as we know the Spanish PGCs, that is. However, when it comes to writing, Spanish has a few complex PGCs, in which two or more graphemes are used to represent one phoneme.

As it was introduced in the previous chapter, we can divide Spanish PGCs into two main types: consistent PGCs and inconsistent PGCs. Consistent PGCs may be context independent, that is, simple correspondences, where one phoneme is always represented by one grapheme, independently of the context. In context-dependent consistent PGCs, one phoneme may be represented by two or more graphemes, depending on the context of the sound within the word. Inconsistent PGCs are those in which a phoneme may be represented by two or more graphemes but there is no contextual rule to inform the choice. The most salient cases are those of homophones—pairs of words that sound the same but are written differently, such as *rallar/rayar, casa/caza, ves/vez, hola/ola.*[4] But inconsistent PGCs are also found in words that do not have homophones. For example, there is nothing in *pollo* or *calle* that allows us to know that we need to write *ll* instead of *y*, and there is nothing in *mayo* or *ayer* that tells us we need to write *y*, because both *ll* and *y* can appear before any vowel.

Spanish Vowels and Diphthongs

In Spanish there are only five vocalic phonemes, and they are all in consistent PGCs: four of them are simple (context-independent) and one of them is context-dependent:

Simple (context-independent) PGCs

/a/ → *a* *casa, amigo, hola*

/e/ → *e* *ele, elefante, coche*

/o/ → *o* *ola, copa, mano*

/u/ → *u* *una, jugo, tribu*

Complex (context-dependent) PGC

/i/ → *y*, in word-final diphthong: *maguey, ley, soy;*
when it is the conjunction *y;*
→ *i*, in all other contexts:
word-initial: *isla, inútil*
within word: *pino, mirar*
word-final, after a consonant: *casi, así*
word-final, after a vowel, when stressed: *caí, leí, oí*

Contrary to English, vowels do not change their sound when they appear in a diphthong, that is, next to another vowel in the same syllable.[5] Spanish diphthongs result from a combination of an open vowel (*a*, *e*, o) and a closed vowel (*i*, *u*), or two different closed vowels. From these combinations, we obtain fourteen diphthongs, which appear next.

Lowering diphthongs (open + closed)

ai *bailar, caigo, ahijado*
au *aurora, Laura, ahuyentar*
ei *veinte, afeité, rehiciera*
eu *reunión, deuda, rehuyeron*
oi *oigo, coincidir, prohibir*
ou *estadounidense, bou*

Rising diphthongs (closed + open)

ia *viajar, piano, justicia*
ie *pienso, agobies, antihéroe*
io *avión, agobio, semihombre*
ua *cual, persuadir, truhan*
ue *suelo, adueñó, albuhera*
uo *cuota, arduo, buhonero*

Weak diphthongs (closed + closed)

iu *ciudad, viudo, triunfo*
ui *cuidado, Luis, influir*

In rising and lowering diphthongs, the closed vowel is always unstressed; therefore, if in a sequence of an open and a closed vowel, the closed vowel is stressed, as in *María* or *continúo*, these two vowels do not form a diphthong and they belong to two different syllables. The open vowel can be stressed (e.g., *caigo*) or unstressed (e.g., *bailar*). The presence of *h* between the two vowels does not have any effect, since it does not have any sound (e.g., *ahijado*).

The diphthong *ou* is very rare in Spanish because it has not evolved naturally from Latin vowels or diphthongs. It only results from the combination of two words, as in *estado* + *unidense* or in loanwords from other languages, such as *bou*. On the other hand, the diphthongs *ie* and *ue* are very productive in Spanish. They often appear in alternation with *e* and *o*, respectively, in word families with the diphthong appearing in stressed syllables and the monophthong appearing in unstressed syllables. Here we can see this alternation through a few examples, where the stressed syllable is underlined:

cielo celeste, celestial
piedra pedregal, pedrada

sierra	serrar, serrano, serranía
fuera	forastero, forajido
cuello	collar, collarín, colleja
cuerpo	corporal, corpulento, corpachón

The cases where this alternation is most obvious, perhaps, are in what are typically known as "stem-changing verbs." In these verbs the diphthong appears in all the forms where that syllable is stressed, and the monophthong appears in the nonstressed forms, as in these examples:

quiero, quieren, quieran	querer, querido, querés
siento, siente, sientan	sentir, sentís, sentimos
puedo, pueden, puedan	poder, podido, podés
cuento, cuentas, cuenten	contar, contás, contamos

When the two consecutive vowels within a word are open vowels or two equal closed vowels, we do not have a diphthong but a hiatus; that is, each vowel is in a separate syllable:

aa: *contraataque, azahar*
ae: *trae, caer, portahelicópteros*
ao: *bacalao, maorí, ahora*
ea: *marear, pasea, quehacer*
ee: *leemos, paseé, dehesa*
eo: *mareo, peor, rehogar*
oa: *canoa, cloaca, almohada*
oe: *héroe, poema, cohesión*
oo: *zoológico, coordinar, alcohol*
ii: *antiinmigración, chiita, anihilar*
uu: *duunviro, samuhú*

Variation in Vowels and Diphthongs

Although the Spanish vocalic system is relatively simple, especially compared to that in English, the representation of the vowel system offered in the preceding text is somewhat simplified, as there is some dialectal, social, and register variation. Some elements of variation are worth mentioning here, as they may have an impact on spelling:

- The vowels /e/, /i/, /o/, and /u/ get closer to one another in spontaneous speech than in "laboratory speech," "teacher talk," or rehearsed speech, that is, when the speaker makes an effort in pronouncing the words (Harmegnies and Poch-Olivé 1992).

- In many Spanish-speaking countries, speakers reduce /e/ and /o/ in unstressed position, making these vowels much shorter, and in some cases even deleting them.[6]
- In some nonstandard varieties we find both merger and hesitation between unstressed /e/ and /i/ (Penny 2000), in words such as *civil/cevil, morir/murir, lección/licción* (where the first pronunciation is the standard). The nonstandard pronunciation of these words is commonly found in the US Southwest.
- Many speakers pronounce pre-tonic /i/ (i.e., an *i* that appears before the stressed syllable of the word) as /e/ (or /ɪ/, a sound between /i/ and /e/, like the *i* in the English word *pin*); for example, *envitado, enteresante, enteligente.*
- Many speakers pronounce the hiatuses *ea, eo, ee,* and *oe* as diphthongs—*ia, io, ie,* and *ue*—especially in unstressed position, for example, *pasiar, pasió, pasié* (for *pasear, paseó, paseé*), *tiatro* (for *teatro*), *pior* (for *peor*), *puesía* (for *poesía*).

This variation has a clear impact on spelling. Although we could describe this situation as "some people pronounce *invitado* as *envitado* and *pasear* as *pasiar*," from the point of view of the student who speaks that variety and is learning how to spell, what is actually happening is that /e/ is sometimes spelled as *e* and sometimes as *i*, and /i/ is sometimes spelled as *e* and sometimes as *i*. Therefore, in those varieties, these vowels are not in simple PGCs but rather in the following complex PGCs:

/e/ → *e*	*ella, elemento*
→ *i*	*inteligente, invitado*
/i/ → *i*	*niño, isla*
→ *y*	*doy, y*
→ *e*	*pasear, mareó*

This variability in *e-i, o-u,* and diphthongs that include these vowels is reflected in *A Dictionary of New Mexico and Southern Colorado Spanish* (Cobos 2003), which includes words such as *envitar, ensistir, entriega, dijir, disierto, disconsuelo, dirigemos, dispensa, dispertar, incontrar, empedido, empertinente, prencipal, prencipio, siñor, sirvir, sofrir,* and *suidá* (standard: *invitar, insistir, entrega, decir, desierto, desconsuelo, dirigimos, despensa, despertar, encontrar, impedido, impertinente, principal, principio, señor, servir, sufrir, ciudad*). In addition, in stories collected in the late 1930s in Colorado and New Mexico (Rael 1939), we find many words that include *e* where the standard word contains *i*, and vice versa: *envitado, incontrar, voltiar, pasiar, dicir, cairía, nochi.*

A Note on Etymology: [e]-[i] and [o]-[u]

Although most literate adults will find the difference between [e]-[i] and between [o]-[u] very clear, the reality is that the two vowels of these two pairs are very close in articulation:

[e] and [i] are both front vowels; that is, they are pronounced with the tongue to the front of the mouth. The only difference is that the mouth is a little bit more open when pronouncing [e] than when producing [i]. Similarly, [o] and [u] are both back vowels, and the only difference is that with [o] the mouth is a little bit more open. Our perception of how different they are is mediated by our knowledge of how they are written. This articulatory—and perceptual—closeness makes these vowels very prone to variation. Throughout the evolution of Spanish from Latin, these two vowels have been subject to changes. For example:

sapiat > saipat > sepa
caseu > casiu > caisu > queso
veni > vine

The same mechanisms that have resulted in the standard vocalic alternations in verbs (*sentir/siente/sintió; poder/puede/pudo*) are also behind the alternation between some standard and nonstandard pronunciations (e.g., *civil/cevil, medicina/medecina, pasear/pasiar*).

Consonants in Context-Independent Consistent PGCs

The following consonantal phonemes are consistently represented by only one grapheme, independently of the context.

/tʃ/ → *ch* *chocolate, dicho*
/d/ → *d* *decir, conde, verdad*
/f/ → *f* *farmacia, mofa, pilaf*
/l/ → *l* *luna, cola, mal*
/m/ → *m* *mía, loma, álbum*
/n/ → *n* *no, canoa, pan*
/ɲ/ → *ñ* *ñu, caña*
/p/ → *p* *pan, copa, pop*
/ɾ/ → *r* *cara, mira, por*
/t/ → *t* *toma, lote, cénit*

Although these are simple PGCs and should not cause any difficulty in spelling, we need to consider that SHLLs have typically been schooled in English, and therefore different English PGCs might be in competition with the Spanish ones in the learner's mind. The most likely cases are as follows:

- Consonant doubling
  /d/ → *d, dd* *made, added*
  /f/ → *f, ff* *professor, office*
  /t/ → *t, tt* *fate, attention*
  /l/ → *l, ll* *male, collection*
  /m/ → *m, mm* *Roman, comma*
  /p/ → *p, pp* *apart, appear*
- The *ñ* grapheme: Although the /ɲ/ → *ñ* is a simple PGC, the phoneme /ɲ/, along with the letter *ñ*, does not exist in English. Therefore, SHLLs will need to learn that letter, as well as to identify the /ɲ/ sound, which is similar to the sound of *ni* and *ny* sequences in English, as in *companion* and *canyon*.
- The *d* grapheme: In North American English, intervocalic *d* or *t* in words such as *ladle* and *later* are pronounced as [ɾ], which is the sound associated to the letter *r* in Spanish words, as in *loro, cara*. Therefore, for a bilingual speaker, the sound [ɾ] may be associated with the letters *r* and *d*.

Consonants in Context-Dependent Consistent PGCs

In the Spanish orthographic system, we find several phonemes that can be represented by more than one grapheme and for which the choice depends on the context in which that sounds appears in the word. They are presented in table 3.1. The use of different graphemes for the same sound in different phonological and word contexts results in grapheme alternations across morphology; that is, we may find a word spelled with one grapheme and its derived or inflected forms spelled with another. These are some examples:

/r/: Puerto Rico / puertorriqueño; raíz/arraigar
/k/: poco/poquito; taco/taquería; tocar/toqué
/g/: largo/larguero; lago/laguito; pegar/pegué
/gu/: lengua/bilingüe; paraguas/paragüero; averiguar/averigüé

Here we see an important contrast between the English and the Spanish spelling systems. In cases of conflict between morphological and phonological demands, Spanish orthography prioritizes the phonological criterion over a morphological one (Defior and Alegría 2005). Therefore, *taco* and *taquería*, or *pegar* and *pegué*, use different graphemes, despite the fact that they are

TABLE 3.1. Context-dependent consistent PGCs in Spanish

Phoneme	Graphemes	Context within the word	Examples
/r/	*r*	Word-initial	*roca, ritmo*
		After *l* or *r*	*alrededor, enredar*
	rr	After a vowel	*carro, correr*
/k/	*qu*	Before *e, i*	*querer, maqueta, quizás, aquí*
	c	Before *a, o, u*	*casa, roca, costa, poco, cuesta*
		In the consonant clusters *cr* and *cl*	*claro, crema, aclarar, recreativo*
		End of syllable	*lectura, técnica, acción, anécdota, bistec*
/g/	*gu**	Before *e, i*	*guerra, guitarra, llegué, conseguir*
	g	Before *a, o, u*	*arruga, lugar, gota, luego, gusta, laguna*
		In the consonant clusters *gr* and *gl*	*grato, agradable, glotón*
		End of syllable	*dogma, amígdala, agnóstico, blog*
/gu/	*gü*	Before *e, i*	*bilingüe, averigüé, pingüino*
	gu	All other contexts	*guapo, antiguo, gusta, gula*

*Saying that /g/ is represented by *gu* implies that the *u* is silent. The /g/ symbol is used in the International Phonetic Alphabet (IPA) to represent the sound we find in the English words *gift* or *grace* and the Spanish word *gato*. The symbol for the sound we find in English words like *gentle* is /ʤ/, and the symbol for the sound we find in the Spanish words *gente* or *girar* is /x/.

morphologically related, because maintaining the consistency between letter and sound in these PGCs is the priority. However, English spelling is a morphophonemic system, as it prioritizes the consistent spelling of morphemes over that of phonemes (Bowers and Bowers 2018). For example, the past-tense morpheme is always *-ed*, regardless of pronunciation. And *heal-health* and *deal-dealt* are spelled with the same vowels even though they sound very different. A similar thing happens with the *t* in *act-action, opt-option*.

Inconsistent PGCs

Inconsistent PGCs are the cases in which the phoneme can be represented by more than one grapheme, but the grapheme choice is intrinsic to the word (or the morpheme) itself. In those cases, the context of the phoneme (i.e., what letter or sound precedes or follows it) does not give any clue to the writer about which grapheme to use. The following are the inconsistent PGCs of the Spanish orthographic system.

Phoneme /b/ → *b* versus *v*

The phoneme /b/ can be represented by the letters *b* and *v*—or, as many speakers would put it, the letters *b* and *v* sound the same—because the phoneme /v/ does not exist in Spanish. Although there are no contextual rules, there are some patterns that help to predict where we will find one letter or the other, divided into letter sequences, productive suffixes, and common words (shown in table 3.2).[7] Being aware of sequences that contain a certain letter does not necessarily mean that teachers will explicitly teach those sequences to students as "spelling rules." Those might even be the sequences that require less explicit learning because students will be more familiar with them implicitly, through reading. For example, in Spanish there are no words that contain the *vr* or *vl* sequences. That means that the mere image of *vr* and *vl* will seem odd to the eyes of a student, and it would be less likely for a student to misspell *libro* as **livro* (more about this in chapter 4). However, since there are many words with the sequences *b* + *vowel* and *v* + *vowel*, those words are more likely to be misspelled. Misspelled words **vola*

TABLE 3.2. Common sequences, suffixes, and words with *b* and *v*

b	*v*
Sequences	
In the consonant clusters *bl*, *br*: *blanco*, *brisa* At the end of a syllable: *objeto*, *obvio* After *ha-*, *he-*, *hi-*, *hu-*: *haber*, *hebilla*, *hubo*, *prohíbe* Verbs that end in *-bir* and *-buir*: *escribir*, *concebir*, *contribuir*	After *ol-*: *olvidar*, *volver*, *polvo* *lla-*, *lle-*, *llo-*, *llu-*: *llave*, *lleno*, *llover*, *lluvia*
Productive suffixes	
bi-, *bis-*: *bisiesto*, *bisabuelo*, *bianual* *bio-*: *biológico*, *biodegradable* *sub-*: *subterráneo*, *submarino*, *subsuelo* *-aba*: *cantaba*, *miraba*, *dudaba* *-ble*/*-bil-*: *amable*, *amabilidad*, *contable*	*-avo*: *octavo*, *onceavo* *-ivo*: *afectivo*, *despectivo*, *aditivo*
Common words	
haber, *beber*, *caber*, *saber*, *deber*	*mover*, *valer*, *venir*, *ver*, *vivir* *tuv-* forms of *tener* and *estar*: *tuve*, *tuviste*, *estuvo*, *estuvimos*

A morpheme is the smallest unit of the word that provides meaning, for example:

alt- (which is found in *alto, alta, altas, altura, altitud*...)
-eza (which is found in *belleza, tristeza, pureza*...)

A Note about the Name of Letters *b* and *v*
Throughout the Spanish-speaking territories, we find different names for these letters. The most common names in Spain are "be" (*b*) and "uve" (*v*). In some places in Latin America, the letter *v* is called "ve," which sounds like "be." That makes it necessary to add an adjective to distinguish between the two letters, such as "alta"/"baja," "larga"/"corta," "grande"/"pequeña," "grande"/"chica." Some people add "de burro" / "de vaca."

A Note on Etymology: Why Do These Two Graphemes Exist?
The phoneme /b/ that is spelled with a *b* is typically (with some exceptions) the result of the evolution of /p/ and /b/ in Latin. For example, *lupus* > *lobo*; *labrum* > *labrio* > *labio*; *bassus* > *bajo*.

The phoneme /b/ that is spelled with a *v* is typically the result of the evolution of /w/ in Latin, which was represented with the letter *v*. The phoneme /w/ evolved into /b/ but kept the original spelling of *v*. For example, *vasum* (pronounced /wasum/) evolved into *vaso* (pronounced /báso/).

(for *bola*) or **cabar* (for *cavar*) are not as odd to the sight, since the sequences *vo* and *ba* are found in other words, like *volar, votar, acabar*, and *probar*. In fact, there are several homonyms with these sequences (*vota/bota, vaso/baso*). In the case of productive morphemes, those could be perceived simply as "letter sequences," but they are more than that, as they might be recognized through morphological awareness. Also, because they carry meaning, they are connected to vocabulary development, as we saw in the previous chapter. Finally, common or frequent words are helpful to keep in mind, as mastering their spelling is a quick way to reduce the number of spelling errors in essays and give a boost to students' spelling development and confidence (Belpoliti and Bermejo 2020a).

Phoneme /ʝ/ → *y* versus *ll*

In the Spanish-speaking world, we find two types of language varieties with respect to the pronunciation of these graphemes:

- Distinctive varieties: the varieties whose speakers have a different sound for each of these two graphemes:
  /ʝ/ → *y* *cayó, maya, rayar, yo, yunque*
  /ʎ/[8] → *ll* *calle, malla, rallar, llave, lluvia*
  Currently, the varieties that have the phonemes /ʎ/ and /ʝ/ are spoken mostly in Bolivia and Paraguay and some areas in Peru and Ecuador, especially those in contact with Quechua, as well as in some areas in the northern half of Spain. Those speakers do not have much difficulty in choosing between *ll* and *y*, since they pronounce these two letters differently.
- Nondistinctive varieties: the varieties whose speakers only have one sound that is represented by these two graphemes. In most of the Spanish-speaking territory this sound is /ʝ/ (very similar to the sound of *y* in English

A Note on Etymology: Why Do These Two Graphemes Exist?

The reason is in the etymology of these words and the sounds they had in the original Latin words. The sound /ʝ/ that is spelled with *y* is the result of a triphthong in which the letter *i* is found in between two vowels. The vocalic sound /i/ is very difficult to maintain in that position and it becomes /ʝ/. In those cases, it is spelled as *y*. For example, *radius* > *raius* > *rayo*. (Incidentally, note that the words *rayo* and *radio*, and *ray* and *radius*, have the same origin.) This is more obvious in the conjugation of verbs that end in *-aer*, *-eer*, or *-oer*: *caer*: ca-ió → *cayó*; *leer*: le-ió → *leyó*; *roer*: ro-ió → *royó*.

On the other hand, words that are spelled with *ll* have evolved from words in Latin that either had *-ll-* (*callare* > *callar*; *callis* > *calle*) or that started with *pl-*, *cl-*, or *fl-* (*pluvia* > *lluvia*; *clavis* > *llave*; *flamma* > *llama*). (Incidentally, note that this is why we have words like *pluvial*, *clave*, and *inflamar*, related to *lluvia*, *llave*, and *llama*, respectively.) These Latin consonant groups evolved into the sound /ʎ/ in medieval Spanish, and the grapheme *ll* was used to represent that sound. In most areas, the sound further evolved into /ʝ/, but the grapheme *ll* was kept.

These different origins of the sound /ʝ/ explain why we have pairs of homophonic words like *rallo* and *rayo*. *Rallo* originates from Latin *rallo*, whereas *rayo* originates from *radius* > *raius* > *rayo*.

yes). In Argentina and Uruguay, that common sound is /ʃ/—as in English *sh*oe—or /ʒ/, as in English *measure*. Whichever that sound is (/ʝ/, /ʃ/, or /ʒ/), what is relevant here is that speakers of those varieties, which are the majority of Spanish speakers, are the ones who have more difficulties in spelling words with *ll* or *y*, because they have the same sound for the two graphemes and need to choose between them. And there is no contextual rule to inform that choice.

Another dialectal feature involving these graphemes that has an impact on spelling is the deletion of this sound in intervocalic position, especially when next to /i/, as in *silla*, pronounced as /sía/ in Central American Spanish.

Use of Letter *h*

The letter *h* in Spanish does not correspond to any phoneme. Although its appearance in a word is not subject to any contextual rule, there are some patterns that can help predict whether or not a word is spelled with an *h*:

- No words begin with *ua-*, *ue-*, *ui-*, *ia-*, *ie-*.
  RAE's *Ortografía de la lengua española*, as well as many Spanish spelling websites and spelling manuals, offers these two patterns for the use of *h:* (1) before the diphthongs *ua, ue, ui* at the beginning of a syllable: *náhuatl, hueso, deshuesar, huir*; and (2) before the diphthongs *ia* and *ie* in word-initial position: *hiato, hierba, hielo*. However, these syllable- and word-initial sequences are often pronounced as /gwa/, /gwe/, /gwi/, /ʝa/ and /ʝe/, respectively. And there are words that begin with or include *gua, güe, güi, ye,* and *yi*, which is particularly true with *gua* (*guapo, guante, guajiro, agua, aguantar,...*). There is no spelling rule or pattern that tells the writer that we do not write **huapo, *huante, *huajiro, *ahua, *ahuantar*. In fact, there are only a few words that begin with *hua-*, mostly Quechua and Nahuatl loanwords, such as *huancaíno, huaje, huaco*, and some words have the two spellings accepted (*huaca/guaca, huipil/güipil, colihue/coligüe, ahuate/aguate*). Similarly, there is nothing that tells the writer to write *yeso* and *yema* and not **hieso* and **hiema*. They sound the same, and we just need to learn their spellings. As before, both spellings are accepted in some words; for example, *hiedra/yedra, hierba/yerba*. Therefore, if we take the sound-to-grapheme point of view, I believe the actual spelling pattern should be no words start with *ua-*, *ue-*, *ui-*, *ia-*, or *ie-*.
- We find *h* in words that begin with the following sequences:
  /erm-/ (*herm-*): *hermoso, hermano, hermético* (but *ermita, ermitaño*)
  /orm-/ (*horm-*): *hormiga, hormigón, hormona*
  /um-/ (*hum-*): *humo, humor, humano, humilde*

RAE's *Ortografía de la lengua española* also includes the beginning sequences *histo-*, *hog-*, *holg-*, *horr-*, *hosp-*, and some Greek roots that begin with *h* (*helico-*, *helio-*, *hema-*, *hemi-*, *hepat-*, *hepta-*, *hetero-*, *hidr-*, *hiper-*, *hipo-*, *homeo-*, *homo-*, among others). However, the words that begin with these sequences and roots are technical, less common, and/or English cognates that are also spelled with h: *hospital*, *horrible*, *helicóptero*, *hepatitis*, *hidrógeno*, *heterogéneo*, and so on.

- Word-initial /alb-/ is spelled without *h* (*alb-*): *alba*, *albañil*, *albergue*, *alberca*.
- Some common words with *h* are *hasta*, *hacia*, *hoy*, *hombre*, *hijo*, *hoja*, *hierro*, *herramienta*, *hablar*, *haber*.[9]

A Note on Etymology: Why Do We Have the Letter *h* When We Do Not Pronounce It?

The *h* grapheme has not always been silent; it did correspond to a phoneme, which has disappeared over time. Although Spanish spelling has been modified a lot to reflect the changes in the spoken language—certainly more than English spelling has—it has not kept up with all the changes. And this is a clear case. This silent *h* has several origins:

- Latin had the sound /h/ (the sound of *h* in *house* or *hat*) in words like *habilis* (> *hábil*), *habere* (> *haber*). But around the first century BCE, this sound disappeared, and the grapheme remained. In fact, this written *h* could have disappeared completely, as during the medieval ages those words were spelled without the *h*. It was later, during the thirteenth through fifteenth centuries, that writers brought back the original written *h*.
- Word-initial /f/ in Latin became softer over time until it became /h/ around the fifth century, although people kept writing those words with *f* until the fifteenth century, when the use of written *h* was generalized. Some examples are: *filius* > *hijo*, *ferrum* > *hierro*, *folia* > *hoja*. In the sixteenth century, the sound /h/ disappeared, but the grapheme still remains.
- The *h* grapheme has also its origins in other languages Spanish has borrowed words from. These include Greek words that begin with *hemi-*, *hiper-*, *hidro-* (*hemicírculo*, *hipermercado*, *hidógeno*), and other morphemes and words from Arabic (*alcohol*, *almohada*), English (*hámster*, *hamburguesa*), and Taino (*huracán*).

Curious Spellings

Why do we have the word *huevo* but *oval*, *huelo* but *oler*, *hueso* but *óseo*, when they are clearly related? In Latin and in Spanish until the sixteenth through seventeenth centuries, the letters *u* and *v* were not used to represent different sounds but were two ways to write the same letter (*v* was uppercase and *u* was lowercase). This *v/u* letter was used to represent the sound /b/ and the sound /w/ (the sound of *u* in a diphthong). Words like *uaso* and *ueso* could represent *vaso or uaso* and *veso or ueso.* To avoid confusion, writers started adding *h* in front of the *u* when it preceded another vowel. This is why words like *hueso, huevo, hueco, huérfano, huelo* begin with an *h*. Their related words that have *o* instead of *u* did not need to incorporate that *h*. This is why we have *hueso* but *óseo; huevo* but *oval, óvulo; huelo, huele* but *olemos, oler, olía; huérfano* but *orfanato.*

When Choosing the Right Letter Is Really Difficult: /s/ and /x/

In this section, I present two additional PGCs that have not been covered in the previous sections, because they carry additional difficulties resulting from a combination of conflicting phonological, morphological, and orthographic requirements.

The Representation of /x/ → j/g

It is difficult to decide whether this PGC is rule-based (context-dependent consistent) or non-rule-based (inconsistent). In a way, it is both. When the root of the word is spelled with *ge* or *gi*, its inflected forms are subject to a contextual rule: *j* before *a, o, u; g* before *e, i*. For example:

recoger → recoge, recogí—recojo, recojamos
rugir → ruge, rugido—rujo, ruja
elegir → elige, eligió—elijo, elijan
dirigir → dirige, dirigimos—dirijo, dirija

In those cases, we see that grapheme consistency across morphology is lost in favor of phonology, that is, the need to maintain the /x/ pronunciation, since, in those cases, maintaining *g* with *a, o* would result in another sound (/g/).

On the other hand, when the root of the word is spelled with a *j*, this letter is maintained across morphology, even when it precedes *e* or *i*, because *j* is always associated with /x/. For example:

trabajar → trabajo, trabajan, trabajé, trabajemos
rojo → enrojecer, rojizo

In fact, in some cases, the root itself is spelled as *je* or *ji*, as in *tejer* and *crujir*.

Therefore, the contrast between *je-ji* and *ge-gi* is inconsistent, since there are not contextual rules that tell us that *crujir* and *jirafa* are spelled with *j*, and *rugir* and *girar* are spelled with *g*. This combination of a contextual PGC and an inconsistent PGC makes the spelling of /x/ particularly complex, since writers need to combine different types of knowledge, as follows:

- Phonological knowledge: making sure to change *ge, gi* to *ja, jo* and avoid writing **recogo*, **eligamos*, as that would change the sound.
- Orthographic knowledge: knowing that *rugir* is spelled with *g* and *crujir* with *j*.
- Morphological knowledge: connecting root words and their inflected and derived forms. For example, when spelling /axito/, we need to consider whether we are writing the diminutive of *ajo* (*ajito*), or the first person of *agitar* (*agito*). And when writing *tejido* or *rugido*, it is useful to connect these words with *tejer* and *rugir*, respectively.

Although there are no contextual rules, table 3.3 presents some sequences that help to predict where we will find one letter or the other when preceding *e, i*.

The Representation of /s/ → *s/z/c*

In most Spanish dialects, the /s/ phoneme can be represented with the following three graphemes: *s*, *z*, and *c*:

- *s* can appear in all contexts.
- *c* is only used to represent /s/ when preceding *e* or *i*. (In all other contexts, the *c* grapheme is used to represent /k/).
- *z* can appear in word-final contexts and when preceding a consonant or *a, o, u*. Although the *ze* and *zi* sequences do not result in another phoneme, they are not allowed by the Spanish orthographic conventions. These PGCs are illustrated in table 3.4.

There are exceptions to the correspondences shown in this overview. First, we find words with initial /s/ that are spelled with *x*, such as *xenofobia*, *xilófono*, and some names, such as *Xitlali*, *Xiomara*, or *Xochitl*. In addition, a few exceptions of *z* preceding *e* or *i* exist for some foreign-origin words, such as *zen*, *zenit*, *nazi*, or *zinc*. The /k/ phoneme is also spelled with *k* in loanwords from other

TABLE 3.3. Common sequences with *ge*, *gi* and *je*, *ji*

ge, gi	*je, ji*
Words beginning in /xe-/	
Most of those words begin with *ge-*, *gi-*: *genio, gélido, gesto, girar, gigante,...*	A few common words begin with *je-*, *ji-*: *jefe, jeringa, jerarquía, jinete, jirafa, jícaro.*
Words beginning in /axe-/	
The most common words are *agenda, agente, agencia* (which are all related) and their derived and inflected forms (e.g., *agentivo, agenciar*).	The most common words are *ajedrez, ajetreo, ajeno.*
Words beginning in /exe-/	
Practically no words begin with *ege-*.	Most of the words that begin with /exe-/ are spelled with *j* (*eje-*). But all these words are, in fact, just derived and inflected forms of these four words: *eje, ejercer* (*ejercicio, ejército, ejercitar...*), *ejecutar* (*ejecutivo, ejecución*) and *ejemplo* (*ejemplificar...*).
Verbs ending in /-xer/ or /-xir/	
Most of these verbs are spelled as *-ger, -gir*: *escoger, recoger, encoger, acoger, proteger, sumergir, elegir, regir, rugir, dirigir.*	There are only seven verbs ending in *-jer, -jir*, of which the only relatively frequent ones are *tejer* and *crujir*. Their inflected and derived forms are also spelled with *j*: *tejí, tejido, cruje, crujiente....*
Words ending in /-axe/	
Practically, no words end in *-age*.	Words with the suffix *-aje* (e.g., *masaje, mensaje, paisaje, drenaje*) and words derived from those words (e.g., *masajear, mensajero*). This suffix is spelled as *-age* in English. Irregular preterit forms: *traer*: *traj-*: *traje, trajiste, trajo...*, *traducir* (*traduje...*), *reducir* (*reduje....*), *decir* (*dije...*), *producir* (*produje*).

TABLE 3.4. Graphemic correspondences of /s/ and /k/ in Spanish

Phoneme	Grapheme	Contexts	Examples
/s/	*z*	before *a, o, u*	*zapato, marzo, cazuela*
		before consonant	*juzgar, Cuzco, diezmar*
		word-final	*paz, voz, juez*
	c	before *e, i*	*cielo, cena, hacer, medicina*
	s	all contexts	*sal, sello, signo, sopa, suelo, mes, mismo*
/k/	*c*	before *a, o, u*	*capa, copa, cuerpo, marcar*
		before consonant	*acto, acné*
	qu	before *e, i*	*quedar, quitar, raqueta, máquina*

languages, such as *kiosco, kimono, kilómetro* (also accepted as *quiosco, quimono, quilómetro*), *koala, kayak.*

But the complexity of this PGC is due not only to the fact that there are three graphemes associated with one phoneme but also to the fact that different grapheme correspondences of the /s/ phoneme result from a combination of being a context-dependent consistent PGC and an inconsistent PGC.

Context-Dependent Consistent PGC: c *versus* z

According to a contextual rule, we write *c* before e, *i*, and *z* in all other contexts (before *a, o, u*, before consonant, and in word-final position). Failing to respect this contextual rule leads to different outcomes:

- Writing *c* instead of *z* before *a, o, u* (e.g., **hico* for *hizo*) causes a change in the corresponding pronunciation, from /s/ to /k/.
- Writing *z* instead of *c* before *e, i* (e.g., **hize* for hice) does not change the pronunciation of this grapheme, since no other phoneme is associated with it, but it breaks a Spanish-specific convention disallowing the *ze, zi* strings.

As with other contextual-dependent PGC rules, we see alternation between these two graphemes across morphology, that is, within words of the same family, as in the following examples:

cazar, cazo, cazador; cacería, cacé
voz, vozarrón; voces, vocero
cocer, cocí, cocinar; cuezo
hacer, hacemos, hicieron; hizo

TABLE 3.5. Common suffixes with *s*, *c*, and *z*

s	*-sión* (English *-ssion* or *-sion*)	*misión, tensión, mansión*
	-s (plural and second person)	*caras, libros, alegres, altas*
		tienes, decías, tengas, hablabas
	-és, -esa (languages and demonyms)	*inglés, francés, irlandesa, finlandesa*
	-ense (demonym)	*canadiense, costarricense*
	-oso (English *-ous*)	*peligroso, horroroso, cariñoso*
	-ísimo (superlative)	*grandísimo, feísimo, listísima*
c	*-ción* (English *-tion*)	*acción, educación, comunicación*
	-encia (English *-ence, -ency*)	*tendencia, agencia, urgencia*
z	*-izar* (English *-ize*)	*localizar, analizar, normalizer*
	-azo	*cabezazo, puñetazo*
	-ez, -eza	*niñez, pequeñez, belleza, riqueza*
	-zco	*conozco, parezco*

Inconsistent PGC: **s** *versus* **c** *and* **s** *versus* **z**

The distinction between *s* and *c* (or between *s* and *z*) is not subject to any contextual rule. One must simply learn whether a word is spelled with either *s* or *z/c*. The grapheme *s* is not found in alternation across morphology with any of the other two graphemes, because *s* is not in a context-dependent relationship. For example:

pensar, pensamiento, pensé
casar, caso, casamos, casé
coser, coso, cosí
mes, meses, mensual

Having two types of PGCs converging into one phoneme makes the grapheme choice very cognitively demanding, as writers need to coordinate conflicting sources of information.

- Phonological knowledge: making sure the word sounds as it is supposed to sound. For example, avoid writing **hico* in order to be consistent with *hacer*, as it would change the pronunciation to /k/.
- Orthographic knowledge: knowing that *cansar* is spelled with *s* and *alcanzar* with *z*. In addition, knowing that the sequences *ze*, *zi* violate a conventional rule.
- Morphological knowledge: being aware of what root word we are writing. For example, when writing */kasé/* considering whether we are writing the past tense of *casar* (*casé*) or of *cazar* (*cacé*).

Although there are not contextual rules, we find some patterns that help writers predict whether to write *s* or *c*/*z*. Within the first 4,000 most frequent lemmas—that is, words as they appear in the dictionary—we find *s* is the most frequent overall:[10] 1,156 words contain *s*, 674 contain *c* (associated to /s/), and only 120 contain *z*. Therefore, *s* could be considered the dominant or default grapheme to represent /s/. However, if we do a more fine-grained distribution of these graphemes in sequences that are in contrast, we see the following frequency patterns:

- Before *e*, *i:* There are almost twice as many words containing *ce*/*ci* (674) than words containing *se*/*si* (341) and only one verb with that sequence (*ser*). (There are only two other verbs ending in *-ser*, which are less frequent—*coser*, *toser*—and one in *-sir*—*asir*.) Therefore, *c* could also be considered the dominant grapheme in /se/-/si/ words and/or *-er*, *-ir* verbs.
  Some verbs ending in *-cer*: *hacer, nacer, crecer, parecer, conocer*
  Some verbs ending in *-cir*: *decir, conducir, reducir, producir, traducir*
- Before *a*, *o*, *u*: There are many more words spelled with *sa*, *so*, *su* (356) than spelled with *za*, *zo*, *zu* (93). However, when it comes to /-sar/ verbs, there is a similar number of verbs ending in *-sar* (30) and *-zar* (36). A few examples:
  Some verbs ending in *-zar*: *empezar, comenzar, alcanzar,* and the suffix *-izar* (e.g., *localizar, analizar*)
  Some verbs ending in *-sar*: *regresar, pasar, cansar, pensar, tensar, pesar*
- Other contexts: There are many more words spelled with *s* + consonant and with word-final *-s* than spelled with *z* + consonant and word-final *z*. A few examples:
  -s: *mes, dos, tres, más, detrás, además, asco, pasto, rosco, rasgo, tosco*
  -z: *voz, pez, paz, juez, vez, mezcla, juzgar, durazno, azteca*

Curious Spellings

Why do we have *pez* spelled with *z*, but *pescado*, spelled with *s*, even though they are related? *Pez* evolved from *piscis*, and *pescar* (which the verb *pescado* is a form of) evolved from *piscare*. Therefore, the two Latin words (*piscis* and *piscare*) are more clearly related than the two Spanish words (*pez* and *pescado*) in their spelling. But whereas the *z* in *pez* is the result of the evolution of *c* in *pis<u>c</u>is*, *pescar* kept both consonants. The connection between the spellings of *pez* and *pescado* still exists: the *z* of *pez* is not related to the *s* in *pe<u>s</u>cado* but to the *c*.

TABLE 3.6. /s/ and /θ/ pronunciation of s, z, and c

Written word	Pronunciation in distinctive varieties	Pronunciation in /s/ varieties ("seseo")
casa	/kása/	/kása/
caza	/káθa/	/kása/
casé	/kasé/	/kasé/
cacé	/kaθé/	/kasé/

Table 3.5 includes some productive suffixes that contain /s/, with one of these three graphemes.

***Variation in* s, z, c**

A minority of speakers pronounce *c* and *z* with the sound /θ/, like the *th* in *thief* or *math*, instead of /s/. Because those varieties distinguish between two sounds, they are called "distinctive varieties." Table 3.6 illustrates the different ways in which speakers of different varieties pronounce words with *s*, *c*, and *z*.

A Note on Etymology: Why Do We Have Three Graphemes for One Sound?

Again, we find the explanation in the sounds that existed in Latin and the way they evolved. In Latin, the sound /s/ was only represented by the letter *s*. The letter *c* represented the sound /k/ in any position: *casa*, *cera* (pronounced as /kera/), *cinis* (pronounced as /kinis/). And *z* did not exist originally and was only later adopted from Greek to transcribe Greek words.

In today's Spanish, words that are spelled with *s* result from the evolution of words that had *s* in Latin. For example: *rosa* > *rosa*, *sanguis* > *sangre*, *casa* > *casa*.

Words that are spelled with *c* or *z* in Spanish result from the evolution of other letters and sounds. For example, the sound /k/ in Latin evolved into /ts/ and then /s/ when it preceded *e*, *i*, like in *cera* or *civil*, but not when it preceded *a*, *o*, *u*. This is why *ce*, *ci* sound like /se/, /si/ but *ca*, *co*, *cu* sound as /ka/, /ko/, /ku/. When *ce* was followed by a vowel, the sound /ts/ was spelled as *ç* first and then as *z*. For example, *lancea* (pronounced /lankea/) > *lança* (/lantsa/) > *lanza* (pronounced with /s/).

This variation has an obvious impact on spelling. While most children in Spain only need to learn the contextual rule *za-zo-zu* versus *ce-ci*, the rest of Spanish-speaking children need to learn that words like *sopa*, *paso*, *casa* are spelled with *s*, while *zorro*, *pozo*, *caza* are spelled with *z*.

In addition, the sound /s/ appears as part of the sequence /ks/, which is typically represented with the letter *x*, for example, *examen*, *máximo*, *tóxico*. Therefore, for speakers of nondistinctive varieties, the sequence /ks/ is sometimes spelled as *x* and sometimes as *cc*.[11] This is particularly noticeable in words ending in *-cción* and *-xión*: *acción*, *conducción* versus *flexión*, *conexión*. There is another dialectal difference related to /s/ that affects spelling. In many varieties, syllable-final *-s* (i.e., before a consonant or at the end of the word, e.g., *hasta*, *mes*, *las*) is aspirated (as /h/) or inaudible. Children who speak these varieties need to learn not only which letter to write but the fact that there *is* a letter to write.

Silent Letters and Silent Morphemes: Beyond *h*

In addition to the silent letter *h*, or even other letters such as the silent *p* in words with the Greek suffixes *pseudo-* and *psico-* (also accepted as *seudo-* and *sico-*) or the silent *g* in words like *gnóstico* (also accepted as *nóstico*), we need to consider those sounds that are phonetically silenced by their phonetic context. Defior and Alegría (2005) talk about "silent morphemes," since those are not simply sounds but constitute morphemes and even entire words.

One of the most salient cases is the preposition *a* in the *ir a* + infinitive. or *empezar a* + infinitive constructions when the verb in the infinitive form begins with *a* (or *ha*). For example, in *voy <u>a ha</u>blar* the preposition *a* is not heard and the sequence sounds as /bojablár/; the same in *empezó <u>a ha</u>blar* (/empesóablár/). The preposition is also silenced by the preceding *a* of *va*, *iba*, or *empieza*, as in *v<u>a a</u> comer*, *ib<u>a a</u> ir*, *empiez<u>a a</u> llover*. This situation also leads to a homophony of words that are not actually homophones, such as *ser*/*hacer*, in *voy a hacer* and *voy a ser*, both pronounced as /bojasér/. Something similar happens with *haber*, *a haber*, and *a ver*, all of which sound like /abér/, in sentences like *Juan va <u>a ver</u> una película*, *hoy va <u>a haber</u> un examen*, and *tiene que <u>haber</u> alguien*. In some cases, in a more relaxed pronunciation, words like *hubiera* might sound like *viera*, as in *si hubiera algo* and *si viera algo*. Another case is that of *ha* and *he* when the following verb begins with *a-* (or *ha-*) or *e-* (*he-*), respectively, as in *Juan <u>ha hab</u>lado*, *Juan <u>ha a</u>ndado*, *yo <u>he he</u>cho*, *yo <u>he e</u>stado*. In most of these cases, silenced morphemes can resurface phonetically by changing the contexts. For example, while *a* is not heard in *iba a ir*, it is clearly audible in *íbamos a ir*. A similar resurfacing happens when we move from *voy a hablar* to *voy a comer*, or from *empieza a llover* to *empezó a llover*.

Another situation in which we might find a silent morpheme is related to variation in the pronunciation of /s/. In some varieties, /s/ is aspirated as [h] or not pronounced at the end of a syllable, which also includes the end of a word, for example, *hasta*, *más*. This affects the plural in nouns and adjectives (*rojos*, *mujeres*) and the second person in verb forms (*tienes*, *comerías*).

All these cases are better understood if we adopt the oral-to-written perspective, which is the perspective of the native/heritage language speaker of a language who is learning how to spell. Highly literate adults who developed their literacy skills in early childhood might not even notice that the *a* in *voy a hacer* or the *ha* in *ha hablado* are not heard. Some even have a hard time accepting that fact and insist they hear the *a*/*ha*. As we saw in the previous chapter, "learning to read is learning to hear speech in a new way" (Olson 1994, 85). But to teach spelling, teachers need to "de-learn" that way of perceiving sounds and be able to hear speech in a way that is not mediated by their literacy skills. This approach also applies to the way we think of language variation. Many people describe variation in pronunciation as "some people do not pronounce the syllable-final -*s*." But from the point of view of those speakers before they learned how to spell, there simply is no *s*, or there is a /h/. In addition, patterns and examples presented in this chapter allow us to see that spelling involves much more than a simple series of correspondences between phonemes and graphemes and that it is tightly connected to the phonology and the morphology of the language. With this understanding of how we learn how to spell and how the Spanish spelling system works, we are ready to understand the spellings SHLLs produce and to devise strategies to improve their spelling.

Reflection Questions

1. Underline the graphemes that represent the same sound as the underlined grapheme in the given word.

   Example: cine: casa, caza, copa, cereza → casa, caza, copa, cereza

   a. copa: peca, cena, queso, koala, máquina
   b. llover: callar, maya, colegio, malla, cayó, hierba
   c. gato: pegar, luego, giré, llegué, gesto, guerra, bilingüe
   d. genio: gusta, jugar, lejos, gerente, paisaje, gato, México

2. Match the following words with their definitions. There are two extra definitions.

a. Context-dependent PGC	a) Letter or group of letters that represent a sound in written language.
b. Etymology	b) The study of the origin of words.
c. Grapheme	c) A spelling system where most letters represent only one sound.
d. Inconsistent PGC	d) A sound-grapheme relationship that is not subject to a rule.
e. Morpheme	e) A language sound.
f. Shallow orthography	f) A sound-grapheme relationship where the letter depends on the following sound or its position in the word.
	g) Smallest meaningful unit of language.
	h) The study of accurate spelling.

3. The following statements are not accurate. Explain why.

   a. Students who pronounce *cayó* and *calló* the same way are mispronouncing at least one of these words.
   b. Orthography is the system that assigns sounds to letters.
   c. Spanish prioritizes the consistent spelling of morphemes over that of phonemes.
   d. Words in pairs like *rallo/rayo*, *vaso/baso*, *agito/ajito* are spelled differently to differentiate their meaning.

4. This activity has the goal of helping you see spelling a little bit more like a learner would. For that reason, we are using pseudowords. That way, you cannot resort to your previous knowledge of the word to do the activity and, rather, need to apply the contextual rule.

   First, conjugate the following made-up verbs in Spanish in the first- and third-person singular of the preterit:

   (a) pucar (b) dugar (c) depizar (d) teer (e) tellar

And conjugate the following made-up verbs in Spanish in the first- and third-person singular in the present tense:

(a) pujir (b) pugir

Second, notice and explain each of the spelling changes you made—or did not make—when conjugating those verbs. In particular, pay attention to these items:

a. the changes in the following letters: *c*, *g*, and *z* (in *pucar*, *dugar*, *depizar*)
b. the similarities and differences between the conjugation of *teer* and *tellar*
c. the different behavior of *j* and *g* in *pujir* and *pugir*

Third, write a few real Spanish verbs that behave in the same way as each of these made-up verbs. For example, *tocar* behaves the same way as *pucar*.

5. Following you will find a list of incorrectly spelled words, with the correct spelling in parentheses. Explain why these words are spelled as they are instead of the way they have been misspelled. In your explanation, make sure to include whether there is a contextual rule or not. If one exists, explain what it is; if there is none, are there any hints or patterns that could help?

Example: *mez (mes)

Mes is spelled with an *s* because of an inconsistent PGC. There is no contextual rule informing us that it needs to be *s* instead of *z*. In fact, there are many words that end in *-z*, such as *voz*, *vez*, *pez*. In addition, misspelling *mes* as **mez* does not affect the pronunciation of the word.

a. *hiso (hizo)
b. *hico (hizo)
c. *raízes (raíces)
d. *lelló (leyó)
e. *trabagé (trabajé)
f. *jenio (genio)
g. *gefe (jefe)
h. *ueso (hueso)
i. *güeso (hueso)
j. *rei (rey)

k. *mariar (marear)
l. *tocé (toqué)

Notes

1. The dictionary of the Real Academia Española (RAE) allows different spellings in some words, like *cebiche/ceviche/seviche/sebiche*, but not in a systematic manner as with *-ize/-ise* spellings of English, and certainly not in a way that adapts to the different pronunciations of Spanish in different varieties.
2. Sign languages are also natural languages, that is, languages that have evolved naturally.
3. I am using the word "grapheme" to refer to an alphabetic unit that represents a phoneme, either letters (*e, d, m, ñ*) or combinations of two letters—or digraphs—such as *ll, ch, rr, gn* (in French) and *ph, ck* (in English). However, RAE considers the words "grafema" and "letra" to be completely synonymous. Therefore, digraphs such as *ll, ch*, and *rr* are not considered graphemes by the RAE. In this book I follow the practice generally used in spelling research and will use the term "grapheme" as an umbrella term that includes both letters and digraphs.
4. Except for *hola/ola*, these pairs of words are homophones only in certain varieties of Spanish, whereas in other varieties the words are pronounced differently. This variation will be discussed throughout the chapter.
5. This explanation is a bit simplified. The two closed vowels become semivowels in a diphthong, a difference that is almost imperceptible: /i/ → [j] and /u/ →[w].
6. Unstressed vowel reduction has been found in Bolivia (Sessarego 2012), Ecuador (Lipski 1990), Peru (Delforge 2009), and Spain (Marín Gálvez 1995). Other authors describe greater degrees of reduction and even deletion of unstressed vowels in central Mexican Spanish (Boyd-Bowman 1952; Matluck 1952; Lope Blanch 1964).
7. These patterns are adapted from Real Academia Española (2010). I have excluded many of the patterns that appear in that book either because they have many exceptions or are not very productive.
8. You can listen to this sound here: https://en.wikipedia.org/wiki/Voiced_palatal_lateral_approximant.
9. I am only including words that are not English cognates.
10. From Davies (2016) database.
11. /ks/ is very rarely spelled as *cs* (e.g., *fucsia*).

FOUR

Understanding Spanish Heritage Language Learners' Spelling Errors

This chapter gives a thorough description of the most frequent misspellings among SHLLs. Before we delve into this analysis, I discuss two things we need to consider when describing the spelling errors that a student population makes. One relates to frequency of errors and what we mean when we say that an error is very frequent or not, and the other concerns the way we describe spelling errors.

Frequency versus Accuracy

There is a general consensus that devising teaching strategies that target the most common or frequent errors is a desirable goal. Most teachers would probably spend less time—if any—teaching how to spell the words *tahúr* and *húsar* than how to spell *hacer*. For that reason, several studies have been conducted to find out the most frequent errors produced by a certain student population. These studies count the total number of misspellings produced in a large written corpus and then calculate which percentage of these errors involve a specific PGC or group of PGCs. This is the type of error analysis conducted by Beaudrie (2012), Belpoliti and Bermejo (2020a), and Contreras-Wise (2020). In these studies, the relative frequency of misspellings in certain graphemes might simply reflect the relative frequency of the words containing these graphemes, and it does not automatically say anything about how difficult it is for students to spell that word or that PGC. For example, Beaudrie (2012) found that around 20% of the errors produced in complex PGCs involved *b/v*, whereas only 6.4% of the errors involved *j/g*. Does that mean that spelling *b/v* is more difficult than spelling *j/g*? Maybe, but not necessarily. It could be that students wrote more words with *b/v* than with *j/g* and, therefore, they had the chance to make more errors there. This example shows a disadvantage of looking at the relative frequency of errors, but if we employ this approach and identify a few sources for many misspellings, we can have a more focused instruction approach that is likely to produce a quicker result. As Beaudrie (2012, 142) says, "Given the limited instructional time available for spelling instruction in the typical SHL course, targeted spelling instruction makes good sense." Also, following on the previous example, even if the reason there are more misspellings in *b*/*v* is that more words have *b*/*v*, teachers might decide to spend more time on *b*/*v* and that way reduce the total number of spelling errors students produce.

Other studies look at the accuracy rate, that is, the percentage of errors in a specific PGC or group of PGCs relative to the total number of instances in which this PGC occurs. For example, Llombart-Huesca and Zyzik (2019) used a dictation task with eighty words containing *c* or *s* and gave the percentage of errors for each of these letters. Beaudrie's (2018) study included, among other tasks, a sixty-item dictation test and looked at the percentage of correct spellings. Although this approach might look at the accuracy in spelling words that might not even appear very frequently in the students' essays, it can tell us what is more challenging to a student—and also what is not. In addition, looking at less-frequent errors might be revealing of what the students know and do not know about the Spanish PGCs, as well as of the strategies they employ.

Frequency studies have been conducted in naturalistic writing, that is, free-writing essays (Beaudrie 2012; Belpoliti and Bermejo 2020a), whereas accuracy studies have been conducted in quasi-experimental settings (Llombart-Huesca 2017a, 2019; Beaudrie 2018; Llombart-Huesca and Zyzik 2019). An intermediate approach is employed by Llombart-Huesca (2022), who examines accuracy in spelling /s/ in different groups of words in a corpus comprised of students' essays.

Looking at accuracy in a free-writing essay has its own limitations, too. To determine the accuracy rate, we need to observe not only when students made an error but also all the possible contexts where the error could have been made and was not. In cases such as addition of *h* when it is not needed, how can we know how accurate students were at *not* adding *h*? In addition, we need to have enough instances of a specific PGC to establish accuracy rate. For example, the corpus used here contained only four instances of words spelled with a *c* corresponding to a *cc* in their English counterpart (e.g., *ocasión*, *acomodar*) and three of these are misspelled. Given the low total number of instances, can we strongly assert that the accuracy rate is 25% for this type of word?

Because of the advantages and limitations of each of these three approaches of looking at spelling errors, these sets of studies provide complementary pieces of information about the spelling development of SHLLs.

Describing a Spelling Error

The second issue in studying spelling errors involves the way we describe these unconventional spellings. When we look at a misspelling—say, **toce* for *toque*, or **teine* for *tiene*—we could say that the student made a "substitution" error (wrote *c* instead of *qu*) in the first case and an "inversion" error in the second. Or we can say that there is an "omission of *h*" error in writing **alcol* (for *alcohol*), **ablar* (for *hablar*), or **a cantado* (for *ha cantado*). This is a surface description of the errors, one that merely states the mismatch between the target grapheme and the grapheme produced by the student. However, educators and researchers might want to ask, "Yes, but why?" Although these descriptions are useful and necessary, they do not shed light on the underlying cognitive causes of the errors, because they do not consider the qualitative differences between each of these PGCs. For example, choosing between *c* and *qu* involves a different cognitive process from writing the letters in the right sequence. Accordingly, classroom instruction to help students who omit the *h* in *he cantado* or *ha ido* will probably involve a different strategy from helping students who omit the *h* in *alcohol* or in *hablar*, as will be discussed later.

In this chapter, we look at spelling errors in SHLLs from all these different points of view. I provide data from the corpus used in Llombart-Huesca's (2022) study. This corpus, which I will refer to as the "LH corpus," is composed of 125 essays written by students who at the time of the data collection were enrolled in a Spanish for Spanish Speakers (I) course and had not taken any other Spanish course at a college level. The essays had a total of 22,479 words, after removing names (people, places, etc.) and words written in English (e.g., the name of a course), which were not analyzed nor counted. In Llombart-Huesca's (2022) study, the words that were considered for analysis were those containing the representation of phoneme /s/. Here, I refer to some of the results published in the study, and I also include the analysis conducted on the rest of the PGCs in that corpus, which have not been published elsewhere. I also contextualize these findings with results obtained from other naturalistic corpora and experimental studies.

Overview of the Most Frequently Misspelled Graphemes

Beaudrie's (2012) error analysis study classifies misspellings into four main categories: (1) misspellings in simple (one-to-one) PGC rules, (2) misspellings in complex PGC rules, (3) syllable and word fragmentation errors, and (4) accent errors. The other large error analysis is that of Belpoliti and Bermejo (2020a), who classified misspellings into three types: incorrect grapheme, accent marks, and syllable/word division (segmentation and contraction). While these analyses

TABLE 4.1. Accuracy rates of rule-based PGCs in the LH corpus

PGC	Accuracy rate
/k/ *c* vs. *qu* in *cua, cui, cuo, que, qui*	97.5%
/r/ *r* vs. *rr*	78.0%
/ge/-/gi/ use of *u* in *gue-gui*	62.5%
Use of umlaut (dieresis) (*ü*) in *güe-güi*	20.8%

distinguish between simple and complex PGCs, they group together complex PGCs that are subject to a context-dependent rule and those that are not, that is, inconsistent PGCs.

Leaving aside the errors involving written accents, which are discussed in the next chapter, Beaudrie's (2012) and Belpoliti and Bermejo's (2020a) studies found that most errors involve grapheme substitution in complex PGCs: /s/, /b/, /r/, /x/, /g/, /ʝ/, /k/, and /i/ and the omission/addition of *h*. It is difficult to compare the results from both studies, because the data are grouped and presented slightly differently. However, the results are consistent, and the aspect in which there is clear consensus is that, after placement of stress marks, the representation of /s/ was the source of most spelling errors. In Beaudrie's (2012) corpus, most spelling errors in complex PGCs were found in spelling /s/, /b/, and *h*. The remaining phonemes (/r/, /x/, /g/, /ʝ/, /k/, /i/) produced only 21.7% of the misspellings in this category. Similarly, Belpoliti and Bermejo (2020a) report that /s/ and *h* accounted for 58% of the misspellings.

When There Is a Rule: Misspellings in Context-Dependent Consistent PGCs

This section looks at the spelling errors produced in the PGCs that are subject to a context-dependent rule. Table 4.1 indicates the accuracy rate in spelling these PGCs in the LH corpus.

Representation of /k/

The /k/ phoneme was the most accurately written rule-based PGC. In *ca, co, cu* contexts, such as in *cantar, cosa, cumplir*, /k/ was only misspelled on three occasions (*nunqua, uniqo*, and *chika*) in the 1,580 instances in which this sequence appeared. Therefore, I focused my attention on the sequences that might become problematic: *cua, cue, cui, cuo*, such as in *cuadro, recuerdo, cuidado, cuota*, and *que, qui*, such as in *queso, quizás*. In the first case, the accuracy rate was of 92.1%, with misspelled words such as **quatro, *quadro, *quando, *aquerdo*. These misspellings are arguably influenced by English spelling, which allows the sequences *qua, quo* (e.g., *quarter, quote*) and where in the sequences *que, qui, u* is pronounced (e.g., *quest, quibble*).

The sequences *que, qui*—which appear in *que, aunque, taquero, chiquito, poquito, quizás,* and so on—were spelled accurately in 98.9% of the cases, with misspellings such as **chicito, *cince* (for *quince*), **ke*, and **cuinto* (for *quinto*).

Representation of /r/

The spelling of /r/ is subject to a contextual rule: it is spelled with one *r* at the beginning of a word (*rato, Ramón*) and after a consonant, which can only be *n* or *l* (*enredo, alrededor*). In all other cases, that is, between vowels, it is spelled as *rr* (*carro, morro*). In the LH corpus, the accuracy rate for *rr* was almost 78%, with misspellings such as **carera* for *carrera*, **corecto* for *correcto*, or **agare* for *agarré*. There were no misspellings consisting of writing *rr* when *r* was needed to represent /r/; that is, no instances of *rr* at the beginning of the word or before a consonant. In Beaudrie's (2012) corpus there were just a few instances of such misspellings, for example, **rrepetir* for *repetir*. Since there are no words starting in *rr*- or with the sequence *rr* + consonant in either English or Spanish, writing *rr* in those contexts requires going against the intuition that comes from visual memory. It requires a conscious choice, and this is more likely to happen at an intermediate level, as it is the case of the students in Beaudrie's (2012) corpus, because students are rearranging their knowledge based on what they have learned in class.

The other vibrant phoneme, the sound /ɾ/, can only be spelled with a single *r*, which would make its representation a simple PGC, and not truly a member of this category. However, students might occasionally represent /ɾ/ with *rr*, probably as a result of overcorrection. Misspellings such as **jugarron* (for *jugaron*) or **querro* (for *quiero*) might be puzzling to an instructor or a reader, but if we consider the large number of instances of /ɾ/ that might appear in their essays, these errors amount to a negligeable percentage (0.4% in LH's corpus).

Representation of /ge/-/gi/

As we saw in the previous chapter, the phoneme /g/ is represented as *g* when it is followed by *a, o, u* and by *gu* when it is followed by *e, i*. This is a grapheme change aimed at preserving the sound /g/ and avoiding /x/, because the Spanish orthographic system prioritizes the phonological criterion over morphology. In the LH corpus, in *ga, go, gu* contexts, /g/ was only misspelled once, in **lleguo* for *llegó*, out of the 148 instances in which these sequences appeared, which puts the accuracy at over 99%. (Incidentally, **lleguo* also appears in Beaudrie's [2012] corpus.) When we look at the spelling of /ge/ /gi/ as *gue-gui*, accuracy certainly drops, to 62.5%.

The spelling of *gue-gui* is a clear example of a mismatch between frequency and accuracy. Despite the low accuracy rate, this PGC does not produce a high number of misspellings overall, because words with these sequences were not very frequent in the corpus. In Beaudrie's (2012) corpus, there was a total of eleven instances of *g* replacing *gu* (e.g., **llege* for *llegue*), and in the LH corpus it appeared in a total of eighteen instances, spread out among only four words (*llegué, investigué, sigue,* and *alguien*), out of only six words that had this sequence. Therefore, no matter how low the accuracy rate of these words, it will not be very noticeable in the overall distribution of errors.

However, paying attention to this low accuracy might help reveal what makes certain PGCs more difficult for SHLLs. On the one hand, the fact that *gue-gui* is not a very frequent sequence may be one of the culprits, as the image of *gue-gui* is not strongly engraved in students' minds. But the most likely contributor is that *gue-gui* sequences appear in alternation with *ga-go* across morphology in words such as *llegar* and *investigar*. In fact, the *gue-gui* word that was misspelled the most was *llegué*—in eight of the ten instances in which it appeared. In addition, because *ge-gi* sequences also exist, albeit with another sound, these sequences are in visual competition with *gue, gui,* which makes this spelling less visually shocking for the writer. The fact that *ge-gi* produces another sound in Spanish is not as weighty in the English-Spanish bilingual, because *ge-gi* may be used to represent /ge/-/gi/ in English (*e.g., get, anger, gift, begin*).

Spelling of *ü*

The use of the dieresis (umlaut) (*ü*) was only required in two words of the LH's corpus (*bilingüe* and *lingüística*), and it was only applied in under 21% of the twenty-four instances in which these words were used. This is another clear example of a mismatch between looking at spelling frequency and accuracy. In Beaudrie's (2012) study, the spelling of *gu* for *gü* does not make a dent in the total number of errors, as it only happened in one word (**pinguino*). Although this author does not report the total number of instances in which *gü* was required, one could speculate that it was not very high, either. As to the reason for the low accuracy in spelling *güe-güi*, the fact that there are not many words spelled with *gü*, relatively speaking, makes the visual image of *güe-güi* not strongly encoded in students' mental-visual lexicon. Also, the fact that in English *güe-güi* does not exist and that the *u* in *gui* might be pronounced (e.g., *penguin, linguistics*) are likely contributing factors.

Just Because: When There Is No Rule

In this section, we examine the misspellings in inconsistent PGCs, that is, PGCs that are not subject to a contextual rule. Table 4.2 indicates the accuracy rate found for these PGCs in the LH corpus.

TABLE 4.2. Accuracy rates of non-rule-based PGCs in the LH corpus

PGCs	Accuracy rates
/ʝ/ → *ll*/*y*	95.5%
/b/ → *b*/*v*	95.0%
h omission	94.8%

The three cases in which two graphemes can be used to represent one phoneme without any phonological rule to indicate which one to choose are *ll*/*y* (to represent /ʝ/), *v*/*b* to represent /b/, and *h*. (The choice between *s* and *c*, *s* and *z*, and, in some cases, *ge-gi* and *je-ji* is also not subject to any rule, but because the situation is more complex, it is discussed separately in the next section.) Intuitively, it would seem that spelling PGCs that are not subject to a rule should be more difficult and lead to more errors than PGCs that are subject to a rule. In fact, as we saw in chapter 2, Spanish-monolingual children achieve a high level of Spanish spelling proficiency in consistent PGCs from a very early age, while proficiency in inconsistent PGC rules is achieved much more gradually (Carbonell de Grompone et al. 1980; Defior, Martos, and Herrera 2000; Defior, Jiménez-Fernández, and Serrano 2009). However, children in dual language, transitional bilingual, or Spanish immersion programs in the United States display lower spelling accuracy in words with context-dependent PGC rules than in words with inconsistent PGCs (Arteagoitia et al. 2005; Ford, Invernizzi, and Huang 2018). After analyzing the LH corpus, it was clear that this is also the case for SHLLs, since these three inconsistent PGCs were not misspelled more often than those that are subject to a rule. In fact, they had a high accuracy rate, of around 95%. In addition, contrary to what happens in rule-based PGCs, accuracy rates for both graphemes in competition are similar, and no dominant grapheme clearly emerges. A closer look at these words gives a clearer picture.

Representation of /ʝ/

Overall, in the LH corpus, /ʝ/ was spelled accurately in 95.5% of the instances in which this phoneme appeared, and the spelling of *ll* yielded a slightly greater accuracy (at 98.5%) than the spelling of *y* (at 94.5%). There were only three misspellings of *ll*: in one case, /ʝ/ was spelled as *y* (**eyos* for *ellos*), but in the other two cases, it was omitted altogether: **fiesio* (for *falleció*) and **arguosa* (for *orgullosa*). In the case of words with *y*, unconventional spellings were found in **lla* (for *ya*), **lellendo* (for *leyendo*), and **alludar* (for *ayudar*). There were some omission cases, in **leendo* (for *leyendo*).

As per the total frequency of these errors, Beaudrie (2012) notes that misspellings of /ʝ/ constituted a small percentage of the total number of errors, which is due not only to a high accuracy rate but also to the relatively small number of target words with that phoneme—a total of thirty-three different words, with a few of them accounting for a great percentage of occurrences, such as *yo, ya, ayudar,* and *ellos.*

Representation of /b/

In the LH corpus, /b/ was spelled accurately in 95% of the cases. But this high accuracy is somewhat distorted by the number of cognate words, in which accuracy was 100%, clearly suggesting that knowing the spelling in English assists with the spelling in Spanish. If we look at the accuracy in noncognate words, we see that *v* is spelled correctly in 96% of the cases, with errors such as **estubo* and **todabía*, and *b* in 94.25%, with errors such as **havia* and **vastante*. However, a more fine-grained look at these words reveals a specific sequence where accuracy is distinctively lower, at 88.5%: the *-aba* ending in *-ar* verbs' imperfect tense (e.g., **hablava, *viajava*).

In terms of frequency, Beaudrie (2021) found that errors in representing /b/ constituted 20% of errors in complex PGCs and that a large majority of these errors consisted of writing *v* instead of *b*. In the LH corpus the ratio of words with *b* and words with *v* was almost 2:1, which would explain a prevalence of *v* for *b* errors. Crucially, Beaudrie also found that most errors (55%) happened in the imperfect tense (*-aba*), conjugations of *haber* and *deber*, and the preterit of *estar* (*estub-* for *estuv-*).

The Grapheme *h*

In the LH corpus, words with *h* were correctly spelled with an *h* in 94% of the cases when looking overall, and in 91% of the cases of noncognate words, such as *hacer, haber, hermano,* or *hasta.* (This count does not include *he/ha*, which are discussed separately.) All the cognate words that also have *h* in English, such as *honesto* or *alcohol*, were spelled correctly.

Beaudrie (2012) found that the vast majority of *h* omissions were found in these three words and their variations: *haber, hacer,* and *hasta*. This also bears out in terms of accuracy, as seen in the LH corpus, where *hacer* and its forms were spelled with an *h* in 84% of the cases; *hasta* with an *h* in 89.7%, *haber* (all forms except *he/ha*) with an *h* in 75%, and *he/ha* with an *h* in 56%. In fact, the accuracy of over 90% in *h* is supported by a few high-frequency words that were spelled correctly: *hambre, hola, hijo,* and *hablar.*

With respect to the addition of *h* in words that do not have *h*, it would be difficult to calculate the accuracy, since, as mentioned earlier in the chapter, *h* could be added virtually anywhere. In terms of frequency, Beaudrie (2012) found that at the beginning of words, it was more commonly omitted when it should have been included than added to a word that does not have *h*, which happened mostly in *era* and *iba*. In the LH corpus the two words that added an *h* the most were *iba* and *así*: *iba* was misspelled as **hiba* in 22% of the cases, and *así* as *haci* in 23.5%, while the addition of *h* in *era* (**hera*) was negligible (0.02% of the cases). As with the overuse of *rr*, addition of *h* reflects overcorrection, which only happens when new elements are introduced. For example, among Mexican children K–3, only third grade students made errors of adding *h*, when they had not done so in the previous years (Zhang et al. 2021).

Between Consistency and Inconsistency: The Spelling of /s/ and /x/

As we saw in chapter 3, the spelling of /s/ and /x/ phonemes is particularly complex because the choices between the graphemes are in some cases subject to a contextual rule and in others not. For that reason, the analysis of students' spellings of these phonemes are presented separately.

Representation of /s/

As we saw in chapter 3, in most varieties /s/, as it is used by the great majority of Spanish speakers, is represented by *s*, *z*, and *c*, but the grapheme choices correspond to two different types of rules: while the choice between *z* and *c* responds to a contextual rule (write *z* before *a*, *o*, *u*; write *c* before *e* or *i*), the choice between *s* and *c* (and between *s* and *z*) does not, and writers need to know the spelling of a certain word.

Some researchers have investigated whether there is a default or dominant grapheme, that is, whether there is a tendency to write one grapheme over the other two (Diuk et al. 2009; Gómez-Velázquez et al. 2014). Intuitively, the *s* grapheme is the most likely candidate to be the default grapheme. Unlike *c*, *s* is uniquely associated with the /s/ phoneme, and, unlike *z*, *s* can appear in all word contexts. As we saw in chapter 3, based on the *Corpus del español* (Davies 2016), within the first 4,000 most frequent lemmas, we find 1,156 words containing *s*, 674 containing *c* (associated to /s/), and 120 containing *z*, which could make *s* the default grapheme.[1] However, as pointed out in Llombart-Huesca (2022, 7), "a more fine-grained distribution of these graphemes" would reveal the distinction is not so clear cut. It is the case that there are many more words containing *s* than words containing *c*, to represent the phoneme /s/. However, when we look at the specific sequences /se/ and /si/, the ones for which the writer needs to choose between *s* and *c*, there are almost double the number of words containing the sequences *ce*/*ci* than words containing *se*/*si*. Also, only one verb has that sequence (*ser*), compared to forty ending in *-cer*, *-cir* (e.g., *hacer*, *crecer*, *nacer*, *decir*, *producir*, *traducir*). Therefore, *c* could also be considered as the default grapheme in *ce-ci* words and/or in -/ser/, -/sir/ verbs.

Beaudrie (2012) found that most errors in the spelling of /s/ were due to the overuse of *s*, which happened in 70.2% of the spelling errors in /s/ (e.g., **hise* for *hice*, **tristesa* for *tristeza*). The other graphemes were incorrectly used in fewer instances: *c* was overused in 15.3% of the /s/ spelling errors (e.g., **cer* for *ser*, **hico* for *hizo*), and *z* was overused in 14.5% of the cases. Belpoliti and Bermejo (2020a) and Contreras-Wise (2020) report similar findings. However, we need to remember that these percentages are relative to the total number of spelling errors in the representation of /s/ and not relative to the total number of words containing the target grapheme. Therefore, the overuse of *s* could be due to the fact that a large number of Spanish words containing /se/ or /si/ are spelled with a *c*, as Beaudrie (2012) notes. Looking at spelling accuracy rates, in a study with primary school children in Argentina, Diuk et al. (2009) showed that children spelled /s/ better in words with the dominant grapheme (s), but this study combined items with *a-o-u* with items with *e-i*, which led to different types of choices. Gómez-Velázquez et al. (2014) evaluated the orthographic proficiency of high school students in Mexico through a battery of tests and found a greater tendency to choose *s* over *c* than vice versa (e.g., **nosivo* for *nocivo*), although in some cases the error was associated with the frequency of the syllable, and not the frequency of the grapheme itself: more words ending in *-sión* were misspelled as *-ción* (**infución* for *infusión*) than the other way around, consistent with the fact that *-ción* is more frequent than *-sión*. In SHLLs' spelling, Llombart-Huesca and Zyzik (2019) examined the accuracy rate of representing /s/ in /se/ and /si/ contexts, through an eighty-item dictation task and found no significant difference in the error rate of *s* and *c* spelling, which would indicate no preference for either grapheme.

SHLLs' accuracy in spelling /s/ in naturalistic writing—in the LH corpus—is investigated by Llombart-Huesca (2022). Table 4.3 shows the accuracy results

TABLE 4.3. Accuracy in spelling /s/ in the LH corpus

	In cognate words	Examples	In noncognate words	Examples
se/si	98.8%	*secundaria, música*	97.3%	*casi, pensé*
ce/ci	92.9%	*acento, decidir*	81.7%	*decir, conocer, empecé*
sa-so-su	100.0%	*interesante*	99.8%	*quiso, mesa*
za-zo-zu	87.5%	*analizar, autorizar*	60.9%	*alcanzar, azul, hizo*
s + consonant	100.0%	*específico, escuela*	100.0%	*este, triste*
z + consonant	—	—	20.0%	*mezcla, conozco*
word final *-s*	—	—	99.5%	*mes, dos, además*
word final *-z*	—	—	75.0%	*arroz, feliz, diez*

Source: Adapted from Llombart-Huesca (2022).

for each category: *se-si*, *ce-ci*, *sa-so-su*, *za-zo-zu*, *s* + consonant, *z* +consonant, word-final -*s*, and word-final -*z*.

The study shows that words containing *s* were spelled more accurately than words with its competing graphemes, *c* and *z*. In /se-si/ contexts—when looking at cognates and noncognates together—words with *s* were spelled accurately in 98% of the instances, whereas words with *c* in only 84.9%. The contrast between *sa-so-su* and *za-zo-zu* is even more striking, as only one misspelled word was found among *s*-words—the noncognate *quiso*, spelled as **quizo*—while in the *za-zo-zu* group, the accuracy rate was at 63.2% (87.5% in cognate words and 60.9% in noncognates). In words where *s* and *z* are followed by a consonant, such as *este*, *mezcla*, and verb forms ending in -*zco* (e.g., *conozco*), the contrast was even greater: there was not a single error in words spelled with *s* + consonant, a fact already noted by Beaudrie (2012), while the accuracy in words spelled with *z* + consonant was very low, at 20%. The clear preference for *s* before consonants is likely due to the fact that words containing *s* + consonant are overwhelmingly more frequent than words with *z* + consonant (Llombart-Huesca 2022), at a ratio of 99:1 among the 4,000 most-frequent lemmas in Davies's (2016) *Corpus del español*. The 100% accuracy rate in this category suggests that participants have grasped the *s*+ consonant pattern due to that high prevalence.

The greater accuracy in *s*-words found in the LH corpus (Llombart-Huesca 2022) is not consistent with Llombart-Huesca and Zyzik's (2019) findings that there was no difference in the accuracy rate for *s* and *c* in /se/-/si/ contexts. This discrepancy might be because the *se-si* and *ce-ci* words students used in their essays are much more frequent than the words used in Llombart-Huesca and Zyzik's dictation task. These less-frequent words used in the dictation may have been perceived by students as "more advanced" and, therefore, requiring a more "sophisticated" spelling (Llombart-Huesca 2022). Another difference between these two studies that could explain the different results is that Llombart-Huesca and Zyzik's (2019) dictation words did not include any *ce* forms resulting from inflecting a -*zar* verb.

In fact, a key finding of Llombart-Huesca's (2022) study is that the morphological alternation of *c*/*z* proves to be particularly difficult and a main source of error. For example, the forms of *hacer* under the *ce-ci* category (e.g., *hace*, *hice*, *hicimos*) had a much higher accuracy rate (87.5%) than its inflected form with *z* (*hizo*) (25%). Spelling *hizo* correctly is particularly demanding because the alternation *c*/*z* requires attending to three sources of information: phonological, morphological, and orthographic (Llombart-Huesca 2017a): spelling *hizo* requires changing the letter used in the main form (*c*) to avoid changing the pronunciation, and to choose the specific letter that is found in orthographic alternation with *c* (*z*), a not very frequent one, as we have seen. In fact, those participants who wrote **hiso*, when they also wrote *hacer*, did so correctly, which suggests that what proved most difficult was the alternation from *c* to *z*, and not spelling *hacer* itself. As stated in Llombart-Huesca (2022, 21), "If the connection between the *c* and *z* graphemes is not strongly engraved in the students' minds, resorting to the grapheme *s* is the least costly solution."

The alternation from *-zar* to *-ce* was also very difficult. Llombart-Huesca (2022) notes that *comencé* and *empecé* were the two most problematic *ce* items, with an error rate of over 50%, clearly more than the error rate of *ce* forms of verbs ending in *-cer* such as *nacer, crecer, conocer,* or *decir.* Further supporting the notion that alternating *-zar* to *-ce* is difficult is that there was graphemic consistency in those cases in which participants wrote forms of *empezar* under both categories: those who misspelled *empecé* as **empezé* spelled that verb correctly in the *za-zo-zu* category (e.g., *empezó*), and the participants who wrote **empesé* also used *s* in the *za-zo-zu* category (e.g., **empesó*). In addition, it seems that the spelling difficulties with *ce* in verbal forms inflected from *-zar* verbs are magnified by the fact that participants had difficulties spelling the *-zar* verbs in the infinitive, such as *alcanzar, socializar, avanzar, comenzar, empezar,* and *analizar.*

Another study, part of a larger study on spelling, looked at both accuracy and consistency in the spelling of /s/ across morphology. Participants were ninety-eight college students in a Spanish for Spanish Speakers I course (age ranging between 18 and 34, with an average age of 20.2). Participants heard thirty target words, which were all verb forms with /s/ in the stem: ten with *sa-so,* ten with *ce-ci,* and ten with *za-zo.* The ten words in each category comprised two forms of five different verbs (e.g., *pasar-pasó, empezar-empezó, conocer-conocieron*). The two words of each pair maintained the spelling of /s/; that is, there were no alternation pairs of the type *empezar-empecé.* Participants were given a sheet with a space to write each word, and they wrote the words as they heard them on dictation. (Words were read both in isolation and with a context sentence to help participants better recognize the words.) The first fifteen words were five with each of the three letters (*s, c, z*), and participants wrote them on the first page. Students then turned to the next page as the dictation continued, with the next fifteen target words, which included the pairs of the previous fifteen words. Participants were instructed not to turn to the previous page. The study looked at two measures: accuracy and consistency. Accuracy was measured by counting the number of correct spellings in each of the ten items of each group—only looking at the spelling of /s/. Consistency was measured by looking at each pair (e.g., *pasar-pasó, empezar-empezó, conocer-conocieron*) and counting as "consistent" those pairs in which the same letter had been used in both words, regardless of whether it was correct or not. For example, if a participant wrote **empesar* and then **empesó,* it would be counted as "consistent." Table 4.4 shows the accuracy and consistency results for each condition.

When looking at accuracy, we see that the *s*-words were spelled significantly more accurately than the *c*-words, and the *c*-words were spelled significantly more accurately than the *z*-words, which is consistent with the findings

TABLE 4.4. Accuracy and consistency in spelling pairs of words with *s*, *c*, *z*

	Examples	Accuracy (Std. variation)	Consistency (Std. variation)
s	*pasar-pasó*	90.3% (12.1)	89.0% (16.0)
c	*conocer-conocíamos*	83.3% (20.8)	84.4% (20.2)
z	*empezar-empezamos*	57.9% (30.7)	73.8% (20.4)

in the LH corpus. Spelling consistency was also greater in the *s*-word pairs than in the *c*-word pairs, and in the *c*-word pairs than in the *z*-word pairs, but the difference between *s* and *c* was not statistically significant. These results seem to confirm the findings that spelling of *z* is the most difficult, which is displayed as low accuracy as well as hesitancy or inconsistency.

The difficulty in spelling *-zar* verbs is not only a matter of accuracy but also has an effect on frequency of errors. As Beaudrie (2012) found, verbs ending in *-zar*, together with the words *vez* and *hacer*, accounted for 68% of misspellings in /s/.

The results of Llombart-Huesca's (2022) study on the accuracy of spelling /s/ in the LH corpus also show that cognate status has a clear effect and favors spelling accuracy. In words containing *s*+ vowel, the effect was negligible because accuracy was at or near ceiling. But in the other two relevant contexts, the effect was clear: 92.9% versus 81.7% in *ce-ci*, and 87.5% versus 60.9% in *za-zo-zu*.[2] These results are consistent with those obtained by Llombart-Huesca and Zyzik (2019), who found that participants spelled /s/ in /se/-/si/ words significantly better in cognates (e.g., *símbolo, desierto, cerámica, inocente*) (87.05%) than in non-cognates (e.g., *semejante, cosecha, cejas, bocina*) (77.25%).[3]

Representation of /x/

The other PGC that is both rule based and inconsistent is the representation of /x/. When the word root is spelled with *ge-gi*, it is subject to alternation to *ja-jo* across morphology (e.g., *escoger/escojo*), to avoid a change of phoneme to /g/ (as in **escogo*); but when the word root is spelled with *ja, je, ji, jo*, the grapheme *j* is maintained (*trabajar/-trabajé*). There is no contextual rule to choose between *ge* and *je* and between *gi* and *ji*.

In the LH corpus, the /x/ phoneme in /xe/-/xi/ sequences was spelled accurately in 85% of occurrences. However, a closer look gives us a more telling story. There were only two cognate words with *j*, *lenguaje* and *mensaje*, but in this case, the opposite letter is used in English (*language, message*), which could explain why *lenguaje* was misspelled with a *g* in one quarter of the cases. On the other hand, the spelling of *je-ji* in noncognate words—such as *dije, dejé, enojé, mujer,* *traje, ejemplo*—and the spelling of *ge-gi* in cognate words—such as *sugerir, generación, general, registro,* and *origen*—exhibited higher accuracy: only one misspelling was found, in one instance of **intelijente*. In all these cases, the spelling of /x/ is not subject to grapheme alternation across morphology. However, spelling accuracy of *ge-gi* sequences in noncognate words such as *dirigir* and *corregir* was much lower, at 76.3%. In these verbs, *g* alternates with *j* across morphology, as in *dirigir-dirijo, corregir-corrijo*. These results seem to confirm the trend that grapheme alternation across morphology in order to preserve the phoneme is a major source of difficulty.

Double Consonants

The use of double consonants when only one is needed (e.g., **classe*, **attención*) is, technically, a case of a misspelling in a simple PGC. For example, in /t/ → *t*, there are no two options to choose from. However, in the grapheme inventory of the English-Spanish bilingual, two choices might exist (*t* and *tt*) because double consonants exist in English. Beaudrie (2012), in her classification of errors in simple PGCs, includes a category called "English transfer," and in that corpus, double consonants constituted 56% of errors in consonants in simple PGCs.

In the LH corpus, all instances of double consonants were, not surprisingly, found in cognate words that had double consonant in English, and the accuracy rate was 87.7%, ranging from 90.1% for *s*, with spellings like **classe* and **profesional*, and 78.5% for *f*, with words like **differente*, **difficil*, and **effecto*. For other consonants, there were not enough instances to allow us to examine accuracy by itself. There were two words with English *tt*, *atender* and *atención*, and only one word with *cc* to represent /k/, *ocasiones*, which was spelled with *cc* in one of the four total instances of the word. (This use of *cc* should be distinguished from the spelling of *acento* as *accento*, which is most likely due to students also pronouncing the word as *accento*, with /ks/, as in English.) The double-consonant sequence that proved to be the most difficult was *-mm-*. Students wrote *-mm-* in all instances in which that sequence corresponds to *-nm-* in Spanish: **i<u>mm</u>igrar*, **i<u>mm</u>ersión*, and **i<u>mm</u>ediato* (for *i<u>nm</u>igrar, i<u>nm</u>ersión*, and *i<u>nm</u>ediato*). The effect of English was clear, because the noncognate *conmigo* was spelled correctly in all cases—probably also aided by the internal structure of the word as *con + migo*. When the word was spelled with *-mm-* in English, but with a single *m* in Spanish, as in *común, comunicar, comenzar*, and *comunión*, accuracy was at 76%.

As a part of a larger study with seventy-three SHLLs participants, whose average age was 19.9, I looked at the effect of cognate status when writing words that contained *f*. Participants wrote several words during a dictation task: nine were cognate words that are spelled with one *f* in English (e.g., *profesor, definir*); nine were cognate words that are spelled with *ff* in English (e.g., *oficina, tráfico*); and

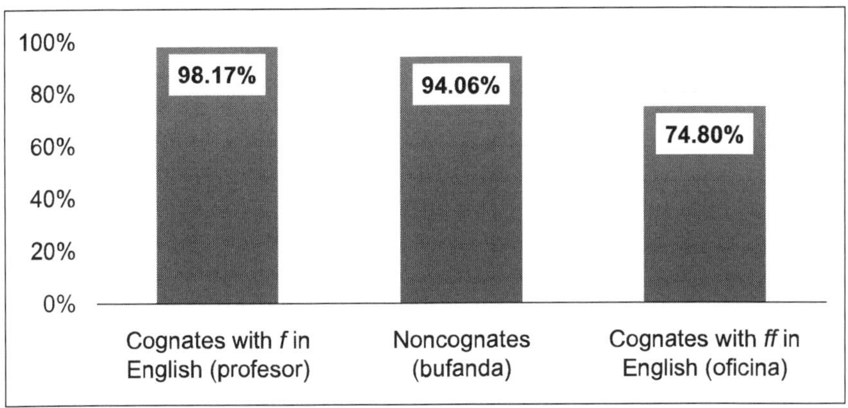

FIGURE 4.1. Accuracy in spelling cognate and noncognate words with *f*

nine were noncognate words (e.g., *afuera*, *bufanda*). The average results for each type of word are represented in figure 4.1.

The difference between the scores in each type was statistically significant.[4] The type of words in which participants had the lowest result when spelling *f* were, not surprisingly, cognate words that are spelled with *ff* in English, such as *oficina* (spelled as **officina*) or *efecto* (spelled as **effecto*). Interestingly, participants spelled cognate words that have one *f* in English (e.g., *profesor*) better than noncognate words (e.g., *bufanda*), and this difference was also statistically significant. Therefore, the single *f* from English spelling had a greater effect than simply considering *f* as the default spelling.

Phonological Awareness and Vowels

Another case of misspellings in simple PGCs involves vowels. Although these misspellings are less frequent than errors in, for example, the representation of /s/, they present a particular challenge to instructors. If the sound /e/ is always represented as *e*, and /a/ as *a*, and so forth, why are these vowels misspelled? In fact, the simplicity in the vocalic PGC system explains why errors in vowels have not been found to be common in monolingual Spanish-speaking children and why students with basic phonological knowledge can achieve vowel spelling accuracy fairly easily (de Manrique and Signorini 1994, 1998). For example, Justicia and colleagues (1999) found that vowels constituted only 2.6% of spelling errors of Spanish monolingual children—ages eight to ten.

However, among English-Spanish bilinguals, the error rate in vowels is much higher. Bahr et al. (2015) found a rate of 19% of vowel errors (such as **pudia* for *podia*) of all errors in the writings of twenty Spanish-speaking middle school students enrolled in an English Language Learners' program in the United States.[5] Errors in vowels were also more frequent in the adult SHLLs' samples analyzed by Beaudrie (2012), at a rate of 23% of the non-accent-related misspellings. Over half of the vowel errors consisted of writing *e* for *i*: **envitados* for *invitados* or **encreíble* for *increíble.* Other cases consisted of writing *i* for *e*, as in **bromiando* for *bromeando*. In the LH corpus, I examined the spelling error rate of vowels and diphthongs in a few high-frequency verbs that have *e* or *o* in their stem. *Tener* (in the *ten-* and *tien-* forms) was misspelled in 7.6% of cases (e.g., **tineya*, **tienía*, and **teinía*, for *tenía*); *querer* (in the *quer-* and *quier-* forms) was misspelled in 19.6% of the cases (e.g., **querio* for *quiero*, **quirea* for *quería*, **quero* for *quiero*); and *poder* (in the *pod-* and *pued-* forms) was misspelled in 10% of the cases (e.g., **puedía* and **pudía*, for *podía*).

The errors involving vowels can be found in these processes: vowel diphthongization, diphthong reduction, inversion, transposition, and substitution.

Diphthongization

Some errors consist of writing a diphthong, that is, two vowels, in a syllable that only has one, mostly *ie* for /e/ and some cases of *ue* for /o/. Diphthongization happened in 11% of the vowel errors in Belpoliti and Bermejo's (2020a) corpus. In the LH corpus, diphthongization was typically found in these situations:

- Verbs that have *e/ie* and *o/ue* stem alternation but in forms that do not have the diphthong; for example, **empiecé* (for *empecé*), **entiender* (for *entender*), **quiería* (for *quería*), **preferiemos* (for *preferimos*), **pueder* (for *poder*)[6]
- Words that have another diphthong in the same word (e.g., **converciación* for *conversación*, **crieciendo* for *creciendo*)
- Words where the diphthong *ie* was written to represent /i/, as in **tieró* (for *tiró*), **aprendie* (for *aprendí*), **cienco* (for *cinco*)

Diphthong Reduction

This is the opposite process: a word that contains a diphthong, usually *ie*, is spelled with a simple vowel. In Belpoliti and Bermejo's corpus, vowel omission—which happened in diphthongs but in other contexts too—constituted 24% of the vowel errors. These are the main categories in which diphthong reduction was found in the LH corpus:

- Verbs that have *e/ie* stem alternation, in forms that should have the diphthong: **quero* (for *quiero*) and **entendo* (for *entiendo*)
- Thematic vowel of *-er* verbs, which take the *-ie-* form in the imperfect subjunctive, gerund, and third-person-plural form of the preterit: **aprendera* (for *aprendiera*), and **dicendo* (for *diciendo*), **aprenderon* (for *aprendieron*)

- Words that had a diphthong in another syllable: **experienca* and **experencia* (for *experiencia*)

Reduction in other diphthongs (*-ie-*, *-io-*, *-ue-*) were less frequent: **quiro* (for *quiero*), **convirtó* (for *convirtió*), **posisón* (for *posición*), **afera* (for *afuera*).

Inversion and Transposition

In some cases, the two vowels in a diphthong are inverted. For example, **peinso* (for *pienso*), **caundo* (for **cuando*), **neuvo* (for *nuevo*), **cuidad* (for *ciudad*). These inversions happened in only 5% of the vowel errors in Belpoliti and Bermejo's (2020a) corpus, and they are also documented by Beaudrie (2012).

In an interesting set of spelling errors involving vowels, a vowel that appears in a sequence with another vowel (diphthong or hiatus) moves into another syllable, creating a diphthong in that syllable, as in the following examples: **queira* and **quiera* (for *quería*), **apriendo* (for *aprendió*), **tempio* (for *tiempo*), **estuidos* (for *estudios*), **confancia* (for *confianza*).

Substitution

Other vowel misspellings involve substitution of one vowel for another, which is most frequent between *i* and *e*. Substitution of *e* for *i* was found in these groups:

- Stressed syllables: **edo*, **escriber*, **ese* (for *hice*), **sentedos*, **aprendé*
- Pre-tonic position: **deficil*, **derejirme*, **enscribir*, **descrebir*, **especialedad*
- Stem-changing verbs (e → i): **sugerieron*, **venieron*, **corregieron*, **corregiendo*

Substitution of *i* for *e* was found in these groups:

- -ea- → -ia-: **bromiando*, **peliar*
- Pre-tonic position: **disafurtadamente*, **imidiata*, **impese*, **intienden*, **linguaje*
- Stem-changing verbs (e → i): **dicer*, **sigia*, **sigido*

In fewer cases, vowel substitution affected *o*/*u*, with almost all instances involving the verb *poder* (e.g., **podiera* for *pudiera*, **pudía* for *podía*) and in a few rare cases, other vowels (e.g., **confendí* for *confundí*).

Now, it is important to think about the reason for these spellings. Vowel misspellings might seem particularly puzzling, since, technically, they are in a one-to-one PGC. Beaudrie (2012) suggests that the vast majority of vowel errors seem to be explained by interference from English spelling. Indeed, this is a plausible explanation for the set of words in which /i/ is spelled as *ie*, as in **aprendie* (for *aprendí*) or **cienco* (for *cinco*), due to transfer from English representation of /i/ as *ie*, as in *thief*, *movie*, or *believe*. English orthographic interference is also likely the reason for spelling /i/ as *e* in stressed syllables, as in **edo* for *ido*, or **sentedos* for *sentidos*, since English /i/ is represented by *e* in stressed position, as in *delete* or *secret*. On the other hand, English interference would not explain the rest of misspellings in vowels, especially in cases of *e* for *i* in unstressed position, such as in **defícil*, **encreíble*, and **envitado* (for *difícil*, *increíble*, and *invitado*), because this is not a position in which /i/ is spelled as *e* in English. In addition, some of these words are cognates, spelled with *i* in English, as in *invite* and *difficult*.

In some of these cases, it is likely that these misspellings are not actual spelling errors but rather can be ascribed to a grammar issue. For example, when students write **fuerta* for *fuerte* (as documented in Beaudrie 2012) or **frecuentamente* for *frecuentemente* (found in the LH corpus), it is likely that students are simply inflecting these gender-invariable adjectives with an *a* to make them feminine. A grammar explanation can probably also be applied to some instances of misspellings in stem-changing verb forms, as **sugerieron* and **entendo*, where students might have failed to apply the vowel change in the stem and wrote *e* as in the stem that appears in the majority of the verb forms.

Other vowel misspellings represent the students' linguistic variety: students write words such as **bromiando*, **envitado*, **divirtir*, or **suidad* because those are the words in their available input, since these words are common in certain varieties of Spanish, as we saw in chapter 3.

Another explanation, which would work in conjunction with the previous one, is that most vowel misspellings, as well as most spelling errors involving syllables—syllable omission and syllable transposition—are the result of underdeveloped phonological awareness (Leal, Matute, and Zarabozo 2005; Llombart-Huesca 2018). The vowel misspellings described in the preceding text involve pairs of vowels that are very close in place of articulation, which makes these vowels an area of intrinsic phonological fragility and variability. This fragility and variability are likely to also affect the way SHLLs perceive and conceptualize the vocalic sounds they hear and produce, particularly in unstressed position and in diphthongs.

In Llombart-Huesca's (2019) study with SHLLs, participants listened to and wrote a series of pseudowords containing *i*, *ie*, and *ea* (e.g., *camilto*, *pariené*, *caleato*). Pseudowords were used so that participants had to rely on what they perceived. (If the dictation is made with real words, students who say *peliar* will most likely write *peliar* even if the dictated word is *pelear*.) The letter *i* in a diphthong *ie* (e.g., *pariené*) had a correct spelling rate of 78.41%, significantly lower than the spelling of *i* in a monophthong (e.g., *camilto*), which achieved a score of 98%. When looking at the misspellings of words with the *ie* diphthong, there were some cases of diphthong reduction to a monophthong, as in **mafenar* (for *mafienar*) and many of these reductions were accompanied by transposition, as in **mafeniar*, which suggests that a diphthong was heard but the participant had difficulty placing it in the correct syllable. These errors are similar to some errors we see SHLLs make in free writing, such as *_gruadar_ (_graduar_), *_querio_ (_quiero_), *_quirea_ (_quería_). The spelling of _-ea-_ pseudowords (e.g., _caleato_ or _poleador_) had an even lower accuracy rate, 65.1%, which suggests that many students conceptualize the sound of [ea] as /ia/.

Llombart-Huesca (2019) suggests that underdeveloped PA and representation of nonstandard pronunciations could be considered together in a unifying account. The processes observed in SHLLs' spelling of vowels—substitution, transposition, insertion, and deletion—are found in children's typical development of phonological awareness (Ingram 1974; Edwards 1992). Exposure to fine-grained phonological distinctions produce increasingly more fine-grained perceptual distinctions (Defior 2004; Defior et al. 2015). For example, being exposed to many words with [ja] (e.g., _enviar, cambiar_) and to many words with [ea] (e.g., _pelear, pasear_) helps to develop the ability to distinguish between those two sequences [ja]/[ea], as well as to conceptualize them as two different phoneme sequences—/ia/ and /ea/. But a speaker whose input and output only contains [ja] and not [ea], because all words containing _ea_ are pronounced with [ja] in their environment, will not develop the ability to perceive these two sequences as phonemically distinct. In addition, lack of development of early literacy in Spanish that would strengthen phonological discrimination and segmentation might further promote a reduced vocalic system.

Phonological Awareness and Consonants

Difficulties with phonological awareness are likely behind other types of misspellings involving consonants. One set of misspellings involve substituting the palatal sounds /ɲ/ (_ñ_) and /ʝ/ (_ll_ and _y_), which are very close in articulation with _ni_ (or _in_) and _li_, as in these cases found in the LH corpus—*_quinceinera_, *_ingeñería_, *_familla_, *_payizes_, *_sabilla_ (for _quinceañera_, _ingeniería_, _familia_, _países_, _sabía_)—or even with one another, as in *_mañoría_ (for _mayoría_). A few involved other similar consonants, as /p/ versus /b/, in *_embese_, *_tamboco_ (for _empecé_, _tampoco_), and /k/ versus /g/, in *_guesta_ for _cuesta_.

Other misspellings resulting from difficulties with PA consist of inversion and transposition of consonants, as in *_ogrullosa_ for *_orgullosa_, *_cuatro_ for _cuarto_, *_otrografia_ for _ortografía_. Similarly, there were cases of repetition of a consonant from a consonant cluster, as in *_halblar_ for _hablar_, *_aprendrer_ for _aprender_, which parallel examples of diphthong repetition we have seen above (e.g., *_converciación_ for *_conversación_).

In other cases, low PA and difficulties in decoding and encoding words also lead to shortening long words. Although some word shortenings are common in informal speech (e.g., *_patrás_ for _para atrás_ and *_onde_ for _donde_, *_prendi_ for *aprendí*, **orita* for *ahorita*, *garrar for *agarrar*), other cases are restricted to SHLLs' attempts to write—and read—long words, such as in **preparon* for *prepararon*, **femino* for *femenino*, **hablavos* for *hablábamos*, or **practido* for *practicado*. Belpoliti and Bermejo (2020a, 28), who report similar misspellings, found that most letter omissions happened in long words, which is likely to be due to the increased difficulty to "maintain a mental representation of the aural expression." Previous studies have suggested that word length has an influence on spelling (Valle-Arroyo 1990; Carrillo, Alegría, and Marín 2013).

In other cases, PA also affects word awareness and the ability to identify the word boundaries, as in these examples from the LH corpus: **aveces/habeces/aveses* (for *a veces*), **alrebez* (for *al revés*), **comunicar me* (for *comunicarme*), **des de* (for *desde*), **halamejor* (for *a la mejor*), **toda via* (for *todavía*), **a reglar* (for *arreglar*).

Morphological and Morphosyntactic Awareness Errors

As it was discussed in chapter 2, successful spelling is not simply about applying the orthographic rules and memorizing the spellings of those PGCs that are not subject to rules. For example, students might quickly learn that "*hacer* is spelled with an *h*" and might even remember to write *h* every time they write *hacer*. But what about *hice, hizo, hace*? And what about *deshice*? And while students might need to memorize the spelling of *tristeza*, is it necessary to also memorize *riqueza, dureza, belleza*, and so on? And what can help students write *niñez* but *inglés*, two words that end in the same sound sequence? In all these examples, it is clear that writers would benefit from an awareness of the morphological structure of the words. Since SHLLs have received no—or limited—literacy instruction in Spanish, have they developed an awareness of the structure of Spanish words and how groups of words share morphemes?

Finding out an answer to this question was one of the goals of Llombart-Huesca's (2017a) study in SHLLs. Participants were given a series of word pairs, in which the two words were somehow related. In some pairs, the words were morphologically related in a transparent way (e.g., *interés-interesante*); in others, they were morphologically related but in an opaque manner (e.g., *hacer-deshago*); and in others, they were related semantically but not morphologically (e.g., *mirar-veo*). Participants were asked to indicate whether the two words of each pair belonged to the same family and were given examples of what constituted the same family. They did this task in both Spanish and English—with different words. Not surprisingly, the results showed that students had the least difficulty when the relatedness of two words was transparent (e.g., *interés-interesante*), although there still was an average error rate of around 15%. The pairs that proved the most difficult were the ones with words that were opaquely related, with an average error rate of 39%. Participants also incorrectly related many morphologically unrelated words, such as *mirar* and *veo*, with an average error rate of 26.5%.

The results of this study suggest that the default strategy employed by the participants was attention to meaning rather than to form, which is the default strategy in speakers at early stages of literacy and metalinguistic awareness development. In addition, while the participants performed similarly in the two languages in the unrelated pairs (*mirar-veo*, *watch-see*), they did significantly better in English than in Spanish in the related pairs. These results support previous findings (Ehri 1979; Bialystok and Ryan 1985; Bialystok 1986a, 1986b) that the ability to pay attention to form is more strongly associated with literacy and linguistic knowledge specific to the language at hand. Since SHLLs have had limited literacy instruction in Spanish, their deployment of the analytical skills that allow relating words such as *hacer-deshago* is limited. In addition, Llombart-Huesca's (2017a) study also found a moderate correlation between the results of this task and a spelling task conducted through a dictation. Interestingly, this correlation was found only when considering the related pairs. This is not surprising, because while incorrectly relating words such as *mirar* and *veo* should not have any negative impact on spelling, failing to notice that words like *hacer* and *deshago* are related is likely to have a negative effect.

The difficulties in maintaining spelling across morphology have been shown earlier in this chapter. Several studies (Beaudrie 2012; Llombart-Huesca 2017a, 2022) have shown that students have a particularly hard time working out the grapheme change across morphology, as in verbs of the *empezar* → *empecé* and *hacer* → *hizo* type. But, as shown earlier, students might also be inconsistent in the spelling of /s/ in two forms of the same verb even when no spelling change takes place, as in *pasar-pasó*, *empezar-empezó*, *conocer-conocieron*. Making strong connections between different morphological forms of a word would allow a stronger connection between the word and the right grapheme.

Underdeveloped morphological awareness also has a detrimental effect on spelling in other situations. There are productive suffixes containing /s/, and having an awareness of them as pieces that can be attached to different stems to form words would help students when spelling those words (e.g., *-eza*: *tristeza*, *pobreza*; *-izar*: *analizar*, *colonizar*). The LH corpus did not include any instance of a word with the *-eza* suffix, but **tristesa* appears as an example in Beaudrie's (2012) corpus, and *analizar* appears as **analisar* in the LH corpus. Another case in which morphological awareness could have an impact in spelling is when writing *-aba* in the imperfect indicative of *-ar* verbs. While /b/ was spelled accurately in 95% of the cases in the LH corpus, *-aba* yielded the lowest accuracy rate in spelling /b/ (88.5%) (e.g., **hablava*, **viajava*), which suggests that SHLLs are not sensitive to this suffix.

Morphosyntactic awareness could greatly assist in the spelling of *ha* versus *a*. In the LH corpus, *ha*/*he* were spelled without *h* in about 44% of the cases. While it is possible that those students had never learned that *haber* is spelled with *h*, this is a misspelling that persists in more advanced levels, as Beaudrie (2012) also found many *h* omissions in *haber* forms in her corpus, which consisted of essays written by SHLLs in an intermediate composition course. Because of the repetitive nature of morphemes, spelling in certain morphemes will have a great impact in the overall number of misspellings in an essay. In fact, Beaudrie (2012, 142) indicates that "the various forms of the words *hacer, haber, hasta, ir, deber, estar, a,* and *era*, together with the *-aba* ending in the imperfect tense accounted for approximately a third of the misspellings" in complex PGCs.

Another clear case in which low morphosyntactic awareness has an impact in spelling involves the spelling of words that have been "perceptually obscured by their phonetic context but whose presence is justified by their morphosyntactic status" (Llombart-Huesca 2018, 218). We see this in sentences where the preposition *a* is preceded by a verb form that ends in *-a* and/or followed by a verb form that begins with *a-* (or *ha-*). For example, in *voy a hablar*, some students omit the preposition *a* and write **voy hablar*. Since the two /a/ are contracted in *voy a hablar* (sounding as /bojabláɾ/), the preposition *a* does not stand out phonetically. In cases like this, the writer can only know that the preposition *a* is there through an awareness of the morphosyntactic structure (*voy a* ________), which would connect *voy a hablar* with *voy a comer*, where *a* is clearly audible. In some cases, the misspelling even leads to the use of a different verb, as in the following example classified as a "syllable omission" in Beaudrie (2012, 140): *#debe ver* for *debe haber*. Other similar cases are *#voy a ser* for *voy a hacer* ([bójaséɾ]), **va ver* for *va a haber* (/babéɾ/), *#haber* for *a ver* (/abéɾ/), *#viera* for *hubiera*.[7]

In the LH corpus, the preposition was omitted in 46.5% of the cases in which this type of structure was used. These are a few examples: **empesamos hablar*, **iba ir*, **va ayudar*, **va salir*. In some cases, *hacer* was used instead of *ser*, when the previous word ended in *a*: **me gustaría hacer más fluente*, **para hacer ingeniero*, **me ha enseñado hacer una persona*. In other cases, *a ser* was used instead of *hacer*—**llegaron a ser un impacto*, **para ser mi cabello*—and there was also a case of *haber* instead of *a ver*: **jugamos haber quien decía . . .*

In a study with thirty-one SHLLs enrolled in a Spanish for Spanish Speakers I class, participants listened to ten short sentences that included the above structures (e.g., *Voy a hablar con mi profesor, Juan empieza a trabajar, Juan ha hablado con ella*) and four control sentences in which the preposition was surrounded by consonants and clearly audible (e.g., *Voy a cenar con mis padres*), and the participants had to write the number of words each sentence had. The results clearly confirmed that they did not count the obscured vowel in a great majority of cases, with an accuracy of only 23.6%. The fact that there was not a single error in word counting in the control sentences confirms that the cause of the miscounting was indeed the phonetically obscured vowel.

Discussion of Findings

In this chapter, we have described and analyzed the spellings produced by SHLLs. There are a few things to consider when we look at misspellings.

How We Elicit the Writing Sample

Researchers have gathered data from SHLLs in two main ways: through essays written by students, which use naturalistic data, and through an experimental (or quasi-experimental) design, where they ask participants to perform tasks with words that have been carefully selected by the researcher with the purpose of investigating a specific aspect of spelling. Typically, naturalistic data produce fewer errors. For example, Beaudrie (2012) found an overall error rate of 11.7% (3.8% when looking only at non-accent-related errors) among intermediate-level students, Contreras-Wise (2020) found an error rate of 4.7% (non-accented-related errors) with participants in four different levels, and Belpoliti and Bermejo (2020a) reported an overall error rate of 15.9%. In contrast, writing produced in experimental or quasi-experimental studies generally produce more errors, because researchers target particular graphemes and/or types of words that are likely to be problematic. However, in essays we observe students' ability to spell words that they are familiar with. For example, Bermejo and Belpoliti (2020a) found that about 90% of the words participants used in their writings were at level-1 frequency (among the 1,000 most frequent words). As Gómez-Velázquez et al. (2014, 59) write, "we have a tendency to write words the spelling of which we are more certain of" (my translation). Therefore, in students' essays we see the errors that students are more likely to make in the words that they are more likely to use, whereas experimental settings put participants in challenging situations. "In a way, free writing shows what participants *do*, while experimental settings show what participants *can* (and cannot) do" (Llombart-Huesca 2022, 11).

Frequency versus Accuracy

Throughout this chapter we have discussed two ways to count misspellings in a specific sequence or PGC: error frequency and accuracy rate. Error frequency tells us the percentage of errors in one PGC relative to the total number of errors found in the corpus. On the other hand, accuracy rate gives us the percentage of errors relative to the total number of instances where errors could have been made.

In terms of frequency, according to Beaudrie (2012), the PGCs that produce the greatest number of errors are the following:

- The spelling of /s/, particularly *vez, hacer,* and verbs ending in *-zar*
- The spelling of *h*, particularly the words *haber, hacer, ir, hasta, a,* and *era*, and their inflected forms

- The spelling of /b/, mostly concentrated in the ending *-aba* of the imperfect tense, the preterit of *estar* (*estuv-*), and the conjugations of *haber* and *deber*
- Vowel substitution of *e* for *i*, which is the main source of error in simple PGCs

In terms of accuracy rate, the PGCs and sequences that seem the most difficult, with an error rate over 10%, based on the LH corpus, are the following:

- *-ba* inflection of the imperfect (e.g., *hablaba, miraba, iban*)
- Verbs ending in *-zar* and their corresponding forms in *-ce* (e.g., *empezar, empecé*)
- The verb *hacer* and its forms, but mostly *hizo*
- Words ending in *-z* and their plural form (e.g., *vez-veces*)
- Words with *-z* + consonant—namely, *-zco* endings (e.g., *mezcla, conozco*)
- Cognate words that have *ff* and *mm* in English (e.g., *oficina, inmigración*)
- The sequences *ge-gi* in noncognate words, mostly verbs in *-ger/-gir* (e.g., *corregir, escoger*)
- The ending *-aje* in cognate words (*-age* in English); for example, *mensaje, lenguaje*
- The sequences *güe-güi* (e.g., *bilingüe*)
- The sequences *gue-gui* (*llegué*).
- Words with /r/
- Vowels in certain stem-changing verbs

What Makes Certain Sequences More Difficult?

When we were examining the different rates of SHLLs' spelling accuracy in different PGCs, we also discussed several PGC and grapheme features that seemed to contribute to the level of difficulty or cognitive demand posed to students when spelling that particular PGC, and those that seemed to facilitate their spelling. Let us review them here.

Rule or No Rule?

As we saw in chapter 2, while Spanish-monolingual children acquire context-dependent consistent PGCs—that is, rule-based PGCs—first and make fewer errors in these words, English-Spanish bilingual children in dual language, transitional bilingual, or Spanish immersion programs in the United States display higher spelling accuracy in words with inconsistent PGCs—that is, those PGCs that are not subject to a rule. This was also observed in the LH corpus, where spelling of inconsistent PGCs was high—around 95%—while spelling accuracy in rule-based PGCs was more variable, ranging between 97.5% in *c-* versus *qu-* and 20.8% in the use of umlaut (*ü*).

One reason we find greater error rates in context-dependent PGGs is that these graphemes occur in alternation across morphology; that is, different graphemes occur in different derived and inflected forms of the same word. For example, accuracy in the spelling of *ge-gi* in *exigir, corregir, escoger,* which are in alternation with forms spelled with *j (exijo, corrijo, escojo),* was much lower than in *je ji* forms, which are not in alternation with forms spelled with *g.* A similar observation was made with *gue, gui* forms, which are in alternation with *ga, go* forms. And the difficulties in changing the grapheme across morphology in *-zar* to *-ce* and *-cer* to *-zo* have been abundantly observed.

The grapheme alternation across morphology that takes place in context-dependent PGCs emerges as a clear contributor to SHLLs' spelling difficulties and errors. This grapheme alternation seems to counteract the potential advantage that the consistency of these PGCs could offer. Grapheme alternation across morphology is cognitively demanding because it requires attending to phonological, morphological, and orthographic information. It requires prioritizing the phonological criterion, instead of the morphological one, which is prioritized in English, where graphemes are maintained across morphology. In addition, while no clear dominant graphemes emerged in inconsistent PGCs, dominant graphemes seemed more clear in rule-based PGCs, where spelling of the grapheme that is only associated with one phoneme is typically the one that leads to more successful spellings: *s* for /s/, *g* for /g/, *j* for /x/.

Cognates versus Noncognates?

Another factor that has a clear effect on spelling is English interference in cognate words, with both a facilitative effect and a hindering effect, depending on the PGC. For example, in Belpoliti and Bermejo's (2020a) corpus, 7.3% of the spelling errors were due to English interference. Cognate words are more likely to be misspelled in these types of words:

- Words with double consonants in English, such as *ss, ff, tt, pp, dd, cc* (with the sound /k/): *professional/profesional, effect/efecto, attention/atención, occasion/ocasión*
- Cognate words with *ce* that are spelled with *ze* in English: *realized/realicé, analized/analicé,* and so forth
- Words ending in *-age* in English, which are spelled with *-aje* in Spanish: *message/mensaje, language/lenguaje, courage/coraje*

However, cross-linguistic transfer needs to be considered both in research and teaching for its facilitative effect and not only as a source of error, as cognate words are spelled more accurately than noncognates in those PGCs where English and Spanish have the same grapheme.

Frequency of Patterns?

Are frequent sequences and syllables more likely to be spelled correctly than infrequent ones? Several studies have shown that children are sensitive to the frequency of certain sequences. For example, French children are more likely to spell *ss* incorrectly in the middle of the word than at the beginning, where we never find *ss* (Alegría and Mousty 1996). Carrillo and Alegría (2014) saw than Spanish children tend to use *v* more in *ve-vi* sequences than in *vu* sequences in pseudowords, reflecting the fact that *ve-vi* are much more frequent sequences than *vu*. Gómez-Velázquez et al. (2014) observed that high school students in Mexico misspelled more words ending in *-sión* as *-ción* (**infución* for *infusión*) than the other way around, consistent with the fact that *-ción* is a more frequent sequence than *-sión*.

SHLLs also seem to be sensitive to some frequencies in Spanish spelling, but this effect is likely due to, or reinforced by, the same frequency patterns existing in English:

- There were no misspellings consisting of the nonexisting sequences **-vr-*, **-vl-* and initial **ue-*, **ua-*, **uo-*, and **rr-*. These sequences do not exist in English, either.
- *s* + consonant (e.g., *puesta*, *mosca*) is much more frequent than z + consonant (e.g., *mezcla*, *juzgar*). This is a pattern that seems to have been grasped by SHLLs, as no errors were found in s + consonant words (Beaudrie 2012; Llombart-Huesca 2022). However, the sensitivity to this frequency pattern could also be due to English, where the same asymmetry holds.
- Verbs ending in *-cer*, *-cir* (e.g., *hacer*, *conocer*, *nacer*) are more frequent than verbs ending in *-ser*, *-sir*. The accuracy rate for these verbs in the LH corpus was 91%, greater than the average for noncognate words with *ce-ci* in general (81%).
- Contrary to what was observed in Mexican high school students, *-sión* words were spelled correctly in many more cases than *-ción* words (96.4% vs. 78.6%) despite *-ción* being more frequent. This is probably due to the fact that the ending *-sión* corresponds to the ending *(s)sion* in English, whereas *-ción* corresponds to *-tion* (in most cases).

Reflection Questions

1. The following words contain vowel-related misspellings. For each of them

   a. Describe the spelling error: substitution, diphthongization, diphthong reduction, inversion, transposition. Notice the specific pattern of the affected grapheme (e.g., a stem-change verb, a pre-tonic syllable . . .).

b. Explain the most likely cause(s) of the error: English interference, low phonological awareness, grammar error, representation of a nonstandard pronunciation. (Focus only on the vowels.)

teinía (for tenía) peliar (for pelear) nacie (for nací)
estuidos (for estudios) pudía (for podía) defícil (for difícil)
fuerta (for fuerte) quero (for quiero)
difierensa (for diferencia)

2. The following words contain consonant-related misspellings. For each of them do the following:

   a. Describe the spelling error (e.g., omission of *h*, substitution of *g* for *j*).
   b. Explain the likely cause of the error.

mescla (for mezcla) quantificar (for cuantificar)
realize (for realice) officina (for oficina),
cantava (for cantaba) tocer (for toser) naser (for nacer),
familla (for familia) parré (for paré) mensage (for mensaje)
educasión (for educación) comunicion (for comunicación)
Voy a ser la tarea (for Voy a hacer la tarea)
Juan va hablar (for Juan va a hablar)

3. What can you infer from each of the following situations? In the same essay, a student writes the following:

   a. *empesar and *empesé
   b. hacer and *hiso
   c. hacer and *hico
   d. hacer and *desaser
   e. riqueza and *bellesa

4. This chapter has presented the spelling areas where we find more errors as well as the spelling elements where the accuracy is lower. The areas of overlap are probably the spelling aspects instructors would like to focus on. Identify those areas.

Notes

1. This count should not be considered exact, since these frequencies are based on the occurrences of these sequences in lemmas, and, as we have seen, graphemes

s and *z* change across morphology. For example, although *hacer* has a verb form spelled with a *z* (*hizo*), it is counted here as one of the 674 lemmas containing a *c*. Likewise, *empezar* is counted as one of the 120 lemmas containing *z*, even though some of its verb forms are spelled with a *c* (e.g., *empecé*).

2. There were only eight tokens (i.e., total number of instances) of *za-zo* in a total of five cognate words. The 87.5% accuracy rate is the result of only one misspelling (**analisarlo*), which could also be influenced by the word *análisis*.
3. Llombart-Huesca and Zyzik (2019) give these results as scores over a maximum score of twenty.
4. When using an ANOVA with repeated measures, the mean scores for *f* spelling accuracy had statistically significant differences ($F (2, 71) = 77.61$, $p = < 0.001$; Partial Eta-Squared = 0.656). Pair-wise comparisons with a Bonferroni correction show that the difference between the results in each type was statistically significant ($p < 0.001$).
5. Bahr et al.'s (2015) study did not look at errors related to stress marks in these essays.
6. The words were written without the stress mark, and they were spelled with the correct consonant or with *s* (*empiese* and *empieso*, for *empecé* and *empezó*). However, here I spell them correctly except for the relevant grapheme, the vowel, to highlight the element I am focusing on.
7. The symbol # indicates that the spelling is correct but not for the intended word.

FIVE

Stress Marks in Spanish

Why Does Spanish Have Stress Marks?

Some teachers, in their interest to highlight the importance of "acentos" (stress marks) and encourage their learning, emphasize their ability to help with distinguishing between words. For example, if we miss the stress mark in *papá* (*papa*), we are talking about a potato! Although there are many pairs of words that are distinguished only by the stress mark, such as *canto/cantó, seria/sería, rio/río, el/él*), the main function of the stress mark is to unequivocally indicate to the reader which syllable receives the stress in the word. On the other hand, because Spanish is a free stress language, that is, the stress may fall in any syllable of the word, stress may become a contrastive factor in distinguishing words, such as in the examples just mentioned.[1]

Most Spanish words have one stressed syllable. Native speakers typically do not have any trouble stressing the right syllable in normal speech, and they do so by applying an extra muscular energy to that syllable, which acoustically manifests in higher pitch, longer duration, and higher intensity (Ladefoged 2001). A syllable is only stressed in contrast with the sound of the other syllables of the word. For example, in the word *elefante*, *fan* is perceived as the stressed syllable in that word, but it is not possible to isolate *fan* and notice whether it is stressed or not. Some words do not have any stress. Most of them are monosyllabic, such as articles (*el, la, las*), conjunctions (*y, o*), relative pronouns (*que, cual*), pronouns (*la, lo, le*), and some possessive pronouns (*mi, tu, su*), and some are polysyllabic, such as conjunctions (*pero*).[2] But not all monosyllabic words are unstressed; in fact, the majority of monosyllabic words are stressed, such as *pon, sal, ven, ten, dé, sol, pan, col.* However, because syllables cannot have stress by themselves, but in contrast with others, we can only know whether a monosyllabic word is stressed or not when heard in a sentence; for example:

ÉL VIno (he came)
el VIno (the wine)

(In written form, the stress mark in *él* makes the contrast obvious, but the contrast also exists in pronunciation.)

Since the function of stress marks is to indicate to the reader which syllable of the word is the stressed one, monosyllabic words are, as a general rule, not marked, even when they are stressed: *pon, ten, ras, juez, guion, vio, crio, fue.* Stressed monosyllabic words are only marked when a similar nonstressed word exists. This is the "diacritic stress mark," which we see in words such as the following:

Té (tea), to distinguish it from *te* (unstressed pronoun)
Mí (prepositional pronoun), to distinguish it from *mi* (unstressed possessive pronoun)
Dé (form of the verb *dar*), to distinguish it from *de* (unstressed preposition)
Él (subject pronoun), to distinguish it from *el* (unstressed article)
Quién (interrogative pronoun), to distinguish it from *quien* (unstressed relative pronoun)
Sé (I know), to distinguish it from *se* (unstressed pronoun)

This is not an exhaustive list. The goal here is to show that stress marks in monosyllabic words only appear when both of the following two conditions apply:

1. The word is stressed (to be more accurate, we should say: the only syllable of the word is stressed)
2. There is another word that looks the same that is unstressed

The forms *fui, fue, dio, vio* had a stress mark until 1958, when the *Nuevas Normas de Prosodia and Ortografía* (Casares 1958) report appeared. Words like *guion, crie,* and *truhan* are not marked because they are monosyllabic, since their two vowels form a diphthong. Many speakers pronounce these words as two syllables (as *gui-on, cri-e, tru-han*) and might feel that this rule does not apply. In fact, before 2010, the stress mark in these words was optional, but the 2010 edition of RAE's *Ortografía de la lengua española* ended this optionality and stated that regardless of the speaker's pronunciation, those words are monosyllabic and should, therefore, not be marked.

Let us focus now on polysyllabic words, that is, words that contain two or more syllables. Polysyllabic words have only one stressed syllable, and the marking rules have been established to accomplish two goals. First, they aim to be unequivocal about the way a word should be stressed even by a reader who has never heard the word, in line with the general principles of the Spanish orthographic system, which allows readers to know how to pronounce any word just by the way it is written. One way to be unequivocal about what syllable is stressed would be to mark all words in their stressed syllable. But the system has also been established to mark as few words as possible. To achieve that, the system considers what the most common stress patterns in Spanish are.

In most Spanish words, the stressed syllable is the second to last. These words are called paroxytones (known in Spanish as "llanas" or "graves"), and most of them end in a vowel, *-n*, or *-s*. Most nouns and adjectives fall under that group. Just look around, and name the things you see and the adjectives that describe them (in my case: *puerta, ventana, mesa, silla, libro, cuaderno, computadora, pantalla, vaso, planta, cuadro, maceta, amarilla, grande, pequeña, verde,*...). And when we make those nouns and adjectives plural, they are still paroxytones, and they end in *-s* (*puertas, ventanas, mesas*, etc.). When we conjugate verbs, in many cases they are paroxytones and end in a vowel, *-n*, or *-s* (*tengo, sabe, bailaba; tienen, saben, bailaban; tienes, sabemos, bailabas*). Therefore, the most economic rule is to *not* mark those words. A reader who sees a word that ends in a vowel, *n*, or *s* and sees that it is not marked will know that it should be pronounced with the stress in the penultimate syllable, as most Spanish words are. (You may try that with these made-up words: *un polino, mi castena, estos adrufites, ellos patigan.*) As a consequence, we need to mark the words that have these endings but whose stressed syllable is the last one, called oxytones (known in Spanish as "agudas"), such as *sofá, camión, además*. Since many oxytone words end in a consonant, mostly *-r* and *-d* (*cantar, leer, vivir, verdad, ciudad*), we avoid having to place many stress marks. And if we were to see an unknown word—such as *pocantel, peritor, malidad* (my made-up words)—we would know how to pronounce them without the need of any stress mark. Finally, all words that are stressed in the third-to-last syllable, called proparoxytones (known as "esdrújulas" in Spanish), need to be marked. But since those are a minority, we still have the most economic option. Through this logic, we obtain the following stress mark rules:

- Oxytone words ("agudas") need to be marked if they end in a vowel, *-n*, or *-s*; for example, *creyó, avión, también, revés.*
- Paroxytone words ("llanas," "graves") need to be marked if they do *not* end in a vowel, *-n*, or *-s*; for example, *fácil, lápiz, Óscar.*
- Proparoxytone words ("esdrújulas") are always marked; for example, *música, parábola, número, íbamos.*

TABLE 5.1. Distribution of frequent stress-marked lemmas in the first 1,000 Spanish words

Oxytones	Paroxytones	Proparoxytones	Diphthong-breaking	Diacritic marks	Total
56	6	33	12	10	117
47.86%	5.13%	28.20%	10.25%	8.55%	100.00%

However, there is a set of cases that fall through the cracks and are not unequivocal. Look at the following words, which are written here without any stress marks but with the stressed syllable in capital letters: *SEria, seRIa, RIo, RIO*. In *SEria*, the penultimate syllable is stressed, and the last syllable contains the diphthong *ia*. Because the word ends in a vowel, we do not mark it. In *seRIa*, the stressed syllable is also the penultimate, with the stress falling on *i*, the weak syllable, which breaks that diphthong, and the last syllable is *a*. (Recall that in a diphthong, the closed vowel is unstressed. Therefore, whenever the closed vowel is stressed, the two vowels belong to different syllables.) Because the word ends in a vowel, it is not marked, either. Consequently, according to the rules presented above, if we saw the word *seria*, we would not know if it should be pronounced *SEria* or *seRIa*. Therefore, the main rules do not allow us to unequivocally know how to pronounce these words. To escape from this catch-22 situation, a new rule is implemented: whenever there is a stressed closed vowel next to an open vowel, we must mark the closed vowel. Therefore, we obtain the following words: *SE-ria: seria; se-RI-a: sería; a-le-GRI-a: alegría; far-MA-cia: farmacia.*

This complete set of rules proves to unequivocally indicate what syllable to stress in any given polysyllabic word. And it does so by marking as few words as possible. For example, among the first 1,000 most frequent lemmas in Davies's (2016) Spanish corpus, there are 117 words with a stress mark, that is, merely 11.7%. The marked lemmas are distributed as table 5.1 shows.[3]

In addition to these rules, we find some productive suffixes and word patterns that are stress marked, shown in table 5.2.

As Lord (2002) explains, while morphologically related words in English tend to share stress patterns—as in *recite-recital, divine-divinity*—this is not the case in Spanish, which prioritizes phonological requirements over morphological ones. Thus, in Spanish we see pairs such as *coche-cochecito, régimen-regímenes, canto-cantamos*, where the stress falls on a different syllable in each of the two words. In fact, derivative suffixes may have their own stress and produce a stress shift in the derived word, as *-al*, in *norma-normal*, *-eza*, as in *bello-belleza*.

TABLE 5.2. Frequent stress-marked suffixes, word patterns, and words

Pattern	Examples
In oxytone words	
First- and third-person singular preterit forms of regular verbs	*hablé, comí, salí, habló, comió, salió*
Future tense forms (except first-person plural)	*hablaré, comeré, iré, saldrán, tendrás*
Suffix *-ción* (but only in singular)	*acción, nación, educación*
Suffix *-sión* (but only in singular)	*misión, pensión, fusión*
Suffix *-és* (in languages and demonyms) (but only in masculine singular)	*inglés, irlandés, escocés, japonés*
The forms *está, estás, están* of the verb *estar*	
In proparoxytone words	
First-person plural of *-ar* verbs in the imperfect indicative	*hablábamos, mirábamos, pasábamos*
First-person plural of verbs in the imperfect subjunctive	*habláramos, comiéramos, tuviéramos*
Adjectives and nouns ending in the suffix *-ico/-ica*	*fantástico, médico, biológico, pánico, música, técnica*
Adjectives and nouns ending in *-culo/-cula*	*artículo, espectáculo, película, ridículo, partícula*
Some frequent nouns	*página, número, miércoles, próximo, título, análisis, rápido*
In paroxytone words	
Last names ending in *-ez*	*Fernández, Gómez, Martínez, Pérez*
Adjectives ending in *-il*	*fácil, difícil, móvil, útil, débil*
Some frequent nouns	*árbol, cárcel, dólar, carácter, lápiz*
Diphthong-breaking words	
Imperfect indicative of *-er, -ir* verbs	*leía, querías, decíamos, salían*
Conditional verb forms	*hablaría, comerías, diríamos, tendríamos, pensarían*
Suffix *-ería* to indicate stores	*panadería, pescadería*
Suffix *-logía* and *-grafía* to indicate academic subjects	*psicología, biología, geografía*
Some frequent words	*día, país, mayoría, todavía, policía, teoría, economía, compañía*

Stress Mark Errors in SHLLs' Writings

Marking stress in words has been identified as a very difficult task in both monolingual children and SHLLs. Defior, Jiménez-Fernández, and Serrano (2009) show that in first-to-fourth grade monolingual children in Spain, the most difficult type of spelling complexity was stress marks. In first grade, children hardly used this orthographic mark, and by the end of the fourth grade they had reached no more than 50% correct responses. Among Mexican high school students, Backhoff Escudero et al. (2008) also singled out stress marks as the most frequent spelling error, and the researchers noticed that 98% of the more than 5,000 students observed made at least one stress mark error. Similar results have been reported in other Latin American countries in students of different socioeconomic status and with parents of different educational levels.

In SHLLs, the use of stress marks has been identified as the most difficult aspect of spelling, and stress mark mistakes typically constitute more than half of the spelling errors SHLLs make (Beaudrie 2012; Belpoliti and Bermejo 2020a). Most stress mark errors consist in omitting the mark, with a much lower percentage of errors involving misplacing the mark or adding it in a word that did not need it (Beaudrie 2012; Belpoliti and Bermejo 2020a; Fernández Parera and Lynch 2021). In addition, Belpoliti and Bermejo (2020a) observed a high level of consistency in the stress mark errors; that is, a student who omitted the stress mark in one word did so in every instance of the word they wrote.

What explains the high number of the stress mark omissions in SHLLs? Accurately placing stress marks in naturalistic writing entails several actions: identifying the stressed syllable and applying the specific rule that corresponds to the position of that syllable—including the diphthong-breaking context—and doing so in an automatized manner, as it needs to happen for every single word of the essay. In addition, writers need to consider diacritic words.

Identifying the stressed syllable is a challenging task. Stress is a complex acoustic phenomenon comprised of three different elements in combination: pitch, duration, and intensity—pitch being the most relevant factor. Duration and intensity have a different effect on stress perception depending on the type of word (oxytones, paroxytones, and proparoxytones) and depending on whether the word is heard in isolation or in context. Llisterri and colleagues' (2016) study suggests that syllable duration helps stress perception in paroxytones and oxytones in context but only in paroxytones when in isolation. On the other hand, intensity contributes to stress perception in proparoxytones when in context and in oxytones when in isolation.

It is no wonder, then, that the scarce literature on stress marking in SHLLs has focused on the ability to identify the stressed syllable and has found it to be extremely challenging for this student population. Carreira (2002) gave

Pronounce these three sentences—taken from Llisterri et al. (2016)—using regular speech, and notice the stress in the three "limite" instances:

> Calculas el límite mal.
> No le limite los gastos.
> No limité los tabiques.

The difference between *límite-limite-limité* in that sentence context is not as striking as when these three words are said in isolation. Still, in Llisterri et al.'s (2016) study, Spanish native speakers were able to identify their stress remarkably well, both when they were presented in context and when they were presented in isolation. But when these words were recorded within their sentence, extracted from the original recording, and then presented in isolation, participants had a hard time identifying the stressed syllable.

twenty-five SHLLs two lists of words and asked them to identify the stressed syllable. For the first list, students read the printed words silently, and for the second students read the printed words while listening to the recording of a native speaker reading them aloud. Their error rate was around 53% in both situations, showing that SHLLs lacked strategies to explicitly identify the stressed syllable as the word sounded in their mind, as well as to use aural input to identify the stressed syllable. These students later read aloud a list of twelve familiar words that were very similar to the ones in which they could not identify the stress in the previous task, and they performed extremely well in pronouncing them. The students were also asked to repeat twelve pseudowords one at a time after they heard them and also performed very well. Likewise, Kim (2015) observed that SHLLs performed similarly to native speakers in a task that required accurately perceiving Spanish lexical stress. Therefore, the difficulty lies not in *perceiving* the stress but rather in "access(ing) their implicit knowledge of Spanish stress for purposes of making explicit linguistic judgements" (Carreira 2002, 249).

Beaudrie (2017) gave seventy-seven intermediate-level SHLLs three tests, each consisting of twenty written disyllabic and trisyllabic words. In one test, students had to circle the stressed syllable in each word. In the other two, students had to add the stress mark to words requiring them: in one test the stressed syllable in each word was underlined, and in the other it was not. In the stress identification task, participants' average accuracy was 62.7%.[4] In the written stress mark portion, students performed better when the stressed syllable was underlined. These results support the idea that difficulty in stress identification hinders

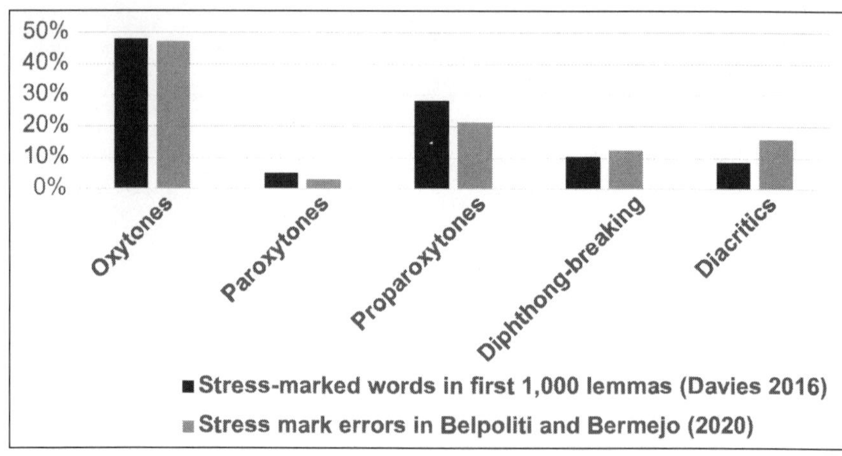

FIGURE 5.1. Stress-marked pattern versus stress mark error pattern

students' performance in placing the stress mark. After six weeks of training, the scores in stress identification were significantly greater (70.95%), proving that training had had an impact on stress perception. However, the scores are not near 100%, a worrisome fact if we consider that stress identification itself is not even the end goal but a prerequisite to learning the stress mark rules.

Difficulties in identifying the stressed syllable also reveal another weakness that has not been explored: failure to predict the stressed syllable based on common patterns (Carreira 2002). Belpoliti and Bermejo (2020a) observed that 47% of stress mark omissions happened in oxytones, 21.3% in proparoxytones, 15.8% in monosyllabic words, 12.3% in diphthong breaking, and only 3% in paroxytones. Fernández Parera and Lynch (2021) observed a very similar pattern. As with frequency data on other misspellings, these numbers are helpful for identifying the sources of most stress mark omissions. Perhaps teachers will find it more efficient to devote more time to oxytone words and, that way, reduce more stress mark errors in a shorter time. But does that mean that students find oxytone words more difficult than paroxytones? Not necessarily, since these percentages correspond to their relative frequency in a set of written texts, and not to accuracy scores. In fact, the distribution of stress mark omissions follows very closely the relative frequency of words that require stress marks. The 117 marked words we find in the first 1,000 lemmas in Davies's (2016) Spanish corpus are distributed the following way: 47.86% are oxytones, 28.2% are proparoxytones, 10.25% have a diphthong-breaking mark, 5.13% are paroxytones, and 8.55% have a diacritic mark.[5] The comparison between the pattern of stress-marked words among the first 1,000 lemmas and the pattern of words with stress mark omissions found in Belpoliti and Bermejo (2020a) can be seen in figure 5.1.

Stress mark omission errors happen in a very similar relative frequency pattern to that of stress-marked words. This pattern strongly suggests that the fact that most omitted stress marks happen in oxytone and proparoxytone words reflects the fact that those are the most frequent words students used in their writing. In addition, a more detailed description of the groups of words where most stress mark omissions take place also reveals a parallelism with frequent groups of words students might use in an essay. For example, Beaudrie (2012) observes that most mark omissions in verbs happened in the past tense: preterit (**enseñe*) and imperfect—both the diphthong-breaking type *ía* (**tenia*) and the paroxytone mark (**cenabamos*). The remainder of the omission in verbs happened in the conditional (**deberia*), the future tense (**olvidare*), and other less-frequent forms (**tuvieramos*, **pasandosela*). There were also omissions in diacritics, which were mostly concentrated in **mas*, **mi*, **si*, **el*, and **como*.

The parallelism between the relative frequency of stress-marked words and the relative frequency of stress mark omissions strongly suggests that SHLLs' accuracy levels are very similar across word types and patterns and, therefore, that students are not making predictions based on common patterns. Sensitivity to these patterns would fall under the purview of morphological awareness. Morphological awareness aids writers in noticing the relationship between forms such as *hablé*, *canté*, *decidí* or *quería*, *decía*, *leía*. The role of morphological awareness in stress marks is also evident in the use of diacritic accents, as writers need to be sensitive to whether a word is a determiner or a pronoun (as in *el*/*él* or *mi*/*mí*), or a pronoun or a verb (*se*/*sé*), for example. Using the metalanguage of technical words as "pronoun" or "determiner" is not a requirement, but it is necessary to develop a sensitivity to the different uses of the words that have a diacritic accent. Therefore, although the prevalence of stress mark errors reveals difficulties in phonological awareness, it also shows the effects of limited morphological awareness.

In chapter 2 we also discussed another component of spelling development—visual memory and the development of a mental visual lexicon. Instead of proceeding step by step from identifying the stressed syllable followed by the application of the spelling rule, writers benefit from the visual memory of words with their stress mark placed on them. And this leads us to wonder whether our mind places its attention on the stress marks when we read in order to know how to pronounce and accurately stress the word. Two main mechanisms have been identified for reading: a lexical route, by which we identify words by a few cues and match them with the words that we have stored in our mental lexicon, and a sublexical route, by which we decode every segment of the word.

Although there are different proposals to explain how exactly this takes place, it is generally agreed that skilled readers are able to employ both mechanisms. Some studies have been conducted to elucidate whether these mechanisms also include processing of the stress mark when reading.

Schwab (2015) conducted a study in which participants were presented a series of words where the stress mark was correctly placed, omitted, or misplaced (e.g., *lápiz, lapiz, lapíz*). Words that do not include a stress mark were presented correctly without it, with the stress mark on the stressed syllable, or with the stress mark on another syllable (e.g., *dulce, dúlce, dulcé*). Similar pseudowords were also presented. Participants had to quickly indicate whether the words they saw were real words or not and were instructed to consider words with stress-marking errors as real words. (For example, *dúlce* and *dulcé* would be real words, while *dulpe* would not.) Reaction times were measured, with the assumption that significant delays in making the decision with words containing a stress-marking error would indicate that attention was being placed on how the words were marked. The results indicated that omission of the stress mark does not create a significant processing cost compared with the process of reading correctly spelled words. This suggests that the letter without the accent mark (e.g., *a* in *lapiz*) is conceptualized as a variant of the letter with the accent mark (*á* in *lápiz*). Thus, when readers see *lapiz*, the word *lápiz* is activated in their mind. On the other hand, the misplacement of the accent mark on the nonstressed vowel involves a processing cost with respect to the correctly spelled word. This suggests that seeing a word like *cómer* activates words that are similarly marked, such as *cómic*, which slows down the recognition of *comer* as a real word.

Schwab's (2015) results are consistent with similar studies conducted in Greek with children and adults and reported in Protopapas (2016), who concludes that although readers do not need to process the accent mark to identify and pronounce the word correctly, the accent mark becomes part of the orthographic image of the words, in such a way that its misplacement may affect orthographic processing. One reason readers do not process the stress mark when reading is that it brings very little information, since we read by recognizing the words, which are stored in our mental lexicon with the information about their stress pattern included. This makes processing the stress mark a "needless burden" (Protopapas 2016, 254). In addition, processing the stress mark is also cognitively demanding, because stress assignment is a suprasegmental feature concerning the syllables, whereas the mark is processed at a segmental level, that is, the specific letter where it appears. Finally, Protopapas (2016) also discusses the possible role of the learning experience, in which children have been able to read successfully without decoding the stress mark.

It must be noted that these studies have been conducted with L1 students who had been schooled in their L1 and who have learned the stress rules. In addition, the words did not contain a contrastive stress mark, that is, there were no words in which attention to the stress mark was actually necessary to disambiguate meaning—as in *límite, limite, limité*. Although this research has not been conducted in SHLLs, it is likely that their attention to the diacritic in reading would be even lower in this population, since the ability to employ a dual route in reading (lexical and sublexical) is associated with the more skilled readers.

In the context of L2 teaching, some strategies have been proposed to direct learners' attention to the stress mark. For example, Gascoigne (2006) found that first-semester learners of French and Spanish were better able to place accent marks accurately on a handwritten dictation task if they had practiced by transcribing the text using a computer keyboard that required typing an alphanumeric code than if they had practiced transcribing the text by hand. Sturm (2013) conducted a similar experiment but asked participants in the handwriting group to write the accented letters in a different color ink in order to call their attention to the accent marks. In that occasion, there were no significant differences observed between the participants who had practiced writing the words by hand and those who had typed them. This result suggests that any significant differences between practicing by typing and by handwriting that have been observed in previous studies would be eliminated by adding this extra step also in handwriting. While these studies have been conducted in the L2 context, the idea of creating an extra burden to type or handwrite stress marks on a word is a promising option to help redirect learners' explicit attention to the stress marks and promote a higher level of recall.

Teaching Stress Marks

The common approach to teaching accent marks used in textbooks starts with syllabification, followed by the accentuation rules for oxytone, paroxytone, and proparoxytone words. These rules are explained in the same lesson/chapter, and the explanation is typically followed by activities that ask students to identify the stressed syllable and to place the mark when it is required. However, we have seen that a major deterrent is the difficulty SHLLs have identifying the stressed syllable (Carreira 2002; Beaudrie 2017; Fernández Parera and Lynch 2021). Both Carreira and Beaudrie conducted studies that examined the effect of training specifically directed to the task of identifying the stressed syllable, by listening to recordings where that stress was emphasized and giving students pairs of words only differentiated by the stressed syllable (e.g., *paPA* vs. *PApa*).

Although this training is absolutely necessary, we do not need to choose between jumping directly to the teaching of the accentuation rules and devoting time exclusively to training the ear to identify the stressed syllable before moving on to the accentuation rules. After all, students still make mistakes in accentuating the words when the stressed syllable is underlined and, therefore, identified for them.

Instead, I propose employing an approach in which accentuation is taught throughout a period of several weeks, together with other spelling patterns.[6] The first section of the chapter gives several lexical and morphological patterns where we find written accent marks. For example, among oxytone words that are marked, we find the following:

- First- and second-person-singular preterit forms of regular verbs (e.g., *hablé, comí, habló, comió*)
- Suffixes *-ción* and *-sión* (e.g., *nación, tension*)
- Suffix *-és*, in languages and demonyms (e.g., *inglés, japonés*)

Each of these patterns can be introduced on a different day. One day, verbs in the preterit are presented, for example, in the context of a short story or a biography, where students are directed to notice all the preterit forms in the first and third person. Those forms can be isolated and read aloud, in order to notice the pronunciation pattern together with the accent mark. It is easy to design activities to practice this particular pattern in a way that pays attention to both the form (the accent mark) and the function (talk about the past). For example, students can write five sentences about what they did yesterday (in the first person), and then convert them into the third person; students can be asked to write a few

Even though I am proposing working with grammatical patterns such as the preterit tense, I am not proposing that the preterit tense conjugation be studied as such. In addition, when a student omits the accent mark in a preterit tense (for example, *canto* for *cantó*), we need to avoid correcting this absence with the notation "wrong tense" just because the absence of the stress mark produces a change in the tense. It is important for instructors to put themselves in the mind of the student who made the mistake. In the students' minds, the word they wrote is *cantó*, and it sounds as such. The error was not a grammatical error, and marking it as such is only confusing to the student.

sentences about the important things a celebrity did (third person), and then convert them into the first person. The key aspects are that at that point, students (1) would only be presented with that pattern, (2) would not even need to be taught that those words are "agudas," and (3) would not learn that the "agudas" that end in *-n* or *-s* are accented.

Another day, the endings *-ción* versus *-sión* are introduced, and students learn both the grapheme (when to write *-ción* and when to write *-sión*) and the accent together, in words such as *nación, creación, pensión, misión*. Having several words with the same ending highlights their stress pattern. Another day, languages and demonyms are introduced: *inglés, francés, irlandés, japonés.*

When these patterns have been introduced and practiced, the concept of "palabras agudas" can be more easily presented. Students have already worked on recognizing the stress pattern and have started associating the endings in vowel, *-n*, and *-s* with the accent mark. Other common words that are frequently misspelled may be presented at that time, such as *así, al revés, a través, también, además.*

Only after some time of working with oxytone words, together with other PGCs, would we introduce paroxytone words, in different days for different patterns. For example, one day students will work with some adjectives ending in *-il*, such as *fácil, difícil, táctil, frágil, ágil, dócil, útil, inútil*. . . . Instructors can create activities that connect these adjectives to one another in a meaningful way, in addition to the formal property to its stress pattern. For example, students can be asked to use these adjectives to describe people and objects. Another day, verbs in the imperfect can be practiced together so that different spelling patterns are studied: *-aba*, with *b*, the most frequent spelling error in the representation of /b/, with the proparoxytone accent pattern in *hablábamos, mirábamos*, and so on and the diphthong-breaking accent mark in *ía* in *tenía, dormía, leía.* Again, meaningful contexts for these words can easily be designed. For example, students may write about things they used to do with their families as children.

These are just a few examples from table 5.2. This approach has several advantages:

- It presents one stress pattern at a time, throughout a longer period of time.
- Words are grouped not only by its stress pattern but morphologically, which combines a certain degree of focus on form and on meaning.
- It allows stacking of spelling rules. Students can learn accent marks together with the representation of different phonemes.
- Students train their ability to notice and identify the stressed syllable throughout a longer period of time while they learn some spelling rules and patterns.

Reflection Questions

1. Explain the reason each of the following words have their stressed syllable marked (or not marked) this way:

   crie creí rehízo huida alegría alergia examen ti fue

2. Read the following pseudowords aloud according to the stress patterns indicated by the stress mark—or lack thereof.

   plai plie alingol palamid maniten padevis padeviz

3. Based on the patterns in table 5.2, write additional words that would fall into each of these patterns.

   a. Suffix -ción: *nación*
   b. Suffix *-sión: misión*
   c. Suffix *-és: inglés*
   d. Adjectives in *-ico/-ica: mágico, mágica*
   e. Adjectives and nouns ending in *-culo/-cula: espectáculo*
   f. Adjectives ending in *-il: fácil*
   g. Suffix *-ería: panadería*
   h. Suffix *-logía: sociología*
   i. Suffix *-grafía: fotografía*

4. Mark the stress in the underlined pseudowords based on your intuition about how they would be pronounced. (The related pseudoword appears in italics.) Justify each of your stress mark choices.

   a. Ayer fui a comprar unos *gántaros* a la gantareria.
   b. Voy a *sadintar* porque ayer no sadinte.
   c. Cuando era niña, mi familia y yo sadintabamos los fines de semana.
   d. Cuando era niño, Luis siempre se dulipia en la escuela.
   e. Necesitas *samacar* esto de nuevo, porque la samacion que me diste tenía errores.
   f. Voy a estudiar dibujologia.
   g. Esta conversación fue totalmente miranicula.

5. The objective of this activity is to force you to make spelling decisions without using your previous knowledge of Spanish words. Instead, simply follow a rule, like a student who is just learning the stress marks. Mark the stress in

the real words that appear in these sentences based on the following made-up rules:

- Oxytone words ("palabras agudas") must be marked when ending in *-z, -r,* and *e, i.*
- Paroxytone words ("palabras graves") must be marked when *not* ending in *-z, -r,* or *e, i.*
    a. Yo le hable con el corazon pero eso no le hizo feliz.
    b. El Sr. Perez me hablo ayer para aclarar la situacion.

Reflect on the challenges presented by this task and connect them with the challenges a student who is learning the actual stress-marking rules may have.

6. In this activity you will have the opportunity to reflect on your ability to recall diacritics and the use of some strategy to redirect your explicit attention to them. Below is the French paragraph used in Gascoigne's (2006) study.

    Step 1. Looking at the paragraph, transcribe it by hand on a sheet of paper. When you start transcribing a letter that includes a diacritic, change pens and write that letter and the diacritic in a different color. Then, change pens again and resume the transcription.
    Step 2. Ask a peer to dictate the original paragraph to you, and write it on another sheet of paper. (For this exercise it is not really necessary to find someone who speaks French.)

    Did you find that stopping your transcription to change pens helped you pay attention to the diacritics? How many mistakes did you make when writing the diacritics?

    Bonjour, Je m'appelle André. Je suis algérien. J'adore le théâtre, la télévision et l'opéra.
    Voilà Joëlle, une copine sénégalaise, et son ami Frédéric. Frédéric est français et il habite à Paris avec sa mère.

7. Think of meaningful/communicative contexts where students could be led to use the following patterns:

    a. demonyms ending in *-és/-esa*
    b. future-tense verb forms
    c. words ending in *-logía, -grafía*

Notes

1. There are some limitations to this freedom, as lexical stress must fall within what is known as the "three-syllable window" at the right edge of the word.
2. These unstressed words can be given a stress in a condition of emphasis or contrast. For example, after one person asks, *¿Trajiste las sillas?* someone may respond, *traje LA silla* with a stress in the typically unstressed article *la* to emphasize that there is only one chair and not several.
3. This constitutes only an approximation of the actual words that might appear in a text, since the corpus only includes lemmas. Because the list only includes the infinitive forms of verbs, only one verb is included in that list—*oír*, with a diphthong-breaking mark. Also, proparoxytone words such as *jóvenes*, *imágenes*, *órdenes*, or *orígenes* are not included, even though their singular forms are found among the most frequent 1,000 words, as they are only marked in the plural form.
4. Beaudrie (2017) gives the results in scores: 12.54 out of 20 in the pre-test and 14.19 out of 20 in the post-test.
5. See note 2.
6. See some examples of educational materials that work on stress marks in a way that is integrated into verb tenses in context in Zapata's (2018) open educational resource grounded in the tenets of Learning by Design.

SIX

Pedagogical Proposals

In this chapter I make some practical pedagogical proposals to improve students' spelling. The proposals go beyond the simple fill-in-the-gap activities in which a "spelling rule" is applied after it is learned. We could make a parallelism with how we approach grammar development in L2/FL teaching. Instructors do not simply teach a grammar point explicitly and then assign a fill-in-the gap activity and expect the student to use that grammar point fluently in conversation and essays from that time on. Using that approach to spelling is equally futile. We need to approach spelling development with a combination of incidental learning opportunities, consciousness-raising activities, focus-on-form and noticing exercises, and fluency-building activities. Just like we want L2/FL students to be able to speak fluently while focusing on the content of what they are saying without having to think about the grammar they are using, we want SHLLs to write fluently and to focus on the content of what they are writing without having to think about the spelling rules. In addition, we need to make sure that the right underlying skills that allow spelling learning are developed, such as decoding skills and phonological and morphological awareness.

The following is not a method to implement in a classroom that will provide a "zero spelling error" result but, rather, a set of strategies and approaches that are not commonly used in textbooks, as well as activities that target some less-visible skills underlying the proficiency of spelling—phonological and morphological awareness. Some are adaptations from strategies that have been tested with other types of students, and some are strategies that I have used in my courses based on the research I have conducted with SHLLs. All are activities and approaches I have used in my teaching. But, first, I discuss the debate between incidental learning and explicit learning of spelling.

Do We Know What Teaching Approaches Work?

Because the research on the spelling of SHLLs is relatively new, few published studies exist that employ a robust design to study the effectiveness of different pedagogical strategies with this particular population. In such studies, we would compare the students' proficiency before and after the pedagogical intervention, with a pre-test and a post-test. However, it is well known that many students do better the second time they take a test, even when they do not do anything special between the two tests. Therefore, we also need to have a control group of students that do not receive the pedagogical method, and to examine their proficiency with two tests. That way we can see whether the first group actually improved because of the pedagogical intervention or simply because of the re-test effect. This design also needs to ensure that students in both groups are similar, since a particular method could be helpful for some students and not others (e.g., different skills, different level, and different background). And we need to make sure no other factors are at play in the observed difference. For example, if students in the control group are in a crowded classroom, with a teacher who cancels class half of the time, we would not know if they performed worse than the other group because of these other conditions or because they did not receive the intervention. Finally, even in equal conditions, the results can be a fluke, an effect of chance or unknown factors (how many times do teachers feel that after doing *exactly the same*, one class does better than another one?). To be able to say that is not the case, a large enough number of students are necessary in order to conduct statistical analyses that tell us (to some level of confidence) the differences observed are not likely to be the result of chance.

To Teach or Not to Teach Spelling: Incidental Learning Approaches

Believing that developing good spelling skills is a desirable goal does not necessarily entail agreeing that spelling needs to be taught, and there is a considerable disagreement regarding how spelling skills and competence are best acquired (Graham and Santangelo 2014). On the one hand, we find some proponents (Bean and Bouffler 1987; Krashen 1989; Edelsky 1990; Wilde 1990) of the idea that spelling is "caught" by incidental learning through reading and writing, as well as by modeling correct spelling in class and occasional opportunistic interventions. This position advocates holistic methods, authentic tasks, collaborative activities, and informal instruction (e.g., Smith 1982). On the other side of this debate, we find those who contend that spelling needs to be "taught"—explicitly and systematically—with a clear scope and sequence in place (Allred 1977; Henderson 1990; Loomer, Fitzsimmons, and Strege 1990; Moats 2005).

One of the most acclaimed activities for incidental learning of spelling is reading, which is touted by many as the best, or even the only, way to achieve spelling. Studies conducted with students in grades 7 through 12 (Gilbert 1934) and with college students (Gilbert 1935) found that students' spelling improved as a consequence of reading: words that were embedded in a text that students read before a spelling test were more likely to be spelled correctly than words that were not. Students' ability to catch spellings through reading improved with age, as older students spelled more words correctly after reading the passage than younger students did. However, these studies found that better spellers accounted for most of the gains in spelling and that poor spellers generally did not benefit from reading the passage. In addition, gains were only significant for those students who took a spelling pre-test of the target words immediately prior to reading the passage. This result suggests that the effect of reading on spelling was strengthened because the attention was drawn to those words. The positive effect of directing students to pay attention to the spelling of certain words in reading passages was also observed in Ormrod (1986a, 1986b). The students who were told they would be tested on the spelling of some unusual words as well as on comprehension of the reading had better spelling scores than those who were told they would be tested only on comprehension. (There was no difference between the two groups in comprehension scores.) Again, good spellers profited more from reading than did poor spellers. Ormrod (1986a) also showed that doubling the presence of target words in a passage led to greater recognition of correct spelling—although tripling the amount of exposure did not result in additional gains.

Some proponents of the natural learning approach (Bean and Bouffler 1987; Wilde 1990) claim that children learn new spellings when they receive feedback from teachers or peers on their spellings, as well as when they learn how to spell words "as needed," that is, when they are uncertain about how to spell a word while writing and they ask someone, or when they verify their spelling as they write. However, correlations between writing and spelling are typically lower than correlations between reading and spelling (Graham 2000).

In addition, it has been observed that corrective feedback on spelling is more effective in producing spelling growth when students receive this feedback immediately, while they are writing (Gettinger 1993, cited in Graham 2000). Since students have access to such feedback through word processors, those programs are a potential contributor. However, one would conjecture that the effect of such feedback on students depends on whether students see the word processor's feedback as actual feedback to improve their spelling skills or as a simple editing tool to improve the essay at hand. In addition, spellcheckers require good spelling competence, because poor spelling at times produce words that are too divergent for the spellchecker to suggest the right word (Moats 2005). Many teachers might have found instances of the following words in their SHLLs' typed essays: *ósea* for *o sea*, *varean* for *varían*, *pisaron* for *pizarrón*. The presence of these forms shows that the spellchecker was not capable of detecting the student's intended word and instead suggested a different word. But it also suggests that the student accepted the spellchecker's word without challenging its suitability.

Another noteworthy observation is that students will often correctly write the stress mark in the first- and third-person forms of the preterit of *-er*, *-ir* verbs, such as *escribí*, *corrí*, *creyó*, *salió* (and some *-ar* forms, such as *pensó*, *contó*) but not in preterit forms of most *-ar* verbs (e.g., *dejé*, *miré*, *pasó*, *dibujó*). While the words in the first group do not have a nonmarked version—that is, there is no **escribi*, **corri*, **creyo*, **penso*, and so forth—and therefore the spellchecker automatically corrects those forms, there is an unaccented version of the words in the second group (*deje*, *mire*, *paso*, *dibujo*), which means the spellchecker does not automatically correct these forms. This output suggests that many students are simply relying on this feedback to edit their work, not to improve their spelling skills. There might be too many misspellings to pay attention to those corrections. Perhaps, automatic feedback might prove more helpful when it identifies a few occasional spelling errors and the writer finds it helpful to pay attention to that particular feedback. However, when the spellchecker signals many spelling errors, it might be too difficult to learn anything from that feedback. Anecdotally, I have noticed that some students not only use the spellchecker function but the autocomplete function, which could be detrimental to spelling growth.

In sum, although it is possible to find studies that support the use of incidental learning of spelling, meta-analysis of studies testing spelling interventions in English (Graham 2000; Graham and Santangelo 2014) have found that the assumption that spelling can be acquired without instruction is not supported and that formal spelling instruction indeed improved students' spelling performance.

Explicit Instruction versus Incidental Learning of Spelling in SHLLs Classrooms

The only intervention studies conducted with SHLLs have involved accent marks. Fernández Parera and Lynch (2021) tested the effect of explicit teaching instruction (conducted through regular textbook explanations and practice) on accent mark placement by comparing course sections that had received explicit instruction with course sections that had not. When looking at the students' performance on a dictation task, only students in the explicit instruction sections significantly improved their accent mark scores—students in the sections without explicit instruction either did not improve, or their improvement was not significant. However, when looking at the scores in natural writing (written responses in exams), the results were more nuanced. The effect of explicit instruction was clear in students enrolled in a first-semester college course—students who typically had not taken any Spanish course prior to that one. But in a second-semester course—that is, one with students who had taken two or three years of Spanish courses in high school—explicit instruction did not have an effect. Only high-performing students improved their accent-marking skills throughout the course but in a similar way in both types of courses. Mid- and low-performing students did not improve throughout the semester, both in the explicit instruction course and the nonexplicit instruction one.

Fernández Parera and Lynch's (2021) findings that instruction has different effects on students who have not taken Spanish courses previously than on students who have already taken some Spanish courses have been observed in other studies. For example, Llombart-Huesca (2022) found that college students who had taken one year or more of Spanish courses in high school had better spelling of /s/ compared to students who had not taken any course before or only one semester. However, additional Spanish instruction in secondary school did not bring additional gains. Similarly, Beaudrie's (2018) study found that students' spelling growth from one course level to the next only happened between the first levels.

Therefore, when we consider the effect of different instructional approaches and strategies, we need to consider the specific level of the student: (1) beginning students do not seem to benefit from natural approaches, and (2) among nonbeginning students, only those who are good spellers benefit from instruction.

One can only conjecture the reason for these findings. On the one hand, beginning students might not have the tools to take advantage of natural exposure. As mentioned in chapter 2, the natural linguistic strategy of speakers is to focus their attention on meaning, because this is the primary use of language (Cazden 1974; Hakes 1980). And it has been observed that SHLLs tend to focus on the content of the language materials they encounter in class, instead of the formal elements (Torres 2013). Therefore, beginning SHLLs enrolled in a course that does not offer explicit instruction on spelling might not direct their attention to it, since their focus is directed to conveying meaning and reading for comprehension and content. As we saw in chapter 5, learning stress mark placement requires a series of underlying cognitive-linguistic skills, such as phonological and morphological awareness, the ability to combine lexical and sublexical reading, that is, word identification and decoding, as well as the development of a strong visual memory of the stress marked words.

On the other hand, it seems that less-skilled spellers have not developed the underlying skills to take advantage of new instruction—be it incidental or explicit. A student who has gone through years of Spanish instruction without developing good spelling skills might be reading solely through lexical/whole-word reading without having successfully gone through the necessary decoding stage in which accurate orthographic representations are acquired (Share 1995, 2004). Less-skilled spellers are also likely to not have developed an awareness of the morphological structure of words (Llombart-Huesca 2017a), which would assist students in noticing the spelling's morphological patterns—including accent placement. In addition, students who are poor spellers even after years of Spanish instruction probably have not developed habits that would assist them, such as carefully rereading a new word by decoding each letter into sound before storing it into memory, rewriting a word with a challenging spelling, or using spellcheckers as a source of feedback and not simply as editors.

The hope is that both incidental and explicit learning can be reconciled in a classroom with a rich literate environment where structured and explicit instruction on spelling and decoding takes place. Likewise, it is important to create an environment where spelling is not seen from a purely prescriptive perspective but as the means for students to become curious about language, make connections between words, and become self-reflective about their learning process.[1]

Working with Phonological Awareness

We saw in previous chapters that some spelling errors SHLLs produce are associated with underdeveloped phonological awareness (PA). Those are misspellings related to omission of vowels in diphthongs (*tene* for *tiene*), transposition of vowels into another syllable (*difierensa* for *diferencia*), omission of entire syllables (*comunición* for *comunicación*), and some errors related to similar consonant sounds (*familla* for *familia*, *ensellaron* for *enseñaron*). These misspellings cannot be addressed by teaching a "spelling rule" because those graphemes are in a simple PGC. Memorizing those specific words would not guarantee any improvement, since the underlying cause would be unaddressed. For example, memorizing *comunicación* and *tiene* would not always prevent the student from writing *hablábamos* as **hablavos* or *nuevo* as **nevo*. To address this type of difficulty with spelling—which will probably be reflected in reading too—we need to address PA and decoding abilities.[2]

Phonological awareness does not need to be developed to the degree that it is developed in early literacy education. Even highly literate adults do not always perform well in tasks of phonemic knowledge (e.g., Scholes 1993; Scarborough et al. 1998). For example, Serrano, Defior, and Martos (2003) found that Spanish teacher trainees for primary education and language therapy had low levels of PA, similar to those found in pre-reading children. Although this low PA may hinder some of the tasks these teachers will have to do in their future profession, these authors also suggest that, perhaps, for highly literate people, PA has become implicit after automatization of reading. In this case, PA activities should have a focused aim in the SHLLs' classroom, and only target those areas that can have an impact on reading and spelling proficiency. The following are some targeted activities addressing PA and decoding abilities.

Reading Aloud

Some studies have found that practice in word decoding improves the spelling performance of children, including children with reading difficulties (Ehri and Wilce 1980; Greaney, Tunmer, and Chapman 1997; Lovett and Steinbach 1997). The reading aloud activity should be considered separate from reading a text for comprehension. Reading aloud can also be used to identify reading difficulties. However, some students will have very fluent reading that might not raise any concerns until an unknown or unfamiliar word appears. As we saw in chapter 2, this is because adult readers use nondecoding strategies that allow us to identify words and "say" them, instead of sounding them out. Although this is a great—and necessary—strategy that allows us to read quickly and fluently, when we encounter a new or unfamiliar word—perhaps a technical word or the name of a city—we need to momentarily switch to a decoding strategy to read that word. Readers typically slow down when reading such words, but the time difference would only be detected in a laboratory setting, or it is so insignificant that it does not disrupt fluent reading. But when the readers' decoding skills are very limited, they will stumble in a noticeable way, and on some occasions they might even be incapable of reading the word or will switch to an English pronunciation.

The reading aloud activity should target words that students find particularly difficult to read. They can be long words—but not uncommonly long ones—or words with diphthongs. Ideally, those should be words the instructor has noticed students have had difficulty with, as well as new words and even pseudowords that are pronounceable and follow Spanish-language patterns. One could argue that reading pseudowords is a waste of time, since they will not be used in real reading and writing. But we need to consider the use of pseudowords as brief interventions that only aim at developing decoding skills. (A—perhaps silly—analogy: it is not likely that I will ever find the need to raise a fifteen-pound dumbbell ten times in a row in real life. However, doing so is likely to help me raise a heavy bucket of water when I need it.) In any case, reading aloud for the purpose of helping students improve their decoding skills should include words that students are not likely to use in daily speech:

1. Names of cities that students may have not used in their speech; for example, *Santander, Bilbao, Coatzacoalcos, Antofagasta, Copiapó, Baigorrita*
2. Cognate words that students are likely to have used in English, in an academic setting, but not in Spanish, since oftentimes students switch to English pronunciation even when they encounter these words when reading a Spanish passage; for example, *pirámide, molécula, aerosol, homogéneo, heterogéneo, glaciar, paleolítico*
3. Words with two contiguous vowels; for example, *nieve, ciudad, diferencia, aéreo, veinte, aceite, deterioro, lee, seriedad*
4. Pseudowords with two contiguous vowels; for example, *dees, rielo, goesa, tiega, tuero, fiendo, luenta, piugado, puigado*
5. Long words, especially those that have a repeated letter sequence or two similar syllables; for example, *comunicación, adecuadamente, asesoramiento, duodécimo, ensimismado, pronunciatión*

This activity also has a place in advanced Spanish courses where spelling is not particularly addressed, such as in upper-division literature or linguistics courses. In these courses, new words related to the discipline will appear, and some students might learn to identify them as whole words. Long words that appear in this disciplinary context could be used for reading aloud, to make

A few classroom situations spurred in me an interest in researching students' decoding skills. On one occasion, a fluent Spanish-speaking student was discussing a linguistics article about a study conducted in Santander and Bilbao. I asked the student to read a specific passage aloud and he read these two city names with an English pronunciation, as *standard* and *Balboa*, respectively. I asked him to read them "in Spanish," and he was simply incapable of doing so. He had never seen or heard those two names before and was simply unable to decode them, letter by letter or syllable by syllable. After that encounter, I started paying more attention to the types of words students would have trouble reading.

On another occasion, playing hangman in class, a student wrote twenty-two lines on the board, for his secret word. Many students immediately exclaimed: ¡Parangaricutirimícuaro! Some of them were students who would stumble when reading much shorter words. This shows that when we want students to practice their decoding skills, we need to use pseudowords or words unknown to them. And if we want to use names of cities, they should be cities with names unfamiliar to the students.

sure students actually decode them in reading and later encode them in writing. These are some examples from my linguistics courses: *preposicional, adverbio, implícito, cláusula, subordinada, determinante, infinitivo, subjuntivo, subjetivo.*

Adapted Dictation of Words

The instructor reads a list of words, one by one, while students write them down. The adaptation consists of giving students a paper with one line for each letter of each word. This is more appropriate for words with diphthongs that are not very long. These are some suggestions: *nueve, nuevo, ciudad, graduar, veinte, aceite, diente, tiene, siente, fuera, duele, fuimos*; for example:

1. __ __ __ __ __ (for *nueve*)
2. __ __ __ __ __ __ (for *ciudad*)

An added feature to this activity is to provide one vowel in its place, to direct the attention to the right order of vowels; for example,

1. __ __ e __ __ (for *nueve*)
2. __ i __ __ __ __ (for *ciudad*)

For this option, as with any option where students are not writing the entire word—as in fill-in-the blanks, or when asking students to place a stress mark—I would recommend asking students to rewrite the entire word afterward.

Word dictation can also be adapted to target syllable segmentation. A common PA activity that aims at teaching syllable segmentation is to ask students to clap or tap once for each syllable in a word the teacher says, using the students' names and other familiar words (Denton et al. 2000). One way to adapt this activity to SHLLs in secondary school and at the college level is to ask students to write one line on a piece of paper for each syllable they hear, instead of clapping or tapping. After confirming that the right number of lines were placed, the instructor will read the word again and ask students to write it, with one syllable on each line. This activity can be used for long words for which teachers have noticed a tendency to omit entire syllables. It seems that some syllable omissions happen when similar syllables appear in a word, or when two syllables start with the same letter. Therefore, these are some suggestions: *comunicación, prepararon, hablábamos, femenino, asesoramiento, asesinato.*

Word Games

Some games such as hangman, or Lingo/Wordle are a fun way to direct students' attention to each letter of a word and the order in which they appear,[3] instead of the word as a whole. Since those are popular games, I will not detail the instructions, which are also easy to find online. I would not spend an entire class playing those games, but they are a good way to relax toward the end of the class period and have some fun while still learning. They can be played with the instructor as the "host"—the person thinking of the secret word—and have students guess as a group, or let students play in pairs or small groups where students rotate the role of host. In order to have some control over the words, the instructor may give the secret word to the student host in a piece of paper, but allowing the hosts themselves to think of a word also gives them the chance to reflect about their spelling and the sequence of letters.

Some suggestions for "secret words" in hangman: *ingeniera, ingeniería, diferencia, seriedad, paciencia, siniestro, invitado, interesante, beneficio, experiencia, bromeando, paseaba, especialidad.* Some suggestions for five- and six-letter "secret words" in Wordle: *miedo, medio, serio, seria, luego, tiene, fuera, puesto, veinte, miente, diente, fuimos, ciudad, tiempo.*

Working with Rhymes

Using rhymes is a great strategy for developing sensitivity to sounds, and their presence in many children's songs assists children in developing some preliteracy skills. In the school setting they are used to detect children's sensitivity to rhymes, by asking them whether two words rhyme or not (Defior 1996).[4] For secondary school and college-level SHLLs, sensitivity to rhymes can be used to lead students to notice stress contrasts as in *-ia* and *-ía* (*alegría* vs. *alergia, medía* vs. *media, sería* vs. *seria*), as well as the endings *-ear* and *-iar* (*crear, marear, pasear* vs. *criar, variar, premiar*). For example, the instructor can write two columns each headed by one of the two words from these pairs (e.g., *crear* and *criar*.) The instructor then reads words ending in *-ear* or *-iar* and asks students to place them under their corresponding rhyming word: *marear, variar, hojear, negociar, batear, copiar, bucear, pasear, vaciar, pelear, enviar, tutear, premiar.*

These are other ideas for rhyming sorting:

1. Heading pair: *cansó, canso.* The read words would be *-ar* verbs in the third-person-singular preterit and in the first-person-singular present: *pasó, paso, miró, leyó, lavo,* and so on.
2. Heading pair: *alergia, alegría.* Read words: *manía, ansia, encía, ciencia, bujía, agencia, batería, farmacia, caloría, diferencia, brujería, magia, panadería, afasia.*
3. Heading pair: *taparon, arpón.* Read words: *bailaron, ladrón, dejaron, limón, comieron, varón, apagón, ocuparon, patrón.*

Directing students' attention to rhymes can also be done through poetry reading or in popular sayings, such as these:

Cree el león que todos son de su condición and *En los ojos del patrón, verás siempre su ambición*, where attention can be made to the oxytone sequence *-ón*
Ya comí, ya bebí, ya no me hallo aquí and *Más vale que digan: aquí corrió que aquí murió*, to notice the oxytone pattern
El que se fue a la villa, perdió su silla, to notice the *-illa* ending
Lo que no fue en tu año, no es tu daño, to notice the palatal sound /ɲ/ and its corresponding letter, *ñ*
La pereza es la madre de la pobreza, which shows a rhyme and also the spelling of the *-eza* suffix

A very nice activity involving rhymes consists of asking students to write a poem that includes certain final syllables or sequences, such as *-ción*, *-sión*, *-ia*, *-ía*, *-ez*, *-és*, *-ió*, *-ó*, *-encia*. Instructors may start giving the rhymes students need to choose from and prompting them to brainstorm some words that include these rhymes before writing their poem.

Working with Morphological Awareness

We saw in chapter 2 that successful spelling and reading development are also connected to an awareness of and a sensitivity to the morphological structure of words. Typically, less-skilled readers and writers have more difficulties in naturally noticing spelling patterns that are related to the morphological structure of words (Elbro and Arnbak 1996; Nunes, Bryant, and Bindman 1997). Graphemes in inconsistent PGCs appear in some productive suffixes (e.g., *-eza*, *-izar*, *-aba*), and being aware of the word components will reduce guesswork and the number of words whose spellings we need to memorize. Likewise, being able to recognize that *deshice* is connected to *hice* despite its meaning the opposite will also help with its spelling. In chapter 4 we saw that SHLLs sometimes shorten long words, both in reading and in writing. Because oftentimes long words are comprised of several suffixes, being aware of these word components facilitates reading and writing these words.

While some children develop MA naturally through extensive reading and writing, other children might require more targeted instruction, which is likely the case in SHLLs, because they have not been reading extensively in Spanish, given their English schooling. As reported in chapter 2, training in segmenting words into morphemes results in spelling accuracy improvement (Arnbak and Elbro 2000; Nunes, Bryant, and Olsson 2003; Kirk and Gillon 2009), and training focusing on connecting morphologically related words results in an increase in vocabulary (Bowers and Kirby 2010). Next, I present some activities that have been proposed to develop morphological awareness or are used in research to identify MA in participants, adapted to the SHLLs' classroom. Although these activities target spelling elements, they also help build up vocabulary, and they might be supplemented by other activities, such as asking students to create sentences with some of the words.

Reading Aloud

Some long words students have difficulties reading and writing might be multimorphemic words. They may appear in a variety of literary and nonfiction texts teachers employ in their language courses, as well as in content courses, such as in secondary school social sciences in dual immersion programs, and in Spanish BA linguistics, literature, and civilization courses. As we saw earlier, when presenting phonological awareness and decoding skills, it is important to allow students to decode those words themselves. Instructors can assist by making them notice the internal components (morphemes) and the way the long words are formed by stacking additional components. These are some examples of long words my students have encountered in class texts and have had difficulty reading:

> preposicional, predominantemente, estigmatización, vehementemente, cosmopolitismo

Students can be encouraged to notice that *preposicional* results from *posición* → *preposición* → *preposicional*; *predominantemente* results from *dominar* → *predominar* → *predominante* → *predominantemente*; and so forth.

We saw in previous chapters that many misspellings could be avoided by paying attention to the word's morphological structure, that is, by displaying some morphological awareness. Morphological awareness entails considering semantic aspects together with formal ones, while the default tendency of speakers is to prioritize meaning and neglect attention to formal aspects. The following are some activities that require paying attention to formal aspects.

Morphological-Relatedness Task (1)

In this activity, students indicate whether the two words of several pairs belong to the "same family" (i.e., whether they are morphologically related) or not. In the following examples, in the first two pairs the words are morphologically related to one another, while in the other two pairs, they are not.

1. *Bello/belleza*: These two words belong to the same family, and it is relatively easy to see the connection, because of the semantic and formal similarities.
2. *Hacer/deshice*: These two words belong to the same family, since *deshice* is a form of *deshacer*, which is morphologically related to *hacer*. (It adds a prefix.) If we pay attention to meaning only, we will probably miss the

connection—after all, they mean the complete opposite. In addition, because the two words begin in such a different way, it is also easy to miss their connection. But being able to notice the morphological relatedness contributes to the ability to correctly spell *deshice*.

3. *Ver/mira*: These two words are not morphologically related, despite the meaning connection. Wrongly relating these two words is not likely to be a problem for spelling, but the task of noticing that they are not actually related has a potential positive effect for morphological awareness.
4. *Coser/cocía*: These two words do not belong to the same family, since *cocía* is a form of the verb *cocer*, which is different from *coser*, even though they sound the same. Noticing this distinction requires paying close attention to the spelling.

These are some word pairs that can be used for this activity:

Related: *hacer/rehizo, gordo/engordar, triste/entristecer, triste/tristeza, tengo/tuviera, eléctrico/electricidad*

Unrelated: *tasa/tacita, beso/vaso, vaso/vacío, hago/echo, coser/cocina, oigo/escucha*

Morphological-Relatedness Task (2)

In this activity, students are given the following list for verb forms (or a subset of these):

hice, asir, asiendo, rehacemos, echo, haciendo, asía, azar, asé, haré, aré, hecho, asaba, deshice, hizo, izó, así.

Some are forms of the verb *hacer* (*hice, rehacemos, haciendo, haré, hecho, deshice, hizo*), some are forms of other—less frequent—verbs: *asir* (*asir, asiendo, asía*), *asar* (*asé, asaba*), *izar* (*izó*), *echar* (*echo*), and *arar* (*aré*), as well as the words *así* and *azar*.

First, students are asked to underline those words that are forms of the verb *hacer*. In order to do this, students need to pay close attention to spelling and to meaning at the same time.

Second, students are asked to rewrite the underlined words and write a sentence with each of the *hacer* forms—which reinforces the connection between form and meaning. Note that they are not required to do the same with the other words, since the target here is *hacer*.

Morphological Matchup

This is another widely used activity that targets morphological awareness in relation to spelling. And it is also helpful for vocabulary-building purposes. After showing students that some words are composed of smaller parts that can reappear in other words, such as *horror + oso → horroroso*, and *cariñ(o) + oso → cariñoso*, students are asked to create words by matching roots with affixes. For example:

horror-	
peligr(o)-	-ción
milagr(o)-	-oso
educa(r)-	-tivo
opera(r)-	
trabaj(o)-	
dud(a)-	

(Note that *educa-* and *opera-* can combine with *-ción* and *-tivo*, and the rest with only one of the suffixes.)

Other possibilities:
Roots: *bell(o)-, trist(e)-, pobr(e)-, sincer(o)-, agud(o)-, curios(o)-, normal, pasiv(o)-, dur(o)-*
Suffixes: *-eza, -idad*

Morphological Sorting Task

Here, students are asked to classify words according to their root. For example, each of the following words are forms of either *cocer* or *coser*, and students are asked to rewrite them under the right label: *cocina, cocinero, cosí, cocía, cocían, cocido, cosida*

Another possibility:
Labels: *brazo/brasa*
Words to sort: *braceros, brasero, brasear, abrazar, abrasar, abrazo, abraso, bracito, brasas, braza*

Task for Raising Awareness of Morphological Spelling

In this activity, the instructor reads the following words and asks students to write each word in the appropriate column (see figure 6.1) according to the ending of the word. (The first word of each type has already been written in the column):

imaginación, comunicación, expresión, dedicación, intuición, inteligencia, atención, honor, sencillez, dedicación, persistencia, paciencia, indiferencia, cooperación, motivación, organización, madurez, innovación, iniciativa, adaptabilidad, responsabilidad, liderazgo, obediencia, firmeza, destreza

-ción	-sión	-encia	-ez o -eza	"otras"
imaginación	expresión	inteligencia	madurez	iniciativa

FIGURE 6.1. Task for raising awareness of morphological spelling

This is an awareness-raising task because students have not received instruction on those words or their spelling yet. But when they write them in the appropriate column, they pay attention to the spelling of the given suffix and of the word that is already in place. After the entire list has been read and written, the instructor directs students' attention to the morphological structure and spelling patterns.

Notice that all these words have something in common: they are all qualities a person can have. This is a compromise between decontextualizing language and paying attention to formal aspects, on the one hand, and seeing language in context and paying attention to meaning and use, on the other. This activity may be followed by other meaningful activities that have communicative goals and help increase vocabulary, while paying attention to spelling. For example, the instructor may ask students to list the qualities they possess, or the qualities "a good ____" (e.g., student, waiter, teacher) needs to possess to do their job.

While working with these nouns, it is important to keep making connections with the related adjectives. For example, *Una persona madura actúa con madurez* (a mature person acts with maturity). This type of sentence might sound good to language professionals but not so much to students, who might want to explain how a mature person acts. If we look at this sentence purely from a perspective of meaning and communication, it is a banality. But in this banality rests the ability to notice patterns. Literacy skills are built on the ability to switch between paying attention to these formal patterns and creating more meaningful statements (such as explaining what acting with maturity would be).

Word Buildup Activity

The following activity aims at directing students' attention to the morphemes inside polymorphemic words. Looking at morphemes allows students to notice spelling regularities. For example, verbs such as *independizar*, *señalizar*, *penalizar*, and *realizar* are spelled with *z* not as a coincidence but because all of them contain the same morpheme, *-izar*, which is spelled with a *z*. In this activity,

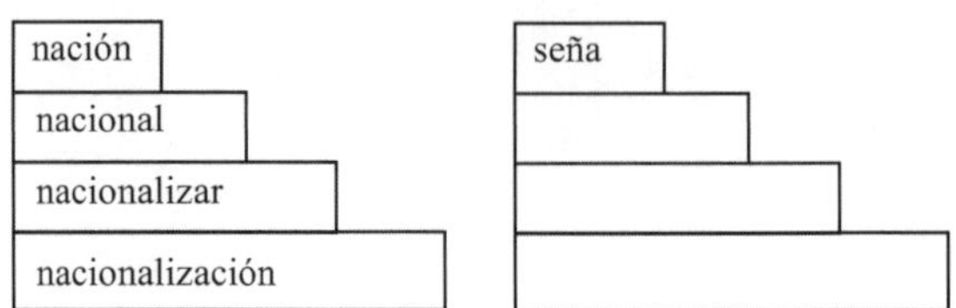

FIGURE 6.2. Word buildup activity

students start with a base word, which becomes progressively longer by adding one morpheme at a time. These words are presented in boxes that also become progressively longer (see figure 6.2) After looking at one progression as a model, students are given other base words and are asked to create new words by adding one morpheme at a time, following the model.

Some base words that work well for this progression are *seña* (*señal, señalizar, señalización*), *persona* (*personal, personalizar, personalización*), *norma, centro, pena, comercio, concepto*.[5]

In this particular progression, students can practice words with the suffixes *-izar* and *-ción*; they contain two different representations of /s/, which, as we know, is in a particularly complex PGC. But this activity, as other activities that target morphological awareness, also helps to develop a sensitivity toward the internal structure of words, which has the potential to extend to other spelling areas that are not targeted here. In addition, becoming aware of the fact that a long word is composed of smaller parts assists with reading fluency and accuracy, as well as with vocabulary building. As with other activities that aim to raise morphological awareness, this activity may be supplemented by asking students to write sentences that include some of these words.

Tongue Twisters

The goal of directing students' attention to the morphemes inside polymorphemic words is also behind certain tongue twisters, such as

> *El cielo está encapotado; ¿quién lo desencapotará? El desencapotador que lo desencapote buen desencapotador será.*

The steps below form an activity that aims to raise morphological awareness by incorporating this type of tongue twister.

Step 1: Students read the tongue twister—in silence first and then aloud. The instructor may provide some help by making students notice the patterns.

Step 2: Students are asked to create another tongue twister using the same format, but with another base word, instead of *capot(e)*. Some ideas: *camino, castillo.*[6]. In addition, instructors can offer the adjective form as a base word. I suggest adjectives derived from verbs with the suffix *-izar*, since it contains *z*, a grapheme we want to give attention to. For example, *idealizado, hechizado, paralizado, escuchimizado.* Instructors could give the first one: *El cielo está idealizado; quién lo desidealizará; el desidealizador que lo desidealice buen desidealizador será.*

A Note on Tongue Twisters

Tongue twisters, as well as the rhyming songs that parents sing to their babies and toddlers, are resources that parents instinctively use to strengthen the linguistic abilities of their children. Some tongue twisters and songs raise awareness of the common syllables of the language and help children become more aware of and able to pronounce particularly challenging sounds, such as that of /r/ in Spanish (e.g., *El perro de San Roque no tiene rabo . . .*) or of consonant clusters, such as in *Tres tristes tigres*. Song games consisting of repeating the same verse using only one vowel at a time help children develop phonological awareness of vowels.

Other tongue twisters are more directed toward developing morphological awareness, such as those where the same word is derived and inflected several times. These tongue twisters make little sense, but they are not completely nonsensical. For example, *desencapotador* does not appear in the dictionary and it does not refer to an actual profession. However, we understand that it means "someone who removes clouds" because it has the prefix *des-*, which we use for undoing acts (e.g., *desatar, desligar, despegar*) and the suffix *-dor*, which we use for "person who does [verb]." This intermediate point where a sentence or a word makes "partial sense" is where morphological awareness resides. If the word were really used in communication, it would be more difficult to pay attention to its morphemes, because we would simply process the word as a whole.

Tongue twisters and rhyming songs are also part of the cultural patrimony of a community and get transmitted from parents to children generation through generation. Although they are collected in children's books, their transmission is typically oral, which causes the tongue twisters to vary from one place to another. For example, some say, *el cielo está encapotado*, others say, *el cielo está enladrillado*, while others know it as *el suelo está enladrillado*.

Working with Specific Spelling PGCs

Most textbooks offer activities that target specific PGCs—the "spelling rules."[7] They explain the spelling changes that happen when a verb that ends in *-gar, -car, or -zar* is conjugated in the past, as in *jugar-jugué, tocar-toqué, empezar-empecé.* I am presenting here additional activities to complement those used in textbooks. More specifically, I present two activities that use pseudowords.

Using Pseudowords (1)

In order to momentarily direct students' focus to a certain contextual rule, we may offer them a combination of familiar and unfamiliar words, as well as pseudowords. The purpose of using pseudowords when working on certain PGCs is to make sure that students are not resorting to their memory of a word and that they actually apply a certain rule. For example, after studying the *c* versus *qu* rule to represent /k/, some students will correctly spell words they already knew how to spell and make mistakes on words they would misspell before learning the PGC. And in reading, while students might read the real words by employing nondecoding strategies, that is, by identifying them, reading pseudowords will require actually paying attention to the specific grapheme. The following are some suggestions for pseudowords:

For *c/qu*: *tucero, tuquero, diquene, ficera, jaquene, ceturo, quelica, coquero, quitape*

Notice that these pseudowords show not only correctly spelled sequences (as in *ca, co, cu* vs. *que, qui*) but sequences for which it is necessary to look at the specific grapheme in order to be able to pronounce the word, as in *tucero* versus *tuquero.* These words might be given to students to read, or in form of a dictation for them to write. Obviously, the emphasis should be put in actual words, but brief interventions with pseudowords will redirect students' attention to the PGC.

The following are some suggestions for other sequences:

For /x/ versus /g/ represented with *g/gu*: *gedepa, guedepa, guelope, fagire, faguimar, manigue, radigé, lagone, naguora, naguera.* (For this series, if students are asked to write the words on dictation, they should be told that none of these pseudowords are spelled with *j*.)

For *güe/güi/gue/gui/gua/guo*: *paguano, logüera, seguota, ligüiña, liguina, tigüera, tiguera*

Using Pseudowords (2)

To work on the spelling of the sound /s/ as *s, c,* or *z,* the following activity helps to develop morphological awareness and the graphemic representation of /s/

across morphology, as in *empezar* → *empecé; pensar* → *pensé.*[8] For this activity, students complete the following sentences with a pseudoword that is the inflected form of the given pseudoword:

> Voy a *turazar* mi libro porque ayer no lo ____. (*turacé*)
> Juan *cubazó* su tarea pero yo todavía no la ____. (*cubacé*)
> Mercedes *pelisó* su auto hoy y yo lo ____ ayer. (*pelisé*)

These sentences can be complemented with similar ones where the given form contains *ce* or *se* and the inflected form needs *z* or *s*. For example:

> Antes yo *nebicé* una tienda, y mi amiga la ____ ayer. (*nebizó*)
> Ayer no *dericé* mi ropa, y la tengo que ____ hoy. (*derizar*)
> Esta mañana *dilusé* unas cosas pero todavía necesito ____ unas más. (*dilusar*)

Although this activity can—and should—be done with real words, using a few pseudowords forces students to look at the grapheme of the base form (*z* or *s*) in order to inflect, since they cannot resort to habit, memory, or what "feels right."

Working with Cognates

Most instructors are aware of the ways in which English spelling can negatively impact Spanish spelling. Those errors have been documented in the analysis of the spelling errors students produce, such as consonant doubling (e.g., *effective/efectivo, class/clase, immediate/inmediato, collective/colectivo*) or the *-age/-aje* suffix (e.g., *message/mensaje*). For this type of error, there needs to be a conscious effort to avoid the pull that the visual image of the double consonant in the English counterpart of these words has on the writer. And many textbooks do.

However, as we saw in chapter 4, English cognates also have a positive impact on Spanish spelling when the grapheme is the same in both languages, and this effect is sometimes overlooked. Therefore, except for those cognate situations that have been identified as problematic, when studying different PGCs we should give greater emphasis to noncognates, in terms of examples and activities. Beaudrie (2012, 142) points out that textbooks "are designed around standard orthographic rules for common Spanish patterns . . . rather than being targeted to the specific spelling features that present the greatest difficulty to SHLs," such as the use of *s* in words ending in *-sta*, a pointless rule to teach because no misspellings of *s* in this context appear in her corpus—as is also the case in the LH corpus. Likewise, some textbooks give an exhaustive list of sequences and morphemes that require a certain grapheme, but oftentimes this sequence requires the same grapheme in English and is not likely to produce misspellings. A few examples of this are *br-, bl-, ob-, -ivo,* where the same grapheme occurs in English and Spanish. And this is why, with /b/, accuracy was 100% in cognates.

On the other hand, the facilitative effect of cognates is not fully exploited by our students, and I would like to point out a few areas where instructors can emphasize the English-Spanish connections. One is semicognates, words in English and Spanish that have evolved from related words, with a slightly different meaning or that belong to a different part of speech. Sometimes, the Spanish version will be relatively common and the English counterpart will be rarer. For example: *azul-azure, cerebro-cerebral.* The following activity aims at strengthening the connection between Spanish-English words allowing students to benefit from spelling similarities. It asks students to find a similar word in the other language—even if the meaning is slightly different. These are some of these words:

From Spanish to English:

asesino silencio mansión artificial cerebral explosión
horizontal grave edificio maravilloso

From English to Spanish:[9]

religious insect adherence pensive palace azure television
alcohol grace adolescence ceramics arbor

It is obvious that English *grave* and Spanish *grave* do not have the same use and that the English word *edifice* is not very common; however, the goal of this activity is not to work on meaning but on formal properties. The ultimate goal is to use students' knowledge of English spelling to facilitate Spanish spelling. This activity is one in which we may use a different approach in SHLLs from the approach we would use in a Spanish L2/FL setting. When a SHLL writes the word *asesino*, the word *murderer* will be closer to it in the student's mind than *assassin*, since *murderer* is the better translation for *asesino*, while *assassin*, although related, has a different use. For a SHLL, meaning and communication supersede formal characteristics. However, that student will not take advantage of the fact that *asesino* is spelled with *s*—and not *c*—as in English. A Spanish L2/FL student who hears the word *asesino* in a Spanish class for the first time will quickly connect it with *assassin*. In fact, this is why Spanish L2 instructors focus on the opposite process: to explain the different meanings of these "false friends."

However, for SHLLs, momentarily leaving meaning considerations aside to be able to notice formal similarities is a literacy task that will aid with spelling.

Another set of words in which the connections between Spanish and English are not obvious are those that have a *c* in English and *z* in Spanish. For example: *race-raza, trace-trazar, lace-lazo, dance-danza, piece-pieza, embrace-abrazar, chance-chanza, force-fuerza, finance-finanza, menace-amenazar, balance-balanza.* The *c-z* connection across languages can be done together with the *c-z* connection across morphology within Spanish (*empezar-empecé, raza-racista, amenazar-amenacé*).

Finally, another way in which English can be used to facilitate Spanish spelling is to address misspellings where students shorten long words, when those are cognates, as in **comunicion* for *comunicación*. Instructors may direct students to notice each one of the syllables both in Spanish and English.

Conclusion

The activities proposed in this chapter are not meant to be comprehensive but rather suggestions to complement or adapt the activities that appear in the textbook. They can also be seen as approaches for instructors to design their own spelling activities either in isolation or to complement vocabulary and reading activities. The activities presented here also target the underlying skills that facilitate spelling learning: phonological and morphological awareness. Developing those skills also adds depth to learning spelling, since students become more aware of the structure of language, instead of simply seeing spelling from its conventional nature and as a surface level of writing relegated to editing. Finally, delving into the structure of words and becoming aware of language patterns allow instructors to not have to choose in the "caught vs. taught" debate but rather move back and forth between focus on form and focus on meaning, where decontextualizing language is, in itself, a rich literate experience.

Notes

1. For more ideas on how to approach the teaching of spelling in the SHLL classroom, see Belpoliti and Bermejo (2020b).
2. Phonological awareness is the ability to manipulate the sounds of language without the presence of the written word, while decoding activities involve written words.
3. Lingo was the name of a TV game show, and Wordle is the online version of the game. I do not know whether there is a common name for the game itself.
4. Defior (1996) mentions the following authors as researchers who have worked with rhymes to increase phonological awareness in children's literacy development: Lundberg, Olofsson, and Wall (1980); Lenel and Cantor (1981); Blachman

(1983); Calfee, Chapman, and Venezky (1972); Lundberg, Frost, and Petersen (1988); Stanovich, Cunningham, and Cramer (1984); Yopp (1988).

5. I have noticed that some students write *señalar* instead of *señalizar* in this activity. This error suggests that they are not actually focusing their attention on the internal structure of the word but rather processing the word as a whole. Although the word *señalar* exists, it is not the word required in this activity, and noticing this distinction redirects the student's attention to the actual suffix (*-izar*) and, in turn, to its spelling.
6. *El cielo está encaminado, quien lo desencaminará; el desencaminador que lo desencamine buen desencaminador será.*
7. I have looked at several textbooks for Spanish for Spanish Speaking courses to see the explanations on spelling they present and the different types of activities they offer. I do not refer to specific textbooks here, as I do not mean this chapter as a textbook review or critique. For a review of textbooks' approach to spelling, see Burgo (2015).
8. This activity was used in Llombart-Huesca's (2017a) study, which was referenced earlier in the book.
9. From Spanish to English: *assassin, silence, mansion, artificial, cerebral, explosion, horizontal, grave, edifice, marvelous.* From English to Spanish: *religioso, insecto, adherencia, pensativo/pensar, palacio, azul, televisión, alcohol, gracia/gracias, adolescencia, cerámica, árbol.*

Glossary

Allophone. One of the phonetically distinct variants of a phoneme; each of the ways a phoneme is pronounced depending on its position within a word (initial, medial, final) or the preceding or following phoneme. For example, in Spanish, the phoneme /b/ has two allophones: [b] and [β]. The allophone [β] is the one speakers use after a vowel or a non-nasal consonant, as in *cabo* or *carbón*. It is a fricative sound, that is, one that is produced by partially obstructing the airflow, in this case between the lips. The allophone [b], a stop sound that is produced by totally closing the airflow and then letting the air go, is used in word-initial position and after a nasal consonant, as in *barco* or *cambio*.

Cognates. Words in two languages that have a similar form (pronunciation and spelling) and similar meaning. True cognates are word pairs that are very similar in form and have an equivalent meaning (*hotel-hotel*, *rose-rosa*, *prison-prisión*). Semicognates are word pairs that have similar spellings and pronunciation but some differences in meaning (*assassin-asesino*). In both cases, the similarity in spelling, pronunciation, and meaning is not coincidental but due to their common etymology.

Context-dependent consistent PGC. A phoneme-grapheme correspondence (PGC) in which one phoneme may be represented by two or more graphemes and there is a rule based on the context of the phoneme within the word. For example, in Spanish, /k/ → *c* (before *a*, *o*, *u*) and *qu* (before *e*, *i*).

Context-independent consistent PGC. A simple correspondence between one phoneme and one grapheme. For example, in Spanish, /l/ → *l*.

Digraph. A combination of two letters used to represent one sound. For example, in English, *ch*, *wh*, *gh*, *sh*, *ck*.

Diphthong. The combination of two vocalic sounds in one syllable (e.g., *ai-re*, *tie-ne*, *se-rio*).

Dominance (Language dominance). The relative proficiency of a bilingual person in the two languages.

Etymology. The history of how a word has evolved through time, both in form and meaning.

Explicit knowledge. Declarative knowledge of the language, that is, the knowledge of facts about the language, such as the fact that the verb agrees with the subject or that an adjective is a part of speech that is used to modify a noun.

Grapheme. An alphabetic unit that represents a language sound. It is an umbrella term for both letters (*a, m, r, c*) and digraphs (*ll, ch, rr, ck, ph*). However, it should be noted that the Real Academia Española considers the words "grafema" and "letra" to be completely synonymous and to exclude digraphs.

Hiatus. A sequence of two vowels appearing in two different syllables (e.g., *le-er, te-ní-a, te-a-tro*).

Implicit knowledge. The procedural knowledge of the language. It relates to the ability to speak without consciously thinking about the formal aspects of the language, such as agreement rules or verb conjugations.

Inconsistent PGC. A phoneme-grapheme correspondence in which a phoneme is represented by two or more graphemes and there is no rule to inform the choice (e.g., /b/→ *b* and *v*).

International Phonetic Alphabet (IPA). A set of symbols used to represent the sounds of all languages in an unequivocal manner regardless of the specific grapheme(s) used in each language. For example, the symbol [f] represents the initial sound of *fun, pharmacy, farmacia*, and the final sound of *laugh*, and [ð] is used to represent the *d* sound in Spanish *lado*, as well the *th* sound of *leather*, since they are the same sound.

Lemma. The form of a word that is included in the dictionary, which has been conventionally chosen to represent all the inflected forms of a word. In Spanish, the verbal lemma is the verb in its infinitive form. For example, the lemma of *comer, comí, comió, comes, coma*, and so on is *comer*. The adjectival lemma is the adjective inflected in the singular masculine form. For example, *rojo* is the lemma of *rojo, roja, rojos, rojas*. Derived forms (e.g., *comedor* and *rojizo*) are different lemmas.

Metalinguistic awareness. The ability to analyze, think about, or manipulate language as an object separate from its meaning in or out of context. Metalinguistic awareness is manifested in the different components of the language, such as phonology (phonological awareness), morphology (morphological awareness), syntax (syntactic awareness), and pragmatics (pragmatic awareness).

Morpheme. The smallest unit of the language with meaning. A morpheme may be free, that is, capable of standing alone as a word (e.g., *sing, for, yellow* in English; *feliz, por* in Spanish), or bound, when it must be attached to another morpheme to form a word (e.g., *in-, pre-, -tion* in English; *cant-, roj-, -ble* in Spanish).

Morphological awareness (MA). A component of metalinguistic awareness. It entails speakers' sensitivity to the morphological structure of words and their ability to think and talk about that structure.

Opaque orthography. Also "deep orthography." An orthographic system in which the relationship between graphemes and phonemes is highly irregular because it includes many cases in which one grapheme represents different sounds and one sound is represented by different graphemes. English, French, and Danish are languages with an opaque orthography.

Oxytone. A word with the stress on the last syllable, such as *regard, assault* in English and *perdón, temblor* in Spanish.

Paroxytone. A word with the stress on the second-to-last syllable, such as *communication, trouble* in English and *ventana, difícil* in Spanish.

Phoneme. The smallest unit of sound that can distinguish one word from another in a given language, such as /m/ in *map*, which distinguishes that word from *rap, cap*, or *lap* in English.

Phoneme-grapheme correspondence (PGC). The correspondence between a phoneme and the grapheme or graphemes that we use in a given language to represent that phoneme. This correspondence can be consistent or inconsistent.

Phonological awareness (PA). A component of metalinguistic awareness. It entails speakers' sensitivity to the sounds of a language and their ability to segment the different sounds of a sequence and discriminate between similar sounds.

Productive. A productive linguistic unit, such as a suffix or a diphthong, is an element that is used to form many new words. For example, the diphthong *-ie-* is a very productive diphthong because it appears in many words.

Proparoxytone. A word with the stress on the third-to-last syllable, such as *magical, elephant* in English, and *mágico, número* in Spanish.

Pseudoword. A made-up word that resembles a real word because it conforms to the pronunciation and spelling of a language but that has no meaning. Pseudowords are used in spelling and reading research because doing so allows researchers to observe how participants process letter sequences without resorting to their previous knowledge of the word. Pseudowords also have pedagogical applications in the classroom.

Semivowel. A speech sound that is articulated as a vowel but is shorter in duration and appears in a syllable with another vowel. In Spanish, there are two semivowels—[j] and [w]—which correspond to the vowels [i] and [u], respectively, when they appear with a vowel in the same syllable, that is, in a diphthong. For example, the *i* in *aire, tiene* and the *u* in *nueve, suave.*

Seseo. The pronunciation of the letters *c* and *z* as [s] in Spanish. The concept of "seseo" is understood in contrast with the pronunciation of these two letters as [θ] in Castillian Spanish.

Transparent orthography. Also "shallow orthography." An orthographic system in which the correspondences between graphemes and phonemes are one to one or close to it. Spanish, Italian, and Finnish are languages with transparent orthographies.

Yeísmo. The pronunciation in Spanish of the digraph *ll* as [ʝ], which gives the same pronunciation to the graphemes *ll* and *y*. The concept of "yeísmo" is understood in contrast with the pronunciation of the digraph *ll* as [ʎ].

References

Achugar, Mariana, and M. Cecilia Colombi. 2008. "Systemic Functional Linguistic Explorations into the Longitudinal Study of the Advanced Capacities: The Case of Spanish Heritage Language Learners." In *The Longitudinal Study of Advanced L2 Capacities*, edited by L. Ortega and H. Byrnes, 36–57. London: Routledge.

Adams, Marilyn. 1990. *Beginning to Read: Thinking and Learning about Print*. Cambridge, MA: MIT Press.

Alegría, Jesús, and Philippe Mousty. 1994. "On the Development of Lexical and Nonlexical Spelling Procedures of French-Speaking Normal and Disabled Children." In *Handbook of Spelling, Theory, Process and Intervention*, edited by G. D. A. Brown and N. C. Ellis, 211–26. Chichester: John Wiley and Sons.

Alegría, Jesús, and Philippe Mousty. 1996. "The Development of Spelling Procedures in French-Speaking, Normal and Reading-Disabled Children: Effects of Frequency and Lexicality." *Journal of Experimental Child Psychology* 63: 312–38.

Allred, Ruel A. 1977. *Spelling: The Application of Research Findings*. Washington, DC: National Education Association.

Anthony, Jason L., and David D. Francis. 2005. "Development of Phonological Awareness." *Current Directions in Psychological Science* 14 (5): 255–59. https://doi.org/10.1111/j.0963-7214.2005.00376.x.

Arnbak, Elisabeth, and Carsten Elbro. 2000. "The Effects of Morphological Awareness Training on the Reading and Spelling Skills of Young Dyslexics." *Scandinavian Journal of Educational Research* 44 (3): 229–51. https://doi.org/10.1080/00313830050154485.

Arteagoitia, Igone, Elizabeth R. Howard, Mohammed Loguit, Valerie Malabonga, and Dorry M. Kenyon. 2005. "The Spanish Developmental Contrastive Spelling Test: An Instrument for Investigating Intra-linguistic and Crosslinguistic Influences on Spanish-Spelling Development." *Bilingual Research Journal* 29 (3): 541–560. https://doi.org/10.1080/15235882.2005.10162851.

Baayen, Harald, Lee H. Wurm, and Joanna Aycock. 2007. "Lexical Dynamics for Low-Frequency Complex Words: A Regression Study across Tasks and Modalities." *Mental Lexicon* 2 (3): 419–63. https://doi.org/10.1075/ml.2.3.06baa.

Backhoff Escudero, Eduardo, Margarita Peón Zapata, Edgar Andrade Muñoz, Sara Rivera López, and Manuel González Montesinos. 2008. *La ortografía de los estudiantes de educación básica en México*. Mexico City: INEE.

Bahr, Ruth H., Elaine R. Silliman, Robin L. Danzak, and Louise C. Wilkinson. 2015. "Bilingual Spelling Patterns in Middle School: It Is More Than Transfer." *International Journal of Bilingual Education and Bilingualism* 18 (1): 73–91.

Barry, Christopher, and Pierluigi De Bastiani. 1997. "Lexical Priming of Nonword Spelling in the Regular Orthography of Italian." *Reading and Writing* 9: 499–517.

Bean, Wendy, and Chrystine Bouffler. 1987. *Spell by Writing.* Portsmouth, NH: Heinemann.

Beaudrie, Sara. 2009. "Receptive Bilinguals' Language Development in the Classroom: The Differential Effects of Heritage versus Foreign Language Curriculum." In *Español en Estados Unidos y otros contextos de contacto: Sociolingüística, ideología y pedagogía*, edited by M. Lacorte and J. Leeman, 325–45. Madrid: Iberoamericana / Vervuert Verlag.

Beaudrie, Sara. 2011. "Spanish Heritage Language Programs: A Snapshot of Current Programs in the Southwestern United States." *Foreign Language Annals* 44 (2): 321–37.

Beaudrie, Sara. 2012. "A Corpus-Based Study on the Misspellings of Spanish Heritage Learners and Their Implications for Teaching." *Linguistics and Education* 23: 135–44.

Beaudrie, Sara. 2017. "The Teaching and Learning of Spelling in the Spanish Heritage Language Classroom: Mastering Written Accent Marks." *Hispania* 100 (4): 596–611.

Beaudrie, Sara. 2018. "On the Relationship between Self-Concept and Literacy Development in the Spanish Heritage Language Context." *Reading and Writing Quarterly* 34: 147–59. https://doi.org/10.1080/10573569.2017.1370623.

Beaudrie, Sara M., and Damián Wilson. 2022. "Reimagining the Goals of HL Pedagogy through Critical Language Awareness." In *Heritage Language Teaching: Critical Language Awareness Perspectives for Research and Pedagogy*, edited by S. Loza and S. M. Beaudrie, 63–79. New York: Routledge.

Belpoliti, Flavia, and Encarna Bermejo. 2020a. *Spanish Heritage Learners' Emerging Literacy.* London: Routledge. https://doi.org/10.4324/9781315646589.

Belpoliti, Flavia, and Encarna Bermejo. 2020b. "Orthography in the Spanish Heritage Classroom." *TeCHS Professional Training Modules.*

Bernal-Enríquez, Ysaura, and Eduardo Hernández-Chávez. 2003. "La enseñanza del español en Nuevo México: ¿Revitalización o erradicación de la variedad chicana?" In *Mi Lengua: Spanish as a Heritage Language in the United States*, edited by A. Roca and M. C. Colombi, 96–121. Washington, DC: Georgetown University Press.

Berninger, Virginia W. 1999. "Coordinating Transcription and Text Generation in Working Memory during Composing: Automatic and Constructive Processes." *Learning Disability Quarterly* 22 (2): 99–112.

Besner, Derek. 1999. "Basic Processes in Reading: Multiple Routines in Localist and Connectionist Models." In *Converging Methods for Understanding Reading and Dyslexia*, edited by P. McMullen and R. M. Klein, 413–58. Cambridge, MA: MIT Press.

Bialystok, Ellen. 1986a. "Children's Concept of Word." *Journal of Psycholinguistic Research* 15: 13–32.

Bialystok, Ellen. 1986b. "Factors in the Growth of Linguistic Awareness." *Child Development* 57: 498–510.

Bialystok, Ellen. 2002. "Acquisition of Literacy in Bilingual Children: A Framework for Research." *Language Learning* 52 (1): 159–99. https://doi.org/10.1111/1467-9922.00180.

Bialystok, Ellen, and Ellen Bouchard Ryan. 1985. "A Metacognitive Framework for the Development of First and Second Language Skills." *In Metacognition,*

Cognition, and Human Performance, edited by D. L. Forrest-Pressley, G. E. Mackinnon, and T. G. Waller, 207–52. New York: Academic Press.

Bialystok, Ellen, Gigi Luk, and Ernest Kwan. 2005. "Bilingualism, Biliteracy, and Learning to Read: Interactions among Languages and Writing Systems." *Scientific Studies of Reading* 9: 43–61. https://doi.org/10.1207/S1532799xssr0901_4.

Blachman, Benita A. 1983. "Are We Assessing the Linguistic Factors Critical in Early Reading?" *Annals of Dyslexia* 33: 91–109.

Borzone de Manrique, Ana M., and Angela Signorini. 1994. "Phonological Awareness, Spelling and Reading Abilities in Spanish-Speaking Children." *British Journal of Educational Psychology* 64 (3): 429–39. https://doi.org/10.1111/J.2044-8279.1994.Tb01114.X.

Borzone de Manrique, Ana M., and Angela Signorini. 1998. "Emergent Writing Forms in Spanish." *Reading and Writing: An Interdisciplinary Journal* 10 (6): 499–517. https://doi.org/10.1023/A:1008019206946.

Bowers, Jeffrey S., and Peter N. Bowers. 2018. "Progress in Reading Instruction Requires a Better Understanding of the English Spelling System." *Current Directions in Psychological Science* 27 (6): 407–12. https://doi.org/10.1177/0963721418773749.

Bowers, Peter N., and John R. Kirby. 2010. "Effects of Morphological Instruction on Vocabulary Acquisition." *Reading and Writing* 23: 515–37. https://doi.org/10.1007/S11145-009-9172-Z.

Bowles, Melissa A. 2011. "Measuring Implicit and Explicit Linguistic Knowledge." *Studies in Second Language Acquisition* 33 (2): 247–71. https://doi.org/10.1017/S0272263110000756.

Boyd-Bowman, Peter. 1952. "La pérdida de vocales átonas en la altiplanicie mexicana." *Nueva Revista Mexicana de Filología Hispánica* 6 (2): 138–40.

Brady, Susan A. 1997. "Ability to Encode Phonological Representations: An Underlying Difficulty of Poor Readers." In *Foundations of Reading Acquisition and Dyslexia: Implications for Early Intervention*, edited by B. A. Blachman, 21–47. Mahwah, NJ: Erlbaum.

Brown, Alan S. 1990. "A Review of Recent Research on Spelling." *Educational Psychology Review* 2 (4): 365–97.

Bruck, Maggie, and Rebecca Treiman. 1990. "Phonological Awareness and Spelling in Normal Children and Dyslexics: The Case of Initial Consonant Clusters." *Journal of Experimental Child Psychology* 50 (1): 156–78.

Burgess, Stephen R., and Christopher J. Lonigan. 1998. "Bidirectional Relations of Phonological Sensitivity and Prereading Abilities: Evidence from a Preschool Sample." *Journal of Experimental Child Psychology* 70 (2): 117–41. https://doi.org/10.1006/jecp.1998.2450.

Burgo, Clara. 2015. "Current Approaches to Orthography Instruction for Spanish Heritage Learners: An Analysis of Intermediate and Advanced Textbooks." *Normas* 5: 133–52.

Calfee, Robert C., Robin S. Chapman, and Richard L. Venezky. 1972. "How a Child Needs to Think in Order to Learn to Read." In *Cognition in Learning and Memory*, edited by L. W. Gregg, 139–82. New York: John Wiley & Sons.

Callahan, Laura. 2010. "U.S. Latinos' Use of Written Spanish: Realities and Aspirations." *Heritage Language Journal* 7 (1): 1–27.

Campbell, Ruth, and Efisia Sais. 1995. "Accelerated Metalinguistic (Phonological) Awareness in Bilingual Children." *British Journal of Developmental Psychology* 13 (1): 61—68.

Carbonell de Grompone, María A., Elida J. Tuana, Mabel Piedra de Moratorio, Elena Lluch de Pintos, and Haydée Corbo de Mandracho. 1980. "Evolución de la ortografía según la clasificación estructural de los errores ortográficos." *Lectura y Vida: Revista Latinoamericana de Lectura* 1 (4): 11—17.

Carlisle, Joanne F. 1995. "Morphological Awareness and Early Reading Achievement." In *Morphological Aspects of Language Processing*, edited by L. B. Feldman, 189—209. Hillsdale, NJ: Lawrence Erlbaum.

Carlisle, Joanne F. 2000. "Awareness of the Structure and Meaning of Morphologically Complex Words: Impact on Reading." *Reading and Writing* 12: 169—90.

Carreira, María. 2000. "Validating and Promoting Spanish in the United States: Lessons from Linguistic Science." *Bilingual Research Journal* 24 (4): 423—42.

Carreira, María. 2002. "When Phonological Limitations Compromise Literacy: A Connectionist Approach to Enhancing the Phonological Competence of Heritage Language Speakers of Spanish." In *Literacy and the Second Language Learner*, edited by JoAnn Hammadou Sullivan, 239—60. Greenwich, CT: IAP.

Carreira, María. 2004. "Seeking Explanatory Adequacy: A Dual Approach to Understanding the Term 'Heritage Language Learner.' " *Heritage Language Journal* 2 (1): 1—25.

Carreira, María, and Regla Armengol. 2001. "Professional Opportunities for Heritage Language Speakers." In *Heritage Languages in America: Preserving a National Resource*, edited by J. K. Peyton, D. Ranard, and S. McGinnis, 109—44. McHenry, Il: Delta Systems / Cal.

Carreira, María, and Olga Kagan. 2011. "The Results of the National Heritage Language Survey: Implications for Teaching, Curriculum Design, and Professional Development." *Foreign Language Annals* 44 (1): 40—64.

Carrillo, María Soledad, and Jesús Alegría. 2014. "The Development of Children's Sensitivity to Bigram Frequencies When Spelling in Spanish, A Transparent Writing System." *Reading and Writing: An Interdisciplinary Journal* 27 (3): 571—90. https://doi.org/10.1007/S11145-013-9459-Y.

Carrillo, María Soledad, Jesús Alegría, and Javier Marín. 2013. "On the Acquisition of Some Basic Word Spelling Mechanisms in a Deep (French) and a Shallow (Spanish) System." *Reading and Writing: An Interdisciplinary Journal* 26 (6): 799—819. https://doi.org/10.1007/S11145-012-9391-6.

Casares, Julio. 1958. "Las nuevas normas de prosodia y ortografía." *Boletín de la Real Academia Española* 38: 321—46.

Cataldo, Suzanne, and Nick Ellis. 1988. "Interactions in the Development of Spelling, Reading and Phonological Skills." *Journal of Research in Reading* 11 (2): 86—109.

Cazden, Courtney B. 1974. "Play with Language and Metalinguistic Awareness: One Dimension of Language Experience." *International Journal of Early Childhood* 6 (1): 12—24.

Champion, Ann. 1997. "Knowledge of Suffixed Words in Reading and Oral Language Contexts: A Comparison of Reading Disabled and Nondisabled Readers." *Annals of Dyslexia*, 47: 29—55.

Chapman, James W., and William E. Tunmer. 2003. "Reading Difficulties, Reading-Related Self-Perceptions, and Strategies for Overcoming Negative Self-Beliefs." *Reading and Writing Quarterly* 19: 5–24. https://doi.org/10.1080/10573560308205.

Chen, Xi, Yu-Min Ku, Emiko Koyama, Richard C. Anderson, and Wenling Li. 2008. "Development of Phonological Awareness in Bilingual Chinese Children." *Journal of Psycholinguistic Research* 37 (6): 405–18. https://doi.org/10.1007/S10936-008-9085-Z.

Cho, Grace. 2000. "The Role of Heritage Language in Social Interactions and Relationships: Reflections from a Language Minority Group." *Bilingual Research Journal* 24 (4): 369–84.

Cho, Grace, Kyung-Sook Cho, and Lucy Tse. 1997. "Why Ethnic Minorities Want to Develop Their Heritage Language: The Case of Korean Americans." *Language, Culture, and Curriculum* 10 (2): 106–12.

Cobos, Rubén. 2003. *A Dictionary of New Mexico and Southern Colorado Spanish*. Santa Fe, NM: Museum of New Mexico Press.

Coltheart, Max, Brent Curtis, Paul Atkins, and Michael Haller. 1993. "Models of Reading Aloud: Dual Route and Parallel Distributed Processing Approaches." *Psychological Review* 100: 589–608.

Colombi, María Cecilia. 2002. "Academic Language Development in Latino Students' Writing in Spanish." In *Developing Advanced Literacy in First and Second Languages: Meaning with Power*, edited by M. Schleppegrell and M. C. Colombi, 67–86. Mahwah, NJ: Lawrence Erlbaum Associates.

Colombi, María Cecilia. 2009. "A Systemic Functional Approach to Teaching Spanish for Heritage Speakers in the United States." *Linguistics and Education* 20 (1): 39–49.

Contreras-Wise, Ángela. 2020. "Análisis de los errores ortográficos en la escritura de los estudiantes de herencia." *Cuadernos de Lingüística Hispánica* 36: 59–78.

Cope, B., and M. Kalantzis, eds. 2000. *Multiliteracies: Literacy Learning and the Design of Social Futures*. London: Routledge.

Cordero, Mariela. 2008. *Integrating Reading, Writing, and Talk in the Spanish for Native Speakers Classroom*. PhD diss., University of Illinois, Chicago.

Correa, Maite. 2011. "Heritage Language Learners of Spanish: What Role Does Metalinguistic Knowledge Play in Their Acquisition of the Subjunctive?" In *Selected Proceedings of the 13th Hispanic Linguistics Symposium*, edited by L. Ortiz, 128–38. Somerville, MA: Cascadilla Proceedings Project.

Craig, Dennis R. 1988. "Creole English and Education in Jamaica." In *International Handbook of Bilingualism and Bilingual Education*, edited by C. B. Paulston, 297–312. New York: Greenwood Press.

Cummins, James. 1979. "Linguistic Interdependence and the Educational Development of Bilingual Children." *Review of Educational Research* 49 (2): 222–51. https://doi.org/10.3102/00346543049002222.

Dale, Philip S., Catherine Crain-Thoreson, and Nancy M. Robinson. 1995. "Linguistic Precocity and the Development of Reading: The Role of Extralinguistic Factors." *Applied Psycholinguistics* 16 (2): 173–87. https://doi.org/10.1017/S0142716400007074.

Davies, Mark. 2016–. *Corpus del español: Web/Dialects*. http://www.corpusdelespanol.org/web-dial/.

Deacon, S. Hélène, and Peter Bryant. 2006. "Getting to the Root: Young Writers' Sensitivity to the Role of Root Morphemes in the Spelling of Inflected and Derived Words." *Journal of Child Language* 33: 401—17.

Deacon, S. Hélène, and John R. Kirby. 2004. "Morphological Awareness: Just More Phonological? The Roles of Morphological and Phonological Awareness in Reading Development." *Applied Psycholinguistics* 25 (2): 223—38.

Deacon, S. Hélène, Lesly Wade-Woolley, and John R. Kirby. 2007. "Crossover: The Role of Morphological Awareness in French Immersion Children's Reading." *Developmental Psychology* 43 (3): 732—46.

Defior, Sylvia. 1996. "Una clasificación de las tareas utilizadas en la evaluación de las habilidades fonológicas y algunas ideas para su mejora." *Journal for the Study of Education and Development, Infancia y Aprendizaje* 73: 9—63.

Defior, Sylvia. 2004. "Phonological Awareness and Learning to Read: A Crosslinguistic Perspective." In *Handbook on Children's Literacy*, edited by P. Bryant and T. Nunes, 631—49. London: Academic Press.

Defior, Sylvia, and Jesús Alegría. 2005. "Conexión entre morfosintaxis y escritura: Cuando la fonología es (casi) suficiente para escribir." *Revista de Logopedia, Foniatría y Audiología* 25 (2): 51—61.

Defior, Sylvia, Jesús Alegría, Rosa Titos, and Francisco J. Martos. 2008. "Using Morphology When Spelling in a Shallow Orthographic System: The Case of Spanish." *Cognitive Development* 23: 204—15.

Defior, Sylvia, Gracia Jiménez-Fernández, Nuria Calet, and Francisca Serrano. 2015. "Learning to Read and Write in Spanish: Phonology in Addition to Which Other Processes?" *Studies in Psychology* 36 (3): 571—91.

Defior, Sylvia, Gracia Jiménez-Fernández, and Francisca Serrano. 2009. "Complexity and Lexicality Effects on the Acquisition of Spanish Spelling." *Learning and Instruction* 19: 55—65.

Defior, Sylvia, Fernando Justicia, and Francisco Martos. 1996. "The Influence of Lexical and Sublexical Variables in Normal and Poor Spanish Readers." *Reading and Writing: An Interdisciplinary Journal* 8: 487—97. https://doi.org/10.1007/BF00577024.

Defior, Sylvia, Francisco J. Martos, and Lucía Herrera. 2000. "Influencia de las características del sistema ortográfico español en el aprendizaje de la escritura de palabras." *Estudios de Psicología* 67: 55—64.

Delforge, Ann Marie. 2009. "The Rise and Fall of Unstressed Vowel Reduction in the Spanish of Cusco, Peru: A Sociophonetic Study." PhD diss., University of California, Davis.

Denton, Carolyn A., Jan E. Hasbrouck, Laurie R. Weaver, and Cynthia A. Riccio. 2000. "What Do We Know about Phonological Awareness in Spanish?" *Reading Psychology* 21 (4): 335—52. https://doi.org/10.1080/027027100750061958.

De Swart, Peter. 2013. "A Single (Case) for Heritage Speakers?" *Theoretical Linguistics* 39 (3-4): 251—58.

Dillon, Anna M. 2009. "Metalinguistic Awareness and Evidence of Cross-Linguistic Influence among Bilingual Learners in Irish Primary Schools." *Language Awareness* 18 (2): 182—97. https://doi.org/10.1080/09658410902928479.

Diuk, Beatriz, Ana M. Borzone, Verónica Sánchez Abchi, and Marina Ferroni. 2009. "La adquisición de conocimiento ortográfico en niños de 1er a 3er año de educación básica." *Psykhe* 18 (1): 61—71.

Durgunoğlu, Aydin Y. 2002. "Cross-Linguistic Transfer in Literacy Development and Implications for Language Learners." *Annals of Dyslexia* 52: 189–204.

Durgunoğlu, Aydin Y., Montserrat Mir, and Sofía Ariño-Martí. 2002. "The Relationships between Bilingual Children's Reading and Writing in Their Two Languages." In *Studies in Writing*. Vol. 11, *New Directions for Research in L2 Writing*, edited by G. Rijlaarsdam (Series ed.) and S. Ransdell and M. Barbier (volume eds.), 81–100. https://doi.org/10.1007/978-94-010-0363-6_4.

Duursma, Elisabeth, Silvia Romero-Contreras, Anna Szuber, Patrick Proctor, Catherine Snow, Diane August, and Margarita Calderón. 2007. "The Role of Home Literacy and Language Environment on Bilinguals' English and Spanish Vocabulary Development." *Applied Psycholinguistics* 28 (1): 171–90. https://doi.org/10.1017/S0142716406070093.

Edelsky, Carole. 1990. "Whose Agenda Is This Anyway? A Response to Mckenna, Robinson, and Miller." *Educational Researcher* 19 (8): 7–11.

Edstrom, Anne. 2006. "Oral Narratives in the Language Classroom: A Bridge between Non-native, Heritage, and Native-Speaking Learners." *Hispania* 89 (2): 336–46.

Edwards, Mary Louise. 1992. "In Support of Phonological Processes." *Language, Speech, and Hearing Services in Schools* 23: 233–40.

Ehri, Linnea C. 1979. "Linguistic Insight: Threshold of Reading Acquisition." In *Reading Research: Advances in Theory and Practice*. Vol. 1, edited by T. G. Waller and G. E. MacKinnon, 63–114. New York: Academic Press.

Ehri, Linnea C. 1980. "The Development of Orthographic Images." In *Cognitive Processes in Spelling*, edited by U. Frith, 311–38. London: Academic Press.

Ehri, Linnea C. 2014. "Orthographic Mapping in the Acquisition of Sight Word Reading, Spelling Memory, and Vocabulary Learning." *Scientific Studies of Reading* 18 (1): 5–21.

Ehri, Linnea C., and Julie Rosenthal. 2007. "Spellings of Words: A Neglected Facilitator of Vocabulary Learning." *Journal of Literacy Research* 39 (4): 389–409.

Ehri, Linnea C., and Lee S. Wilce. 1980. "The Influence of Orthography on Readers' Conceptualization of the Phonemic Structure of Words." *Applied Psycholinguistics* 1 (4): 371–85.

Elbro, Carsten, and Elisabeth Arnbak. 1996. "The Role of Morpheme Recognition and Morphological Awareness in Dyslexia." *Annals of Dyslexia* 46 (1): 209–40. https://doi.org/10.1007/Bf02648177.

Ellis, Nick C. 2011. "Implicit and Explicit SLA and Their Interface." In *Implicit and Explicit Language Learning: Conditions, Processes, and Knowledge in Sla and Bilingualism*, edited by C. Sanz and R. Leow, 35–47. Washington, DC: Georgetown University Press.

Elola, Idoia, Ana Padial, and Paola Guerrero-Rodríguez. 2021. "Social Tools in the HL Classroom: Constructing Learners' Identities as Multiliterate Individuals." In *Aproximaciones al estudio del español como lengua de herencia*, edited by D. Pascual y Cabo and J. Torres, 166–177. London: Routledge.

Fairclough, Marta. 2005. *Spanish and Heritage Language Education in the United States: Struggling with Hypotheticals*. Madrid: Iberoamericana Vervuert.

Fashola, Olatokunbo S., Priscilla A. Drum, Richard E. Mayer, and Sang-Jin Kang. 1996. "A Cognitive Theory of Orthographic Transitioning: Predictable Errors in How Spanish-Speaking Children Spell English Words." *American Educational Research Journal* 33 (4): 825–43.

Fernández Parera, Antoni, and Andrew Lynch. 2021. "The Effects of Explicit Instruction on Written Accent Mark Usage in Basic and Intermediate Spanish Heritage Language Courses." *Journal of Spanish Language Teaching* 8 (1): 16–31. https://doi.org/10.1080/23247797.2021.1913821.

Ford, Karen, Marcia Invernizzi, and Francis Huang. 2018. "The Effect of Orthographic Complexity on Spanish Spelling in Grades 1–3." *Reading and Writing* 31: 1063–1081. https://doi.org/10.1007/s11145-018-9828-7.

García, Ofelia. 2002. "Writing Backwards across Languages: The Inexpert English/Spanish Biliteracy of Uncertified Bilingual Teachers." In *Developing Advanced Literacy in First and Second Languages*, edited by M. Schleppegrell and M. C. Colombi, 245–57. New York: Routledge.

Gascoigne, Carolyn. 2006. "Toward an Understanding of Incidental Input Enhancement in Computerized L2 Environments." *CALICO Journal* 24 (1): 147–62. https://www.jstor.org/stable/24156298.

Gatti, Alberta, and Teresa O'Neill. 2017. "Who Are Heritage Writers? Language Experiences and Writing Proficiency." *Foreign Language Annals* 50 (4): 734–53. https://doi.org/10.1111/flan.12291.

Gertken, Libby, Mark Amengual, and David Birdsong. 2014. "Assessing Language Dominance with the Bilingual Language Profile." In *Measuring L2 Proficiency: Perspectives from SLA*, edited by P. LeClercq, A. Edmonds, and H. Hilton, 208–25. Bristol, UK: Multilingual Matters.

Gettinger, Maribeth. 1993. "Effects of Invented Spelling and Direct Instruction on Spelling Performance of Second-Grade Boys." *Journal of Applied Behavior Analysis* 26: 281–91.

Gilbert, Luther. 1934. "Effect of Reading on Spelling in the Secondary Schools." *California Quarterly of Secondary Education* 9: 269–75.

Gilbert, Luther. 1935. "A Study of the Effect of Reading on Spelling." *Journal of Educational Research* 28: 570–76.

Gironzetti, Elisa, and Flavia Belpoliti. 2018. "Investigación y pedagogía en la enseñanza del español como lengua de herencia (ELH): Una metasíntesis cualitativa." *Journal of Spanish Language Teaching* 5 (1): 16–34. https://doi.org/10.1080/23247797.2018.1469854.

Glushko, Robert J. 1979. "The Organization and Activation of Lexical Knowledge in Reading Aloud." *Journal of Experimental Psychology: Human Perception and Performance* 5 (4): 674–91.

Goldenberg, Claude, Tammy D. Tolar, Leslie Reese, David J. Francis, Antonio Ray Bazán, and Rebeca Mejía-Arauz. 2014. "How Important Is Teaching Phonemic Awareness to Children Learning to Read in Spanish?" *American Educational Research Journal* 51 (3): 604–33. https://doi.org/10.3102/0002831214529082.

Gollan, Tamar H., Jennie Starr, and Victor S. Ferreira. 2015. "More Than Use It or Lose It: The Number-of-Speakers Effect on Heritage Language Proficiency." *Psychonomic Bulletin and Review* 22: 147–55. https://doi.org/10.3758/S13423-014-0649-7.

Gómez-Velázquez, Fabiola R., Andrés A. González-Garrido, Joan Guàrdia-Olmos, Maribel Peró-Cebollero, Daniel Zarabozo-Hurtado, and Daniel Zarabozo. 2014. "Evaluación del conocimiento ortográfico en adultos jóvenes y su relación con la lectura." *Revista Neuropsicología, Neuropsiquiatría y Neurociencias* 14 (1): 40–67.

Goodwin, Amanda P., and Soyeon Ahn. 2013. A Meta-analysis of Morphological Interventions in English: Effects on Literacy Outcomes for School-Age Children. *Scientific Studies of Reading* 17 (4): 257–85. https://doi.org/10.1080/10888438.2012.689791.

Gottardo, Alexandra, Bernice Yan, Linda S. Siegel, and Lesly Wade-Wooley. 2001. "Factors Related to English Reading Performance in Children with Chinese as a First Language: More Evidence of Cross Language Transfer of Phonological Processing." *Journal of Educational Psychology* 93 (3): 530–42. https://doi.org/10.1037/0022-0663.93.3.530.

Graham, Steve. 2000. "Should the Natural Learning Approach Replace Traditional Spelling Instruction?" *Journal of Educational Psychology* 92 (2): 235–47. https://doi.org/10.1037/0022-0663.92.2.235.

Graham, Steve, and Karen R. Harris. 2005. "The Impact of Handwriting and Spelling Instruction on the Writing and Reading Performance of At-Risk First Grade Writers." Paper Presented at the Pacific Coast Research Conference, February, Coronado, CA.

Graham, Steve, Karen R. Harris, and Michael Hebert. 2011. "It Is More Than Just the Message: Analysis of Presentation Effects in Scoring Writing." *Focus on Exceptional Children* 44 (4): 1–12.

Graham, Steve, and Tanya Santangelo. 2014. "Does Spelling Instruction Make Students Better Spellers, Readers, and Writers? A Meta-analytic Review." *Reading and Writing* 27: 1703–43. https://doi.org/10.1007/S11145-014-9517-0.

Greaney, Keith T., William E. Tunmer, and James W. Chapman. 1997. "Effects of Rime-Based Orthographic Analogy Training on the Word Recognition Skills of Children with Reading Disability." *Journal of Educational Psychology* 89 (4): 645–51. https://doi.org/10.1037/0022-0663.89.4.645.

Greenberg, Daphne, Linnea C. Ehri, and Dolores Perin. 2002. "Do Adult Literacy Students Make the Same Word-Reading and Spelling Errors as Children Matched for Word-Reading Age?" *Scientific Studies of Reading* 6 (3): 221–43. https://doi.org/10.1207/S1532799XSSR0603_2.

Hakes, David T. 1980. *The Development of Metalinguistic Abilities in Children*. New York: Springer-Verlag.

Hamachek, Don. 1995. "Self-Concept and School Achievement: Interaction Dynamics and a Tool for Assessing the Self-Concept Component." *Journal of Counseling and Development* 73: 419–25. https://doi.org/10.1002/j.1556-6676.1995.tb01775.x.

Harmegnies, Bernard, and Dolors Poch-Olivé. 1992. "A Study of Style-Induced Vowel Variability: Laboratory versus Spontaneous Speech in Spanish." *Speech Communication* 11 (4): 429–37. https://doi.org/10.1016/0167-6393(92)90048-C.

He, Agnes W. 2006. "Toward an Identity Theory of the Development of Chinese as a Heritage Language." *Heritage Language Journal* 4 (1): 1–28.

He, Agnes W. 2010. The Heart of Heritage: Socio-cultural Dimension of Heritage Language Learning. *Annual Review of Applied Linguistics* 30: 66–82. http://dx.doi.org/10.1017/S0267190510000073.

Henderson, Edmund H. 1990. *Teaching Spelling*. Boston: Houghton Mifflin.

Holguín-Mendoza, Claudia. 2018. "Critical Language Awareness for Spanish Heritage Language Programs: Implementing a Complete Curriculum." *International Multilingual Research Journal* 12 (2): 65–79.

Hulstijn, Jan H. 2011. "Language Proficiency in Native and Nonnative Speakers: An Agenda for Research and Suggestions for Second-Language Assessment." *Language Assessment Quarterly* 8 (3): 229—49. https://doi.org/10.1080/15434303.2011.565844.

Hulstijn, Jan H. 2019. "An Individual-Differences Framework for Comparing Non-native with Native Speakers: Perspectives from BLC Theory." *Language Learning* 69 (1): 157—83. https://doi.org/10.1111/lang.12317.

Ingram, David. 1974. "Phonological Rules in Young Children." *Journal of Child Language* 1 (1): 29—64.

Jensen, Linda, and Lorena Llosa. 2007. "Heritage Language Reading in the University: A Survey of Students' Experiences, Strategies, and Preferences." *Heritage Language Journal* 5 (1): 98—116. https://doi.org/10.46538/hlj.5.1.5.

Jeong, Allan, Haiying Li, and Andy Jiaren Pan. 2017. "A Sequential Analysis of Responses in Online Debates to Postings of Students Exhibiting High Versus Low Grammar and Spelling Errors." *Education Technology Research and Development* 65 (5): 1175—1194. https://doi.org/10.1007/S11423-016-9501-2.

Jiménez González, Juan E., and Roxana Jiménez Rodríguez. 1999. "Errores en la escritura de sílabas con grupos consonánticos: Un estudio transversal." *Psicothema* 11 (1): 125—35.

Justicia, Fernando, Sylvia Defior, Santiago Pelegrina, and Francisco J. Martos. 1999. "The Sources of Errors in Spanish Writing." *Journal of Research in Reading* 22 (2): 198—202.

Kagan, Olga, and Kathleen Dillon. 2001. "A New Perspective on Teaching Russian: Focus on the Heritage Learner." *Slavic and East European Journal* 45 (3): 507—18.

Kalantzis, Mary, and Bill Cope. 2004. "Designs for Learning." *e-Learning* 1 (1): 38—92.

Kemp, Nenagh. 2016. "Children's First Language Acquisition of the English Writing System." In *The Routledge Handbook of the English Writing System*, edited by V. Cook and D. Ryan, 191—204. London: Routledge.

Kim, Ji Young. 2015. "Perception and Production of Spanish Lexical Stress by Spanish Heritage Speakers and English L2 Learners of Spanish." In *Selected Proceedings of the 6th Conference on Laboratory Approaches to Romance Phonology*, edited by E. W. Willis, P. Martín Butragueño, and E. Herrera Zendejas, 106—28. Somerville, MA: Cascadilla Proceedings Project.

Kirby, John R., S. Hélène Deacon, Peter N. Bowers, Leah Izenberg, Lesly Wade-Woolley, and Rauno Parrila. 2012. "Children's Morphological Awareness and Reading Ability." *Reading and Writing* 25 (2): 389—410. https://doi.org/10.1007/s11145-010-9276-5.

Kirk, Cecilia, and Gail T. Gillon. 2009. "Integrated Morphological Awareness Intervention as a Tool for Improving Literacy." *Language, Speech, and Hearing Services in Schools* 40 (3): 341—51. https://doi.org/10.1044/0161-1461.

Kovelman, Ioulia, Stephanie A. Baker, and Laura-Ann Petitto. 2008. "Age of First Bilingual Language Exposure as a New Window into Bilingual Reading Development." *Bilingualism* 11 (2): 203—23. https://doi.org/10.1017/S1366728908003386.

Kuo, Li-jen, and Richard C. Anderson. 2006. "Morphological Awareness and Learning to Read: A Cross-Language Perspective." *Educational Psychologist* 41 (3): 161—80. https://doi.org/10.1207/s15326985ep4103_3.

Krashen, Steven. 1989. "We Acquire Vocabulary and Spelling by Reading: Additional Evidence for the Input Hypothesis." *Modern Language Journal* 73 (4): 440–64.

Krashen, Stephen. 1998. "Language Shyness and Heritage Language Development." In *Heritage Language Development*, edited by S. Krashen, L. Tse, and J. McQuillan, 41–49. Culver City, CA: Language Education Associates.

Kreiner, David S., Summer D. Schnakenberg, Angela G. Green, Michael J. Costello, and Anis F. McClin. 2002. "Effects of Spelling Errors on the Perception of Writers." *Journal of General Psychology* 129 (1): 5–17. https://doi.org/10.1080/00221300209602029.

Ladefoged, Peter. 2001. *A Course in Phonetics*. 4th ed. Fort Worth, TX: Harcourt College Publishers.

Laurent, Angélique, and Clara Martinot. 2010. "Bilingualism and Phonological Awareness: The Case of Bilingual (French-Occitan) Children." *Reading and Writing: An Interdisciplinary Journal* 23 (3): 435–52.

Lázaro, Miguel. 2012. "A Study of Base Frequency in Spanish Skilled and Reading-Disabled Children: All Children Benefit from Morphological Processing in Defining Complex Pseudowords." *Dyslexia* 18 (2): 130–38. https://doi.org/10.1002/dys.1436.

Lázaro, Miguel, Joana Acha, Saray de La Rosa, Seila García, and Javier Sainz. 2017. "Exploring the Derivative Suffix Frequency Effect in Spanish Speaking Children." *Reading and Writing* 30 (1): 163–85. https://doi.org/10.1007/S11145-016-9668-2.

Leal, Fernando, Esmeralda Matute, and Daniel Zarabozo. 2005. "La transparencia del sistema ortográfico del español de México y su efecto en el aprendizaje de la escritura." *Estudios de Lingüística Aplicada* 23 (42): 127–45.

Leeman, Jennifer. 2005. "Engaging Critical Pedagogy: Spanish for Native Speakers." *Foreign Language Annals* 38 (1): 35–45. https://doi.org/10.1111/j.1944-9720.2005.tb02451.x.

Leeman, Jennifer. 2012. Investigating Language Ideologies in Spanish as a Heritage Language. In *Spanish as a Heritage Language in the United States: The State of the Field*, edited by M. Fairclough and S. Beaudrie, 43–59. Washington, DC: Georgetown University Press.

Leeman, Jennifer, Lisa Rabin, and Esperanza Román-Mendoza. 2011. "Critical Pedagogy beyond the Classroom Walls: Community Service-Learning and Spanish Heritage Language Education." *Heritage Language Journal* 8 (3): 293–314.

Lenel, Julia C., and Joan H. Cantor. 1981. "Rhyme Recognition and Phonemic Perception in Young Children." *Journal of Psycholinguistic Research* 10 (1): 57–67. https://doi.org/10.1007/BF01067361.

Lipski, John M. 1990. "Aspects of Ecuadorian Vowel Reduction." *Hispanic Linguistics* 4 (1): 1–19.

Llisterri, Joaquim, María J. Machuca, Antonio Ríos, and Sandra Schwab. 2016. "La percepción del acento léxico en un contexto oracional." *Loquens* 3 (2): 1–13.

Llombart-Huesca, Amàlia. 2017a. "Morphological Awareness and Spelling in Heritage Language Learners." *Linguistics and Education* 37: 11–31.

Llombart-Huesca, Amàlia. 2017b. Rejoinder to "What's Next? Heritage Language Learners Shape New Paths." *Hispania Journal-Special Centenary Focus Issue. Hispania* 100 (5): 277–78.

Llombart-Huesca, Amàlia. 2018. "Understanding Spelling Errors in Spanish Heritage Language Learners." *Hispania* 101 (2): 211–23.

Llombart-Huesca, Amàlia. 2019. "Phonological Awareness and Spelling of Spanish Vowels in Spanish Heritage Language Learners." *Hispanic Studies Review* 4 (1): 80–97.

Llombart-Huesca, Amàlia. 2021. "Conciencia metalingüística en la enseñanza del español como lengua de herencia: El desarrollo de la lectoescritura." In *Aproximaciones al estudio del español como lengua de herencia*, edited by D. Pascual y Cabo and J. Torres, 153–65. London: Routledge.

Llombart-Huesca, Amàlia. 2022. "Default Grapheme and Language Transfer in the Spelling of /S/ in Spanish Heritage Language Learners." *Heritage Language Journal* 19 (1): 1–27. https://doi.org/10.1163/15507076-12340024.

Llombart-Huesca, Amàlia, and Alejandra Pulido. 2017. "Who Needs Linguistics? Service-Learning and Linguistics for Spanish Heritage Language Learners." *Hispania* 100 (3): 348–60.

Llombart-Huesca, Amàlia, and Eve Zyzik. 2019. "Linguistic Factors and the Spelling Ability of Spanish Heritage Language Learners." *Frontiers in Education* 4 (150): 1–12. https://doi.org/10.3389/feduc.2019.00150.

Lonigan, Christopher J. 2007. "Vocabulary Development and the Development of Phonological Awareness Skills in Preschool Children." In *Vocabulary Acquisition: Implications for Reading Comprehension*, edited by R. K. Wagner, A. E. Muse, and K. R. Tannenbaum, 15–31. New York: Gilford.

Loomer, Bradley, Robert Fitzsimmons, and Maxine C. Strege. 1990. *Spelling Research and Practice: Teacher's Edition.* Iowa City: Useful Learning.

Lope Blanch, Juan M. 1964. "En torno a las vocales caedizas del español mexicano." *Nueva Revista de Filología Hispánica* 17(1/2), 1–19. https://doi.org/10.24201/nrfh.v17i1/2.1507.

Lord, Gillian. 2002. "The Second-Language Acquisition of Spanish: Derivational, Analogical, or Lexical?" Unpublished diss., Penn State U.

Lovett, Maureen, and Karen Steinbach. 1997. "The Effectiveness of Remedial Programs for Reading Disabled Children of Different Ages: Does the Benefit Decrease for Older Children?" *Learning Disability Quarterly* 20: 189–210.

Lowther Pereira, Kelly. 2015. "Developing Critical Language Awareness via Service-Learning for Spanish Heritage Speakers." *Heritage Language Journal* 12 (2): 159–85.

Lundberg, Ingvar, Jørgen Frost, and Ole-Peter Petersen. 1988. "Effects of an Extensive Program for Stimulating Phonological Awareness in Preschool Children." *Reading Research Quarterly* 23 (3): 263–68.

Lundberg, Ingvar, Åke Olofsson, and Stig Wall. 1980. "Reading and Spelling Skills in the First School Years Predicted from Phonemic Awareness Skills in Kindergarten." *Scandinavian Journal of Psychology* 21 (1): 159–73.

MacGregor-Mendoza, Patricia. 2000. "Aquí No se Habla Español: Stories of Linguistic Repression in Southwest Schools." *Bilingual Research Journal* 24 (4): 355–67. https://doi.org/10.1080/15235882.2000.10162772.

Mahony, Diana, Maria Singson, and Virginia Mann. 2000. "Reading Ability and Sensitivity to Morphological Relations." *Reading and Writing: An Interdisciplinary Journal* 12: 191–218.

Mann, Virginia, and Heinz Wimmer. 2002. "Phoneme Awareness and Pathways into Literacy: A Comparison of German and American Children." *Reading and Writing: An Interdisciplinary Journal* 15 (7/8): 653–682. https://doi.org/10.1023/A:1020984704781.

Marín Gálvez, Rafael. 1995. "La duración vocálica en español." *Estudios de Lingüística de la Universidad de Alicante* 10: 213–26. https://doi.org/10.14198/ELUA1994-1995.10.11.

Martinet, Catherine, Sylviane Valdois, and Michel Fayol. 2004. "Lexical Orthographic Knowledge Develops from the Beginning of Literacy Acquisition." *Cognition* 91 (2). https://doi.org/10.1016/J.Cognition.2003.09.002.

Martínez, Glenn A. 2003. "Classroom Based Dialect Awareness in Heritage Language Instruction: A Critical Applied Linguistic Approach." *Heritage Language Journal* 1 (1): 1–14.

Martin-Lacroux, Christelle (2017). "'Without the spelling errors I would have shortlisted her . . .': The impact of spelling errors on recruiters' choice during the personnel selection process." *International Journal of Selection and Assessment*, 25 (3): 276–83. https://doi.org/10.1111/ijsa.12179.

Martin-Lacroux, Christelle, and Alain Lacroux. 2017. "Do Employers Forgive Applicants' Bad Spelling in Résumés?" *Business and Professional Communication Quarterly* 80 (3): 321–35. https://doi.org/10.1177/2329490616671310.

Masny, Diana. 1987. "The Role of Language and Cognition in Second Language Metalinguistic Awareness." In *Research in Second Language Learning: Focus on the Classroom. Proceedings From the 6th Delaware Symposium on Language Studies*, edited by J. Lantolf and A. Labarca, 61–72. Norwood, NJ: Ablex Publishing.

Matluck, Joseph. 1952. "La pronunciación del español en el Valle de México." *Nueva Revista de Filología Hispánica* 6 (2): 109–20.

McCarty, Teresa, Lucille Watahomigie, Akira Yamamoto, and Ofelia Zepeda. 1997. "School-Community-University Collaborations: The American Indian Language Development Institute." In *Teaching Indigenous Languages*, edited by J. Reyhner, 85–104. Flagstaff: Northern Arizona University.

Meyer, David E., Roger W. Schvaneveldt, and Margaret G. Ruddy. 1974. "Functions of Graphemic and Phonemic Codes in Visual Word-Recognition." *Memory and Cognition* 2: 309–21. https://doi.org/10.3758/BF03209002.

Mikulski, Ariana M. 2006. "Accentuating Rules and Relationships: Motivations, Attitudes, and Goals in a Spanish for Native Speakers Class." *Foreign Language Annals* 39 (4): 660–82. https://doi.org/10.1111/j.1944-9720.2006.tb02282.x.

Mikulski, Ariana M. 2010. "Age of Onset of Bilingualism, Language Use, and the Volitional Subjunctive in Heritage Learners of Spanish." *Heritage Language Journal* 7: 28–46.

Moats, Louisa C. 2005. "How Spelling Supports Reading: And Why It Is More Regular and Predictable Than You May Think." *American Educator* (Winter): 12–43.

Montrul, Silvina. 2009. "Reexamining the Fundamental Difference Hypothesis." *Studies in Second Language Acquisition* 31 (2): 225–57. https://doi.org/10.1017/S0272263109090299.

Montrul, Silvina, and Kim Potowski. 2007. "Command of Gender Agreement in School-Age Spanish-English Bilingual Children." *International Journal of Bilingualism* 11 (3): 301–28. https://doi.org/10.1177/13670069070110030301.

Morton, John. 1980. "The Logogen Model and Orthographic Structure." In *Cognitive Processes in Spelling*, edited by U. Frith, 118–33. London: Academic Press.

Morton, John, and Karalyn Patterson. 1980. "A New Attempt at an Interpretation, or an Attempt at a New Interpretation." In *Deep Dyslexia*, edited by M. Coltheart, K. Patterson, and J. Marshall, 91–118. London: Routledge and Kegan Paul.

Mozafari, Ahva, Amani El-Alayli, Adrian Kunemund, and Trevor Fry. 2019. "Impressions of Businesses with Language Errors in Print Advertising: Do Spelling and Grammar Influence the Inclination to Use a Business?" *Current Psychology* 38: 1721–27. https://doi.org/10.1007/S12144-017-9735-0.

Nagy, William, Virginia W. Berninger, and Robert D. Abbott. 2006. "Contribution of Morphology beyond Phonology to Literacy Outcomes of Upper Elementary and Middle-School Students." *Journal of Educational Psychology* 98: 134–47. https://doi.org/10.1037/0022-0663.98.1.134.

National Governors Association (NGA) Center for Best Practices and Council of Chief State School Officers. 2012. *Estándares estatales comunes para las artes del lenguaje en español y para la lecto-escritura en historia y estudios sociales, ciencias y materias técnicas*. Washington, DC: NGA.

Nunes, Terezinha, Peter Bryant, and Miriam Bindman. 1997. "Morphological Spelling Strategies: Developmental Stages and Processes." *Developmental Psychology* 33 (4): 637–49. https://doi.org/10.1037/0012-1649.33.4.637.

Nunes, Terezinha, Peter Bryant, and Jenny Olsson. 2003. "Learning Morphological and Phonological Spelling Rules: An Intervention Study." *Scientific Studies of Reading* 7 (3): 289–307. https://doi.org/10.1207/S1532799xssr0703_6.

Olson, David R. 1994. *The World on Paper: The Conceptual and Cognitive Implications of Writing and Reading*. Cambridge: Cambridge University Press.

Ormrod, Jeanne E. 1986a. "Learning to Spell: Three Studies at the University Level." *Research in the Teaching of English* 20: 160–73.

Ormrod, Jeanne E. 1986b. "Learning to Spell While Reading: A Follow-Up Study." *Perceptual and Motor Skills* 63: 652–54.

Pajares, Frank. 2003. Self-Efficacy Beliefs, Motivation, and Achievement in Writing: A Review of the Literature. *Reading and Writing Quarterly* 19: 139–58. https://doi.org/10.1080/10573560308222.

Pan, Steven C., Timothy C. Rickard, and Robert A. Bjork. 2021. "Does Spelling Still Matter—and If So, How Should It Be Taught? Perspectives from Contemporary and Historical Research." *Educational Psychology Review* 33: 1523–52. https://doi.org/10.1007/S10648-021-09611-Y.

Parra Velasco, María Luisa. 2021. "La literacidad múltiple en el aprendizaje del español como lengua de herencia." In *Aproximaciones al estudio del español como lengua de herencia*, edited by D. Pascual y Cabo and J. Torres, 97–110. London: Routledge.

Pascual y Cabo, Diego, and Silvina Montrul. 2021. "Morfosintaxis nominal del español como lengua de herencia." In *Aproximaciones al estudio del español como lengua de herencia*, edited by D. Pascual y Cabo and J. Torres. London: Routledge.

Penny, Ralph. 2000. *Variation and Change in Spanish*. Cambridge: Cambridge UP.

Petrov, Lisa A. 2013. "A Pilot Study of Service-Learning in a Spanish Heritage Speaker Course: Community Engagement, Identity, and Language in the Chicago Area." *Hispania* 96 (2): 310–27.

Phillips, Beth M., Jeanine C. Menchetti, and Christopher J. Lonigan. 2008. "Successful Phonological Awareness Instruction with Preschool Children: Lessons from the Classroom." *Topics in Early Childhood Special Educ*ation 28 (1): 3–17. https://doi.org/10.1177/0271121407313813.

Polinsky, Maria. 2008. "Gender under Incomplete Acquisition: Heritage Speakers' Knowledge of Noun Categorization." *Heritage Language Journal* 6 (1): 40–71.

Post, Yolanda V., Barbara R. Foorman, and Merrill Hiscock. 1997. "Speech Perception and Speech Production as Indicators of Reading Difficulty." *Annals of Dyslexia* 47: 3–27. https://doi.org/10.1007/S11881-997-0018-6.

Post, Yolanda V., Paul R. Swank, Merrill Hiscock, and Anne E. Fowler. 1999. "Identification of Vowel Speech Sounds by Skilled and Less Skilled Readers and the Relation with Vowel Spelling." *Annals of Dyslexia* 49: 161–94.

Potowski, Kim, and María Carreira. 2004. "Teacher Development and National Standards for Spanish as a Heritage Language." *Foreign Language Annals* 37 (3): 421–31.

Potowski, Kim, Jill Jegerski, and Kara Morgan-Short. 2009. "The Effects of Instruction on Linguistic Development in Spanish Heritage Language Speakers." *Language Learning* 59 (3): 537–79.

Protopapas, Athanassios. 2016. "From Diacritics to the Mental Lexicon: Where Is the Stress?" In *Linguistic Rhythm and Literacy*, edited by J. Thomson and L. Jarmulowicz, 237–64. John Benjamins Publishing Company. https://doi.org/10.1075/tilar.17.

Rael, Juan B. 1939. "Cuentos españoles de Colorado y de Nuevo Méjico (Primera Serie)." *Journal of American Folklore* 52 (205/206): 227–323.

Ramírez, Gloria, Xi Chen, Esther Geva, and Heidi Kiefer. 2010. "Morphological Awareness in Spanish-Speaking English Language Learners: Within and Cross Language Effects on Word Reading." *Reading and Writing* 23: 337–58.

Ravid, Dorit, and Steven Gillis. 2002. "Teachers' Perception of Spelling Patterns and Children's Spelling Errors: A Cross-Linguistic Perspective." In *The Relation of Writing to Spoken Language*, edited by M. Neef, A. Neijt, and R. Sproat, 71–95. Tübingen, Germany: Niemeyer Verlag.

Ravid, Dorit, and Liliana Tolchinsky. 2002. "Developing Linguistic Literacy: A Comprehensive Model." *Journal of Child Language* 29: 417–47. https://doi.org/10.1017/s0305000902005111.

Real Academia Española (RAE). 2010. *Ortografía de la lengua española*. Spain: Espasa Libros SLU.

Rothman, Jason, and Jeanine Treffers-Daller. 2014. "A Prolegomenon to the Construct of the Native Speaker: Heritage Speaker Bilinguals Are Natives Too!" *Applied Linguistics* 35 (1): 93–98. https://doi.org/10.1093/Applin/Amt049.

Scarborough, Hollis S., Linnea C. Ehri, Richard K. Olson, and Anne E. Fowler. 1998. "The Fate of Phonemic Awareness beyond the Elementary School Years." *Scientific Studies of Reading* 2: 115–42.

Scholes, Robert J. 1993. "In Search of Phonemic Consciousness: A Follow-up on Ehri." In *Literacy and Language Analysis*, edited by R. J. Scholes, 45–53. Hillsdale, NJ: Erlbaum.

Schreuder, Robert, and R. Harald Baayen. 1997. "How Complex Simplex Words Can Be." *Journal of Memory and Language* 37: 118–39. https://doi.org/10.1006/Jmla.1997.2510.

Schwab, Sandra. 2015. "Accent Mark and Visual Word Recognition in Spanish." *Loquens* 2 (1): 1–21. http://dx.doi.org/10.3989/loquens.2015.018.

Serrano, Francisca, Sylvia Defior, and Francisco J. Martos. 2003. "To Be or Not to Be Phonologically Aware: A Reflection about Metalinguistic Skills of Student of Teacher." In *Literacy Acquisition: The Role of Phonology, Morphology and Orthography*, edited by R. M. Joshi, C. K. Leong, and B. L. J. Kaczmarek, 209–15. Amsterdam: IOS Press.

Sessarego, Sandro. 2012. "Vowel Weakening in Afro-Yungueño: Linguistic and Social Considerations." *Papia* 22 (2): 279–94.

Seymour, Phillip H. K. 1992. "Cognitive Theories of Spelling and Implications for Education." In *Psychology, Spelling and Education*, edited by C. M. Sterling and C. Robson, 50–70. Clevedon, UK: Multilingual Matters.

Share, David L. 1995. "Phonological Recoding and Self-Teaching: Sine Qua Non of Reading Acquisition." *Cognition* 55: 151–218.

Share, David L. 1999. "Phonological Recoding and Orthographic Learning: A Direct Test of the Self-Teaching Hypothesis." *Journal of Experimental Child Psychology* 72: 95–129.

Share, David L. 2004. "Orthographic Learning at a Glance: On the Time Course and Developmental Onset of Self-Teaching." *Journal of Experimental Child Psychology* 87: 267–98. https://doi.org/10.1016/j.jecp.2004.01.001.

Silva-Corvalán, Carmen. 1994a. *Language Contact and Change: Spanish in Los Angeles*. Oxford: Clarendon Press.

Silva-Corvalán, Carmen. 1994b. "The Gradual Loss of Mood Distinctions in Los Angeles Spanish." *Language Variation and Change* 6: 255–72.

Silva-Corvalán Carmen. 2001. *Sociolingüística y pragmática del español*. Washington, DC: Georgetown University Press.

Smith, Frank. 1982. *Writing and the Writer*. New York: Holt, Rinehart and Winston.

Stanovich, Keith E., Anne E. Cunningham, and Barbara B. Cramer. 1984. "Assessing Phonological Awareness in Kindergarten Children: Issues of Task Comparability." *Journal of Experimental Child Psychology* 38: 175–90

Sturm, Jessica L. 2013. "Attention, Awareness, and Accents in L2 French." *Language Awareness* 22 (2): 146–60. https://doi.org/10.1080/09658416.2012.670243.

Tighe, Elizabeth L., and Katherine S. Binder. 2015. "An Investigation of Morphological Awareness and Processing in Adults with Low Literacy." *Applied Psycholinguistics* 36 (2): 245–73.

Titos, Rosa, Sylvia Defior, Jesús Alegría, and Francisco Martos. 2003. "The Use of Morphological Resources in Spanish Orthography: The Case of the Verb," In *Literacy Acquisition: The Role of Phonology, Morphology and Orthography*, edited by R. M. Joshi, C. K. Leong, and B. L. J. Kaczmarek, 113–18. Amsterdam: IOS Press.

Tocaimaza-Hatch, Cecilia, and Laura Walls. 2016. "Service-Learning as a Means of Vocabulary Learning for Second Language and Heritage Language Learners of Spanish." *Hispania* 99 (4): 650–65.

Torres, Julio. 2013. "Heritage and Second Language Learners of Spanish: The Roles of Task Complexity and Inhibitory Control." PhD. diss., Georgetown University, Washington, DC.

Treiman, Rebecca. 1991. "Children's Spelling Errors on Syllable-Initial Consonant Clusters." *Journal of Educational Psychology* 83: 346–60.

Valdés, Guadalupe. 1997. "The Teaching of Spanish to Bilingual Spanish-Speaking Students: Outstanding Issues and Unanswered Questions." In *La enseñanza del español a hispanohablantes*, edited by M.C. Colombi and F. Alarcón, 8–44. Boston: Houghton Mifflin.

Valdés, Guadalupe. 2001. "Heritage Languages Students: Profiles and Possibilities." In *Heritage Languages in America: Preserving a National Resource*, edited by J. K. Peyton, D. A. Ranard, and S. McGinnis, 37–77. Washington, DC: Center for Applied Linguistics / Delta Systems.

Valle-Arroyo, Francisco. 1989. "Errores en lectura y escritura: Un modelo dual." *Cognitiva* 2 (1): 35–63.

Valle-Arroyo, Francisco. 1990. "Spelling Errors in Spanish." *Reading and Writing: An Interdisciplinary Journal* 2: 83–98.

Verhoeven, Ludo, and Charles A. Perfetti. 2011. "Morphological Processing in Reading Acquisition: A Cross-Linguistic Perspective." *Applied Psycholinguistics* 32 (3): 457–66. https://doi.org/10.1017/S0142716411000154.

Vernon, Sofía A., and Emilia Ferreiro. 1999. "Writing Development: A Neglected Variable in the Consideration of Phonological Awareness." *Harvard Educational Review* 69: 395–415.

Villa, Daniel. 1996. "Choosing a 'Standard' Variety of Spanish for the Instruction of Native Spanish Speakers in the U.S." *Foreign Language Annals* 29 (2): 191–200.

Villa, Daniel. 2009. "General versus Standard Spanish: Establishing Empirical Norms for the Study of U.S. Spanish." In *Spanish in the United States and Other Contact Environments: Sociolinguistics, Ideology and Pedagogy*, edited by Manel Lacorte and Jennifer Leeman, 175–89. Madrid/Frankfurt: Iberoamericana/Vervuert.

Wang, Min, Chenxi Cheng, and Shi-Wei Chen. 2006. "Contribution of Morphological Awareness to Chinese-English Biliteracy Acquisition." *Journal of Educational Psychology* 98: 542–53. https://doi.org/10.1037/0022-0663.98.3.542.

Webb, John B., and Barbara L. Miller, eds. 2000. *Teaching Heritage Language Learners: Voices from the Classroom.* Yonkers, NY: ACTFL.

Westwood, Peter. 1999. "The Correlation between Results from Different Types of Spelling Test and Children's Spelling Ability When Writing." *Australian Journal of Learning Disabilities* 4 (1): 31–36.

Wilde, Sandra. 1990. "A Proposal for a New Spelling Curriculum." *Elementary School Journal* 90 (3): 275–89.

Yamauchi, Lois A., Andrea K. Ceppi, and Jo-Anne Lau-Smith. 2000. "Teaching in a Hawaiian Context: Educator Perspectives on the Hawaiian Language Immersion Program." *Bilingual Research Journal* 24 (4): 385–404.

Yopp, Hallie K. 1988. "The Validity and Reliability of Phonemic Awareness Tests." *Reading Research Quarterly* 23 (2): 159–77. https://doi.org/10.2307/747800.

Zapata, Gabriela C. 2017. "A Match Made in Heaven: An Introduction to Learning by Design and Its Role in Heritage Language Education." In *Multiliteracies Pedagogy and Language Learning: Teaching Spanish to Heritage Speakers*, edited by G. C. Zapata and M. Lacorte, 1–26. London: Palgrave Macmillan.

Zapata, Gabriela C. 2018. "Heritage Spanish for Intermediate Learners." Open-Source Materials. https://bit.ly/InterHeritSpan.

Zamudio Mesa, Celia. 2008. "Influencia de la escritura alfabética en la segmentación de sonidos vocálicos y consonánticos." *Lectura y vida* 29 (1): 10–21.

Zhang, Shuai, Alida Hudson, Xuejun R. Ji, R. Malatesha Joshi, Juan Zamora, Fabiola R. Gómez-Velázquez, and Andrés A. González-Garrido. 2021. "Spelling Acquisition in Spanish: Using Error Analyses to Examine Individual Differences in Phonological and Orthographic Processing." *Scientific Studies of Reading* 25 (1): 64–83. https://doi.org/10.1080/10888438.2020.1754834.

Ziegler, Johannes C., and Usha Goswami. 2005. "Reading Acquisition, Developmental Dyslexia, and Skilled Reading across Languages: A Psycholinguistic Grain Size Theory." *Psychological Bulletin* 131 (1): 3–29. https://doi.org/10.1037/0033-2909.131.1.3.

Zutell, Jerry and Virginia Allen. 1988. "The English Spelling Strategies of Spanish-Speaking Bilingual Children." *TESOL Quarterly* 22 (2): 333–40.

Zyzik, E. 2016. "Towards a Prototype Model of the Heritage Language Learner: Understanding Strengths and Needs." In *Innovative Approaches to Heritage Language Teaching*, edited by M. Fairclough and S. Beaudrie, 19–38. Washington, DC: Georgetown University Press.

Zyzik, Eve. 2021a. "How Many Collocations Do Heritage Speakers Know? The Effects of Linguistic and Individual Variables." *Spanish as a Heritage Language* 1 (1): 67–98. https://doi.org/10.5744/shl.2021.1003.

Zyzik, Eve. 2021b. "El conocimiento léxico de los hablantes del español como lengua de herencia." In *Aproximaciones al estudio del español como lengua de herencia*, edited by D. Pascual y Cabo and J. Torres, 53–65. London: Routledge.

Index

About the Author

Amàlia Llombart-Huesca is a professor of Spanish at the California State Polytechnic University Pomona, where she teaches Spanish for heritage language learners, linguistics, and curriculum and methods for Spanish Single Subject Teaching Credential students. She has published numerous journal articles on spelling in Spanish heritage language learners.